IMAGES
of America

ANNAPOLIS AND THE GUALALA RIVER

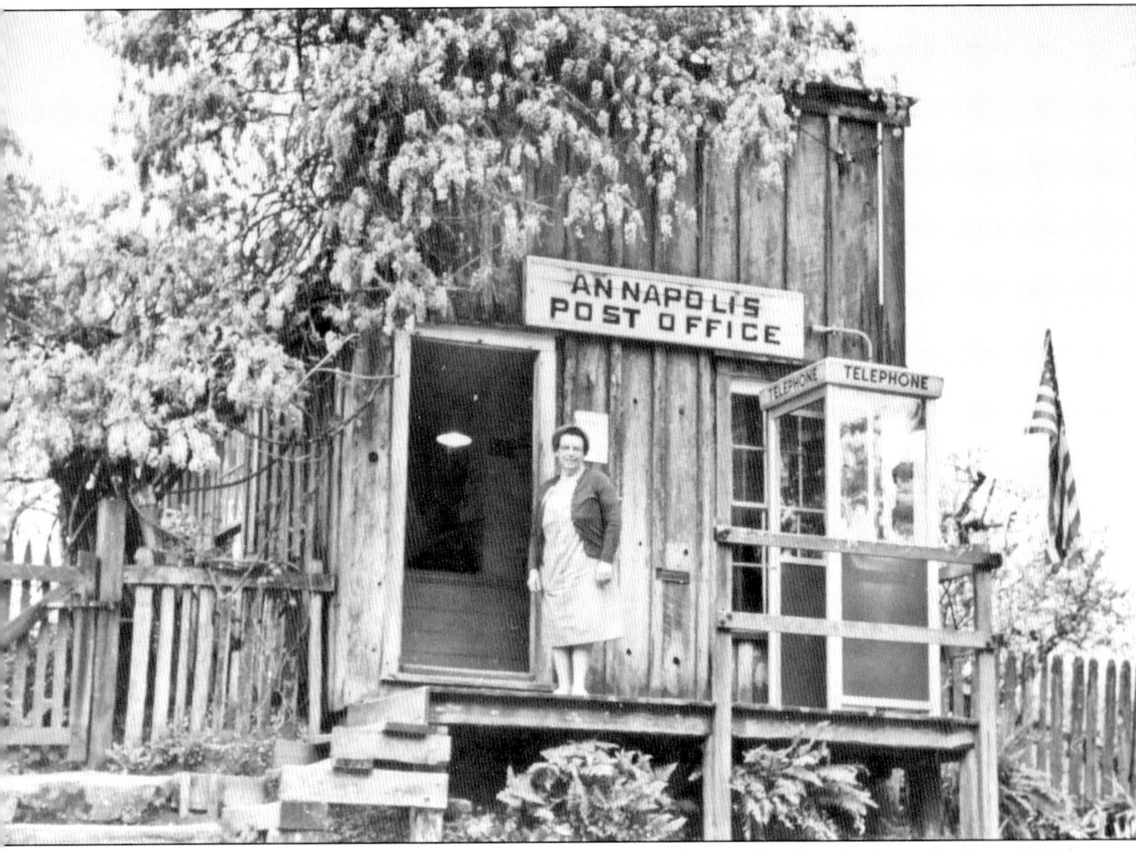

The Annapolis Post Office is probably Annapolis's most famous landmark. It was built in 1901 by Charley Wetmore, and the first postmaster was Henry Wetmore, Charley's father. Molly McMillen Fiscus served the longest period of time as the postmistress (46 years) before her daughter-in-law, Alice Porter Fiscus, took over. Alice, pictured here, was the postmistress beginning in 1942. Often photographed, the post office has remained the town's official center for many years. (Courtesy of Dorothy and Gary Craig.)

On the Cover: Taken in 1919, three-year-old Arline Hamilton goes on a boat ride with her great aunt Thelma Hitchcock near the mouth of the Gualala River, where it meets the Pacific Ocean. The town of Gualala is in the distance. (Courtesy of Arline Hamilton and William McMillen Kramer.)

IMAGES
of America

ANNAPOLIS AND THE GUALALA RIVER

Tammy Durston and Steve Oliff

ARCADIA PUBLISHING

ISBN 978-0-7385-8114-9

Published by Arcadia Publishing
Charleston, South Carolina

Printed in the United States of America

Library of Congress Control Number: 2010923452

For all general information, please contact Arcadia Publishing:
Telephone 843-853-2070
Fax 843-853-0044
E-mail sales@arcadiapublishing.com
For customer service and orders:
Toll-Free 1-888-313-2665

Visit us on the Internet at www.arcadiapublishing.com

To Arline Hamiton Chambers "Nana," Dorothy and Gary Craig in memory of Grandpa George Fiscus, David McMillen Kramer and the kids

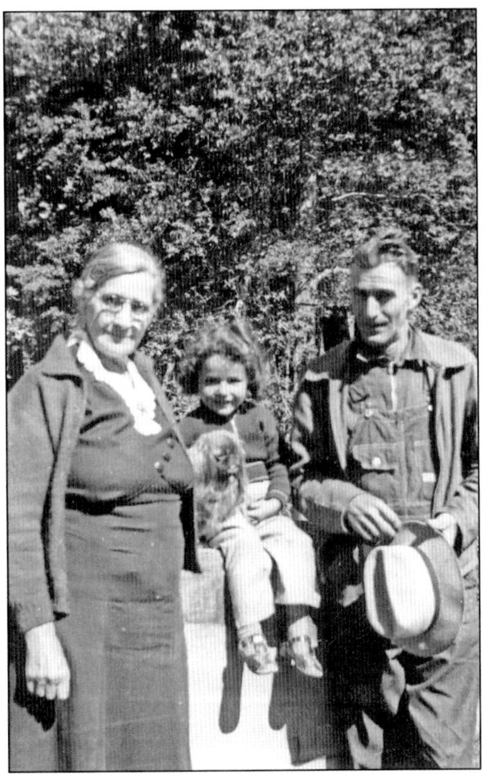

Dorothy Fiscus Craig is seated in between her grandmother Mary "Molly" McMillen Fiscus and her father, Charley Fiscus. Her grandfather George Fiscus took most of the photographs in this book. (Courtesy of Dorothy and Gary Craig.)

Contents

ACKNOWLEDGMENTS

This book would not have been possible without Dorothy and Gary Craig and their extensive collection of glass-plate negatives taken by Dorothy's grandfather George Fiscus. George Fiscus was an amazing man who documented the early times of Annapolis and the area through his camera. He also was a talented woodworker and builder who came to Annapolis as a bark peeler in the 1870s. Dorothy and Gary generously invited me into their home for many hours of scanning. Thanks also to William McMillen Kramer for providing many photographs from his collection of McMillen and Hamilton family photographs. Charlene and Junior Ohlson were a great help with photographs and explanations, as were Sandra Petersen, Bill Richardson, Chris McMillen, and Ken Spacek. Thanks also to Tony Hoskins and Katherine Reinhart at the Sonoma County Library and Lee Torliatt of the Sonoma County Historical Society. Last but not least, a special thanks to Arline Hamilton, who inspired the idea.

Several excellent history books document the surrounding areas: Lynn Hay Rudy's *The Old Salt Point Township*, Annette White-Parks's *q awala-li*, *The Sea Ranch* by Susan Clark, *Fort Ross and the Sonoma Coast* by Lyn Lalani and Sarah Sweedler, and of course, *The Early Days of Point Arena* by Steve Oliff and Cheri Carlstedt. For that reason, as well as the desire to publicly show (many for the first time in print) George Fiscus's turn-of-the-century photographs, the major focus of this book is strictly on Annapolis and the Gualala River in the late 1880s through early 1900s.

We apologize in advance for not including photographs of every early Annapolis family. Efforts were made to include everyone we could, and in our next effort we will endeavor to further our research efforts.

Unless otherwise noted, all images appear courtesy of Dorothy and Gary Craig.

INTRODUCTION

"Annapolis? Where is that?" This is usually what one hears when the name of Annapolis is mentioned. Annapolis, California, is located 6 miles inland from Highway 1 on the Sonoma coastline, 113 miles north of San Francisco and 65 miles northeast of Santa Rosa.

The first inhabitants of this area were the Southern Pomo (Kashaya). There were Kashaya settlements all along the coast, including Black Point, Stewarts Point, Fisk Mill, and near Gualala. There were additional settlements near Rockpile Creek and along the southern fork of the Gualala River. One of these settlements, called Huckleberry Heights, is located where the present Kashaya reservation lies.

The Pomo made good use of the natural materials of the area, including redwood. Bark covered their homes. They relied on the oceans, rivers, and streams. In the Gualala River, they caught silver salmon or steelhead. Little did they know their forests would soon be invaded.

The Gualala River, which actually flows north in some areas, is 32 miles long and extends from Sonoma County into Mendocino County. Where the river meets the ocean is the dividing line between the counties. Early explorers quickly realized the splendor of the river. C. F. Menefee wrote the following in 1873: "It flows through a very heavily timbered country and is a favorite resort of hunters who love tramping over steep mountains and across deep gorges."

The early draw for Anglo settlers to Northern Sonoma County was the timber. The coast redwoods can reach diameters up to 30 feet and produce a huge volume of high-quality lumber. Besides being strong, redwood is fire, pest, and rot resistant. Many early loggers came to California from the woods in Maine or on the East Coast. Gold miners who failed to find gold discovered the value of timber. The San Francisco area was in desperate need of building materials. Sawmills popped up all over the area until the area ran out of redwood and builders had to look elsewhere. By 1884, there were approximately 400 sawmills in California's north counties. Logging in Northern Sonoma County and Mendocino County began in the 1850s.

Easy trees that lined rivers were harvested first. As the woodsmen ventured farther into the forests and up the river, they discovered a vast amount of timber was available. These unique trees, the coast redwoods, grow exclusively along the ocean at elevations less than 2,000 feet. Fog and moist sea air feed them. Redwood is a very useful wood and was in great demand. This virgin timber represented food ready to be picked.

With the advent of the Homestead Act, settlers came and claimed land. They soon learned that the area way up on the ridge via windy, narrow roads, later known as Annapolis, had an ideal climate for growing orchards. Most people say that Annapolis was named for the Annapolis Orchards, grown by the Wetmore family, early Annapolis farmers who originated from Nova Scotia. Henry Wetmore established the first post office and therefore was given the chance to name the settlement. There is another story that Annapolis got its name because there was a less than successful harvest—there was "one apple less."

Annapolis is still known for being a bit inaccessible due to narrow, windy roads. Growing has turned to more vineyards than apples or prunes. However, the town has maintained its preference toward more rugged living and its can-do attitude.

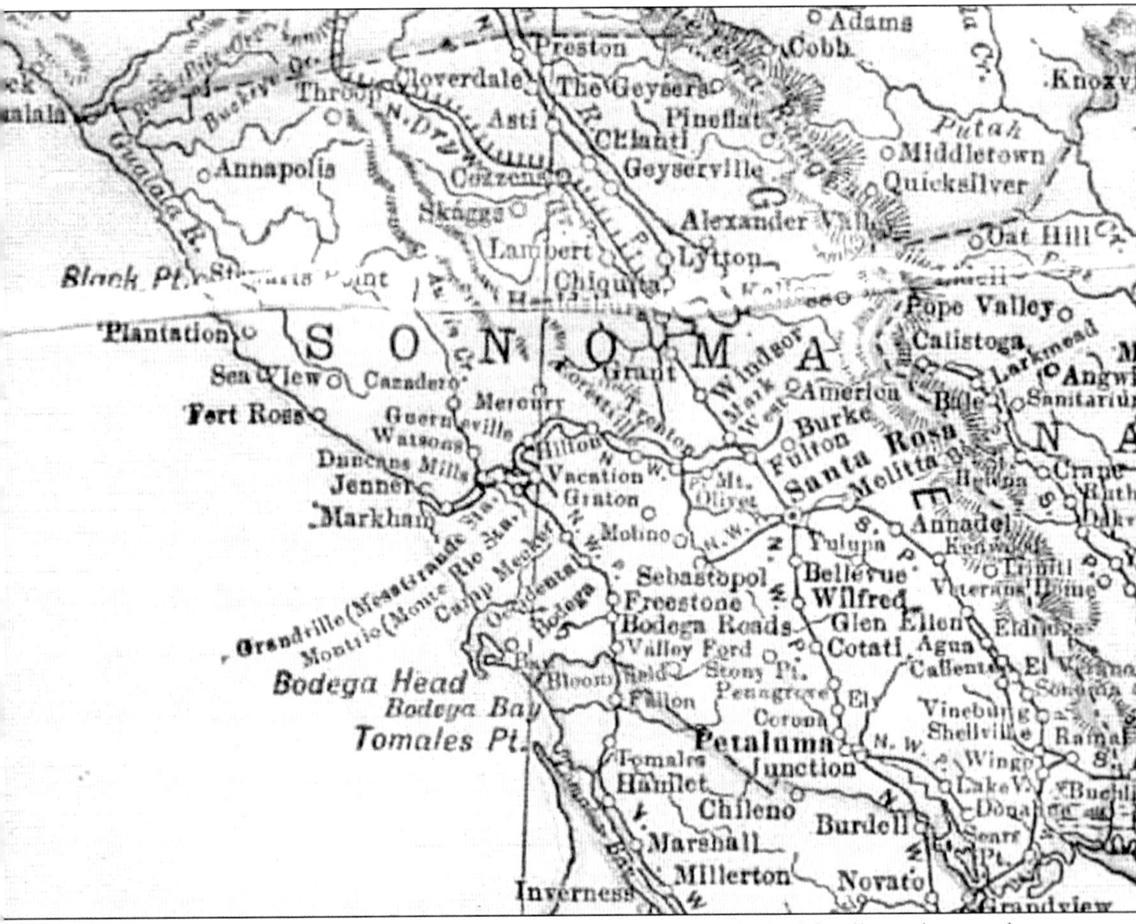

Where is Annapolis? This map from 1914 shows that Annapolis had finally made it on the map. Early maps do not list Annapolis as a town. George Batt, an early Annapolis columnist for local newspapers, wrote the following in 1911: "Annapolis is still on the map and every day convinces the wide awake people here that there is a great future for this neighborhood."

One

The Early Times

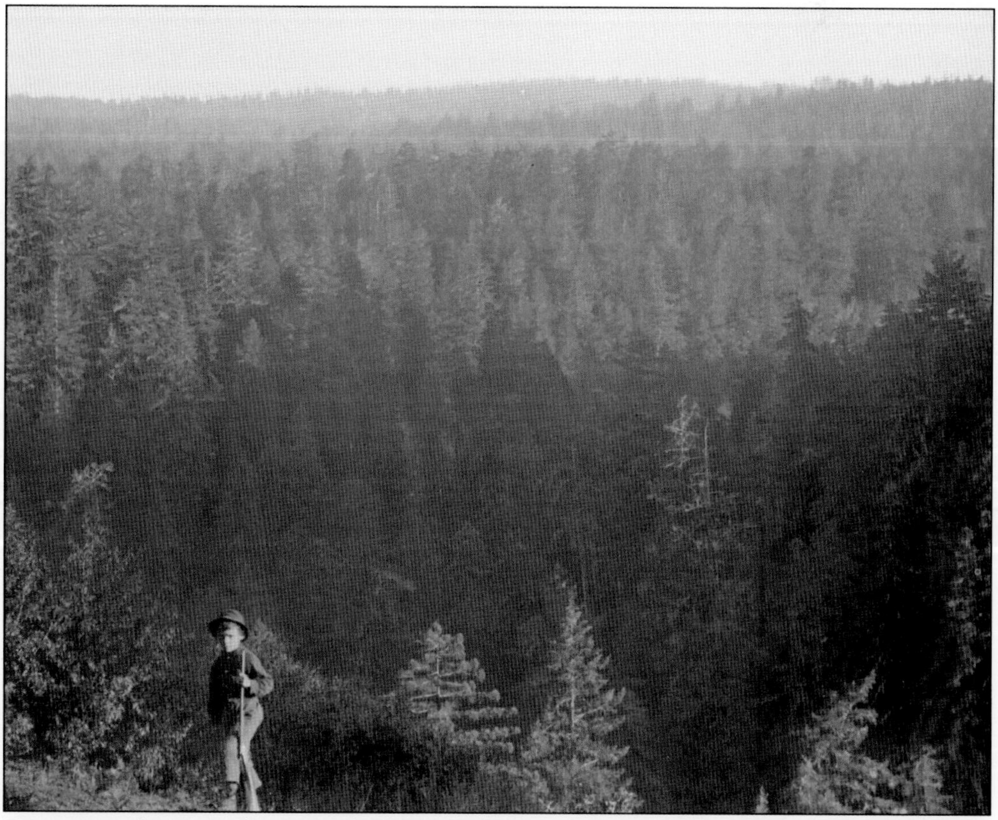

Trees everywhere! Settlers named ridges after them, including Beatty Ridge and Miller Ridge. Early explorers noticed the ridges of trees and used them for navigation. Ridge lines are still used today in Annapolis as people explain where homes or landmarks are located.

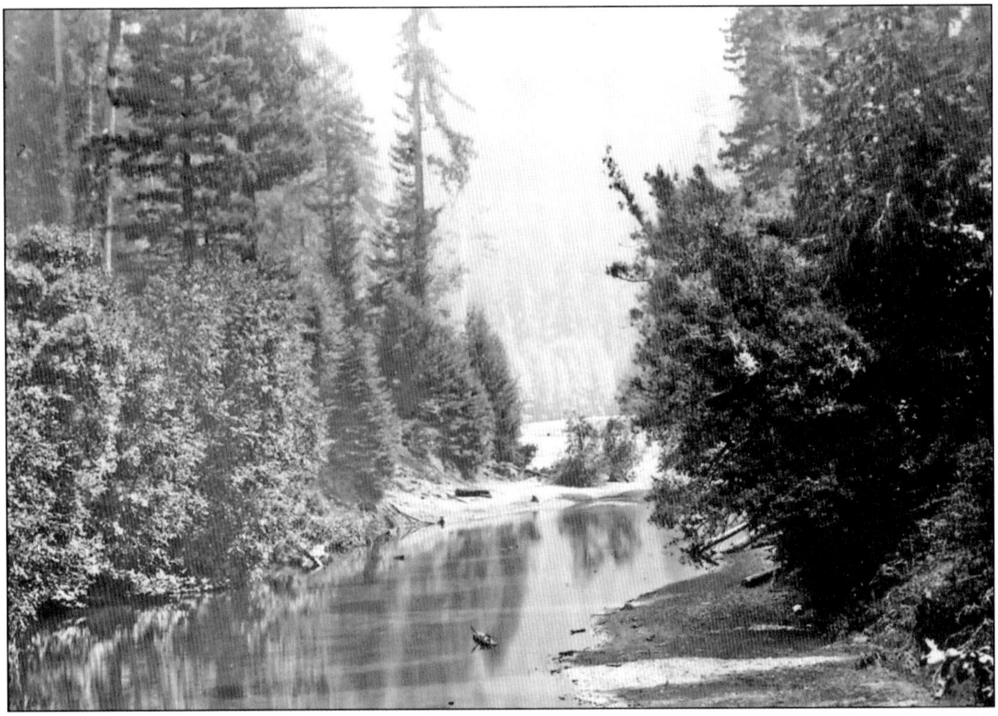

Winding through Annapolis is the Gualala River. There are three forks of the river: the Wheatfield, the South Fork, and the North Fork. The river has always been an important part of the area.

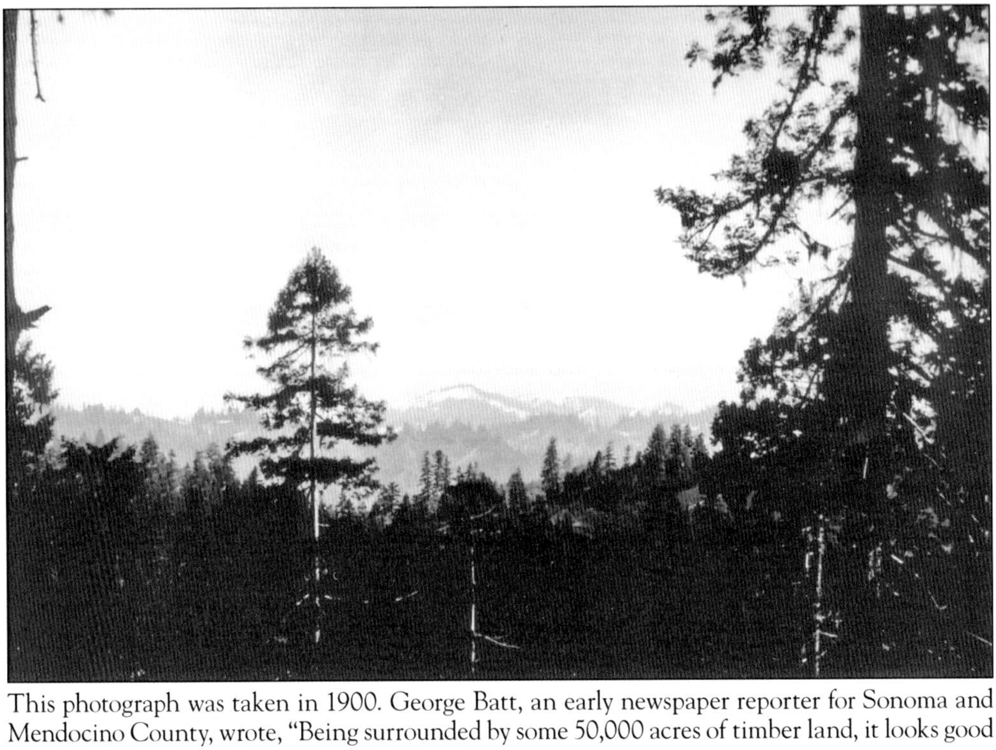

This photograph was taken in 1900. George Batt, an early newspaper reporter for Sonoma and Mendocino County, wrote, "Being surrounded by some 50,000 acres of timber land, it looks good to us."

The coast redwood is one of the world's largest trees. They thrive on the Northern California coastline due to the combination of sunlight, rainfall, and fog. A young tree can add two inches in diameter in one year. Many large trees were discovered in Mendocino and Sonoma Counties, including some over 20 feet in diameter.

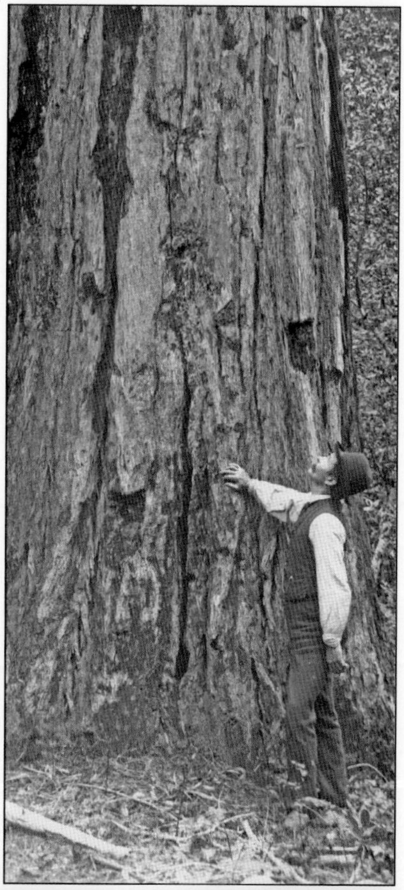

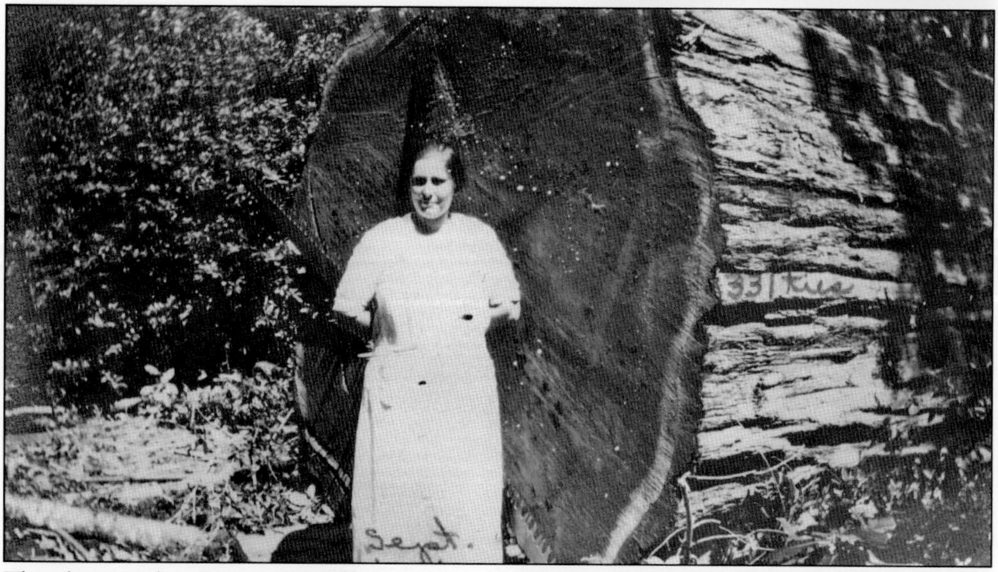

This photograph, taken in 1919 of Eva Hunter, has a notation that 331 ties were created from the tree. The Homestead Act of 1862 encouraged settlement of public land in 160-acre parcels. Settlers quickly filed claims. The living was rugged but worth the effort. (Courtesy of Arline Hamilton.)

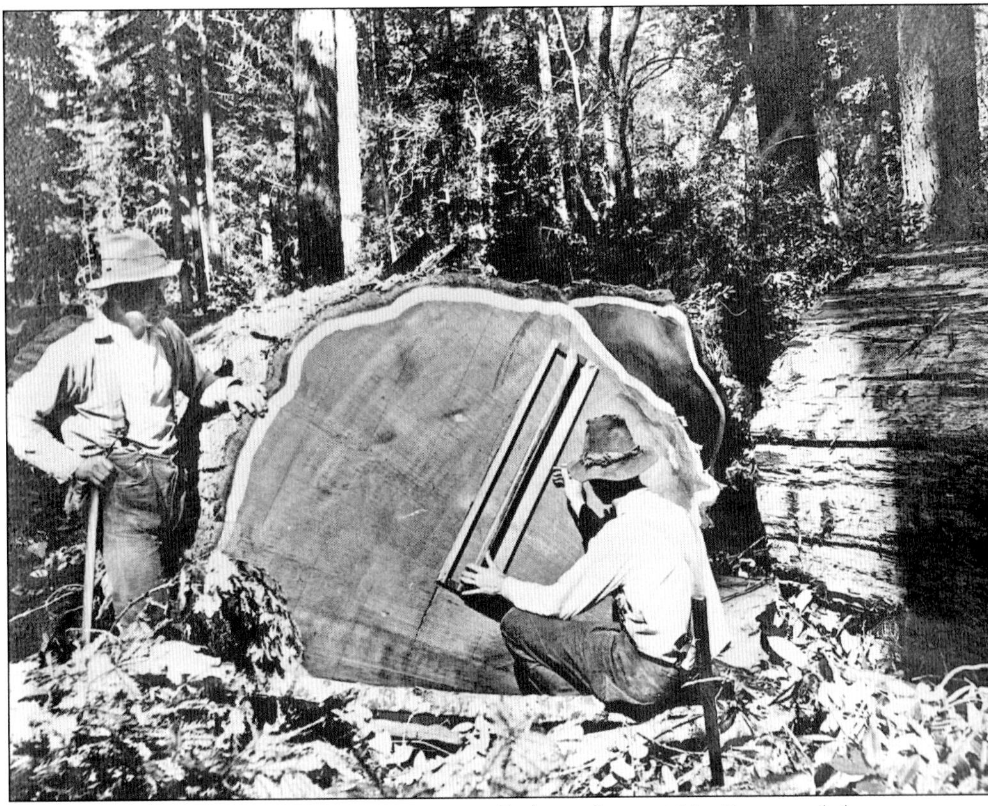

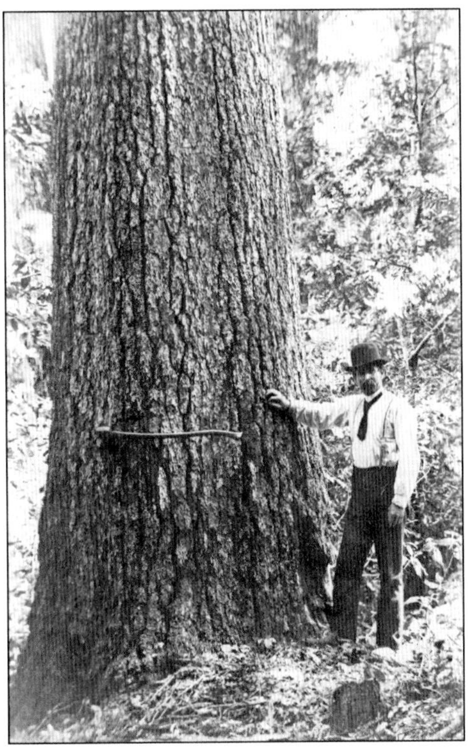

Early settlers quickly discovered that timber was plentiful with such large trees. Lovel Hamilton (left) and Silas McMillen are shown laying out how to split a fallen tree. (Courtesy of Arline Hamilton.)

E. Hickman examines a large tree near the beginning of the 20th century. The Hickmans were one of the early families in the area. Other early landowners were J. C. Beatty, Levi Dresser, George Miller, Henry Parks, William Boyd, James Throop, the Hausers, the Johnsons, the Fisks, the Clarks, the Rasmasons, and the Coles.

Two

LOGGING THE TIMBER

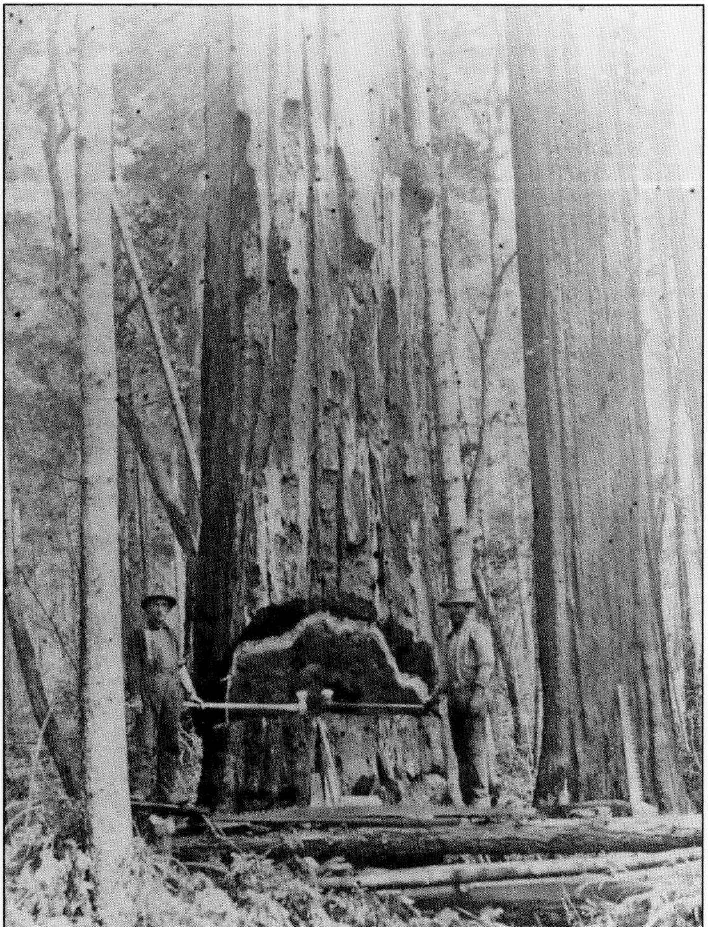

Early logging was challenging with limited tools and massive trees. It sometimes took days of chopping to fell a large tree. After the tree fell, there were even more hours of chopping to be done. (Courtesy of Sonoma County Library.)

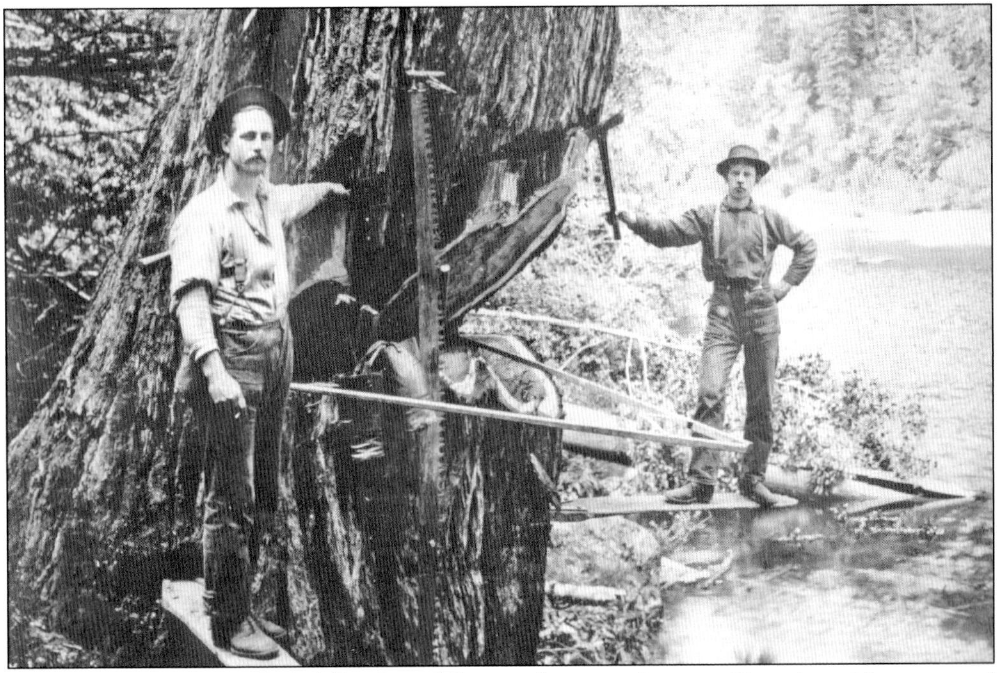

Here, two woodsmen, called "fallers," are felling timber near the river. Gunning sticks were used to site the tree's fall. They form a "V" from the undercut line up to where the tree is to fall. Felling a tree accurately was very important, as transporting an unbroken tree was much easier.

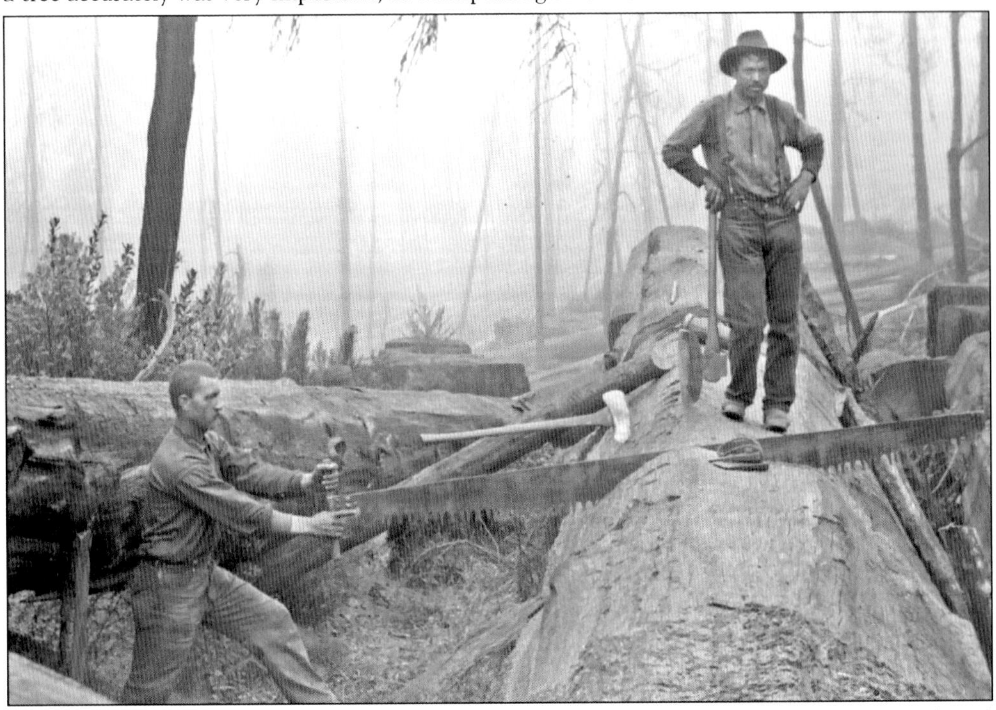

Two men use a crosscut saw on a log that has been peeled of all bark. Redwood bark is tough and thick and caught on the saw, so it was necessary to peel logs before sawing. "Peelers" used special peeling bars to pry the bark off the trees.

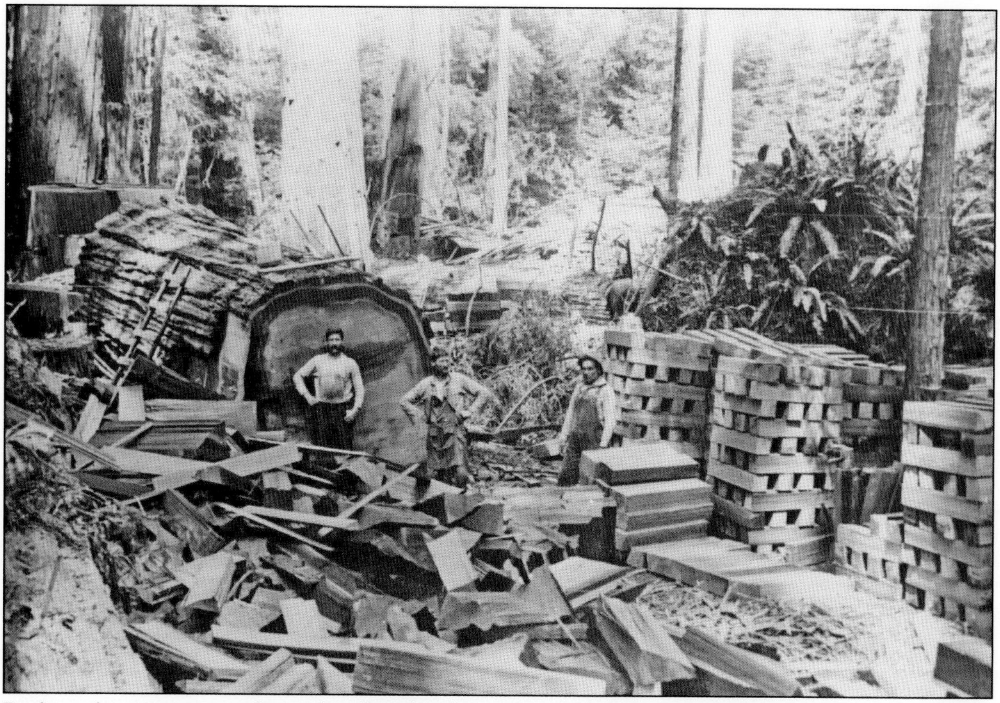

Redwood ties were another side of timber harvesting. Woodmen could make ties—sometimes called splitters—and sell them by the piece. Tie-makers would stack up their ties as shown. The ties would then be either sold to a local tie dealer or transported by wagons to a shipping point. The ties were used for redwood shake roofs, shingles, and fence posts as well as other uses.

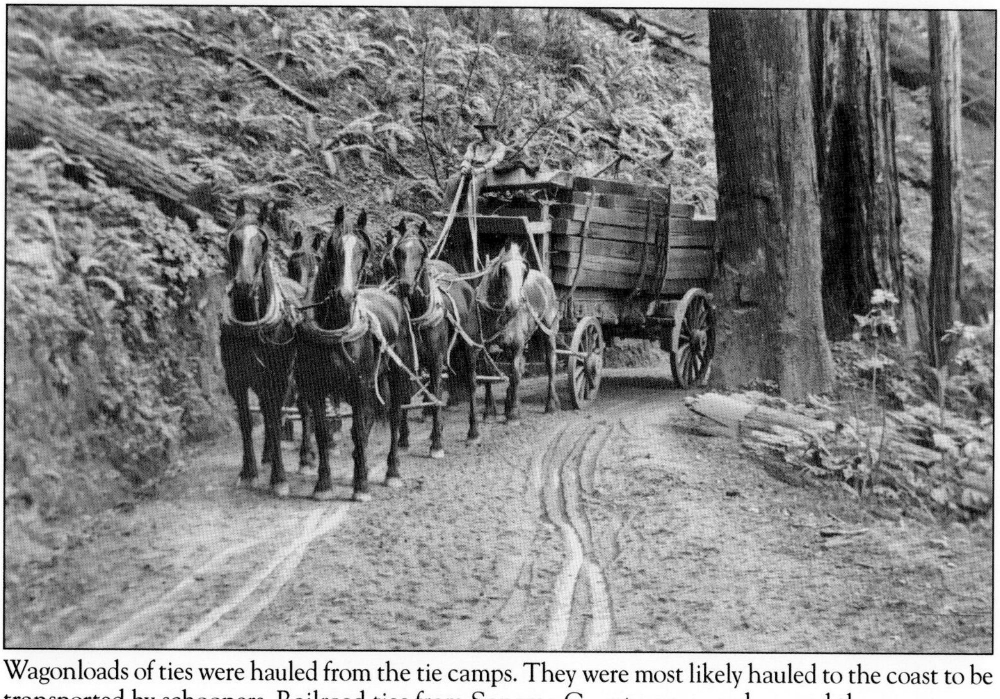

Wagonloads of ties were hauled from the tie camps. They were most likely hauled to the coast to be transported by schooners. Railroad ties from Sonoma County were used around the country.

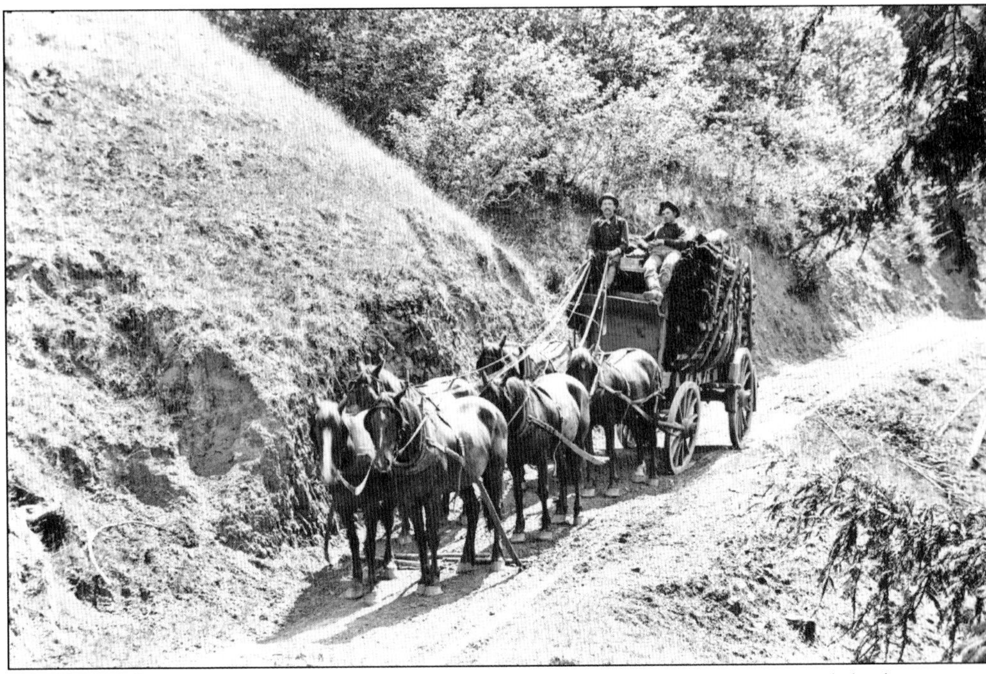

Early logging efforts also involved collecting the bark of tan oak trees. Tan oak bark was used widely for tanning leather and was in high demand for many years. Wagons loaded with tan oak made the trek to waiting schooners.

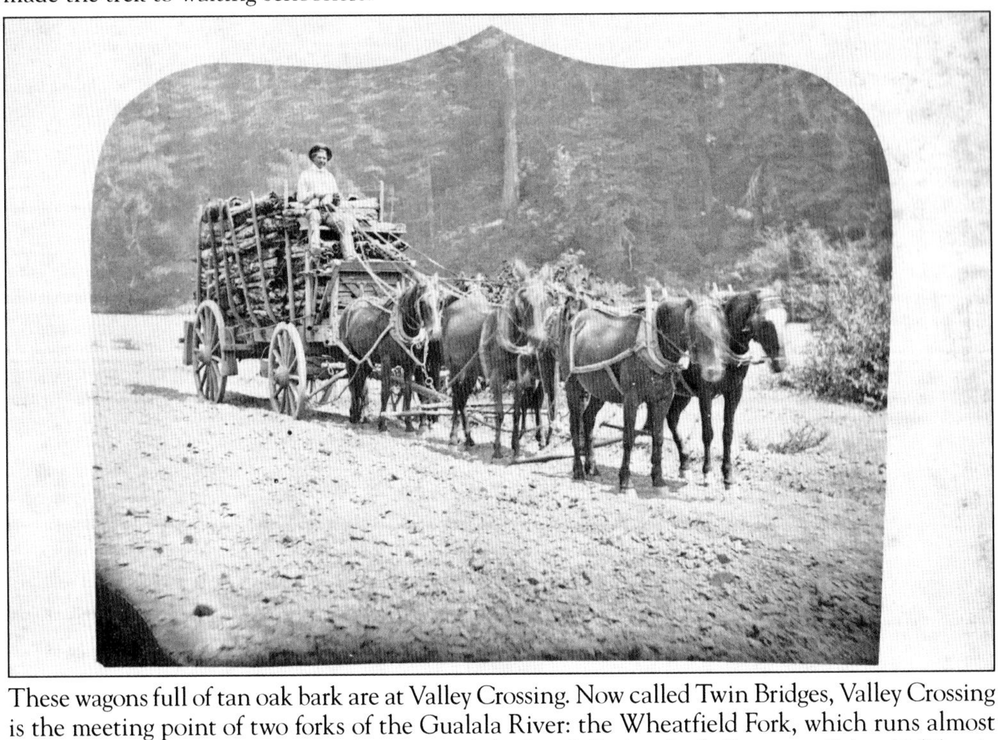

These wagons full of tan oak bark are at Valley Crossing. Now called Twin Bridges, Valley Crossing is the meeting point of two forks of the Gualala River: the Wheatfield Fork, which runs almost parallel to Annapolis Road from the east, and the South Fork, which flows parallel to California Route 1. The South Fork stems all the way from Black Mountain in Cazadero.

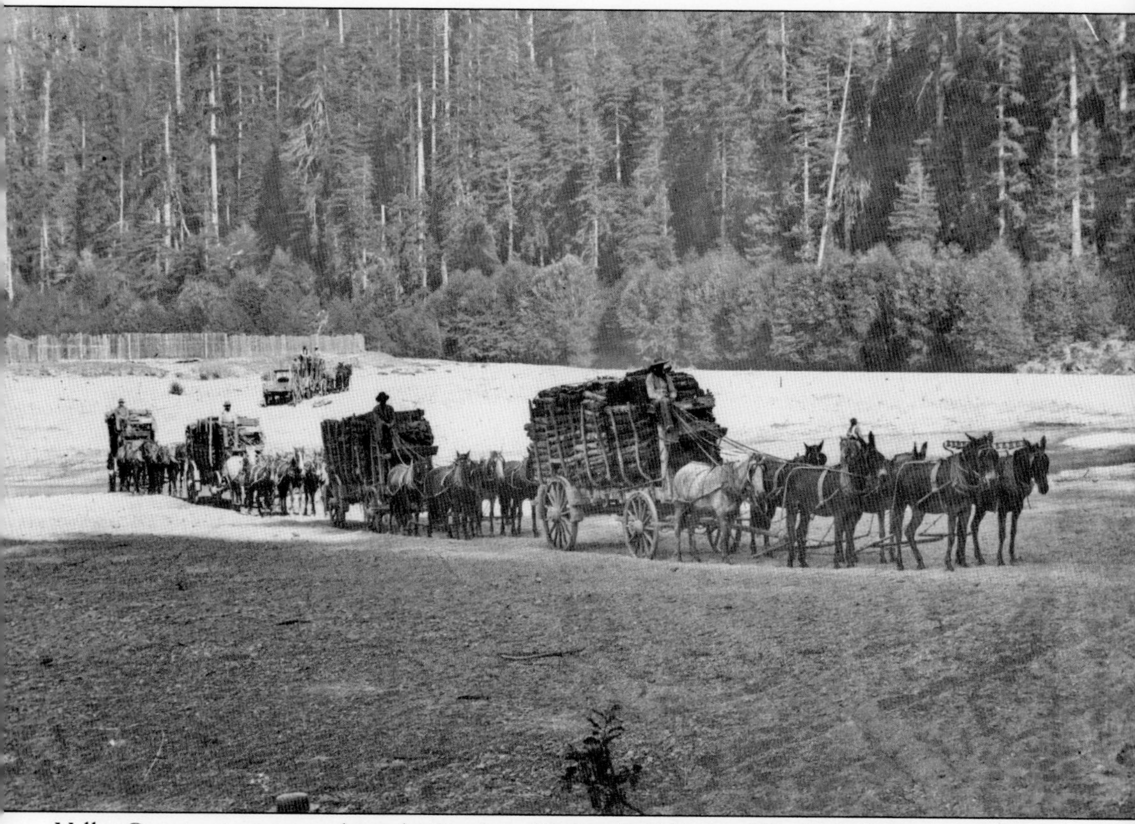

Valley Crossing is an area where the South and Wheatfield Forks of the Gualala River meet. It is now known as Twin Bridges. Although easy to ford in the summer, Valley Crossing was challenging to cross in the rainy season. With no bridge, wagons had to ford the river, so if the river was high, it was impossible to cross. An early resident, George Batt, drowned delivering the mail here in the early 1900s. Many times the river was too deep to pass, and that meant Annapolis was cut off from the coast. There was a big effort by the residents to get bridges built, and they were finally put into place around 1915. Since timber was so readily available, small mills were set up in this area, as well as a small store and saloon. The lumber railway was even extended to the area.

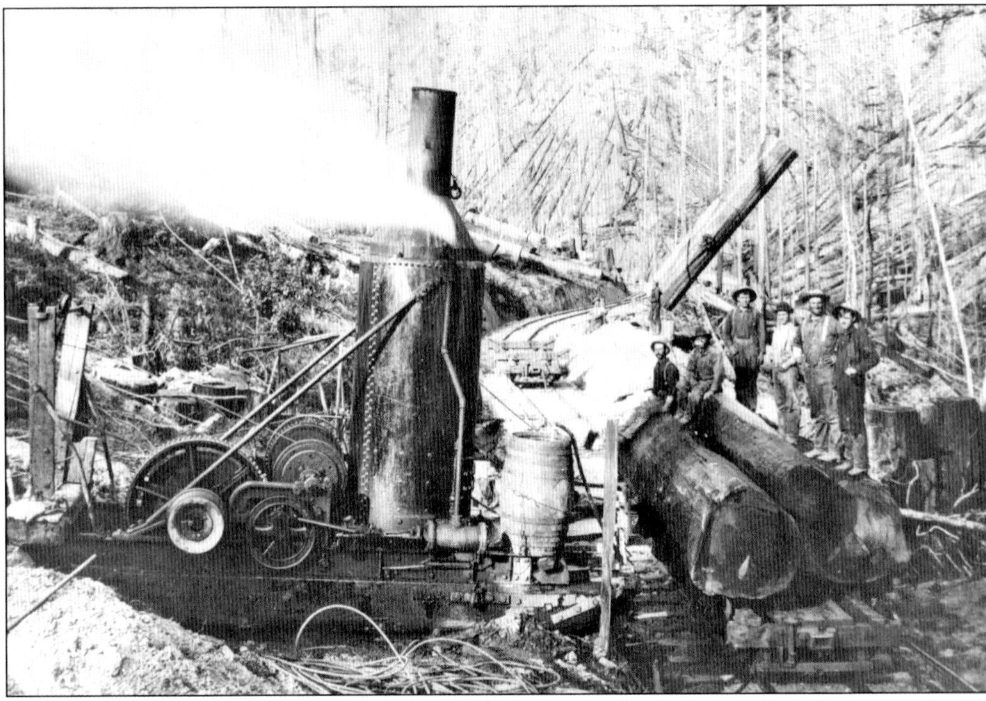

After felling the trees, the massive logs had to be put into place. Moving large logs proved to be a difficult task. Teams of oxen were used to haul the logs onto skid roads. The development of the steam donkey by John Dolbeer in 1882 greatly assisted the loggers. A small boiler supplied steam, which powered the engine, to winch the logs. Cables were wound around a vertical capstan. Steam donkeys were used to roll the logs onto the skid roads and later for loading logs onto the railways.

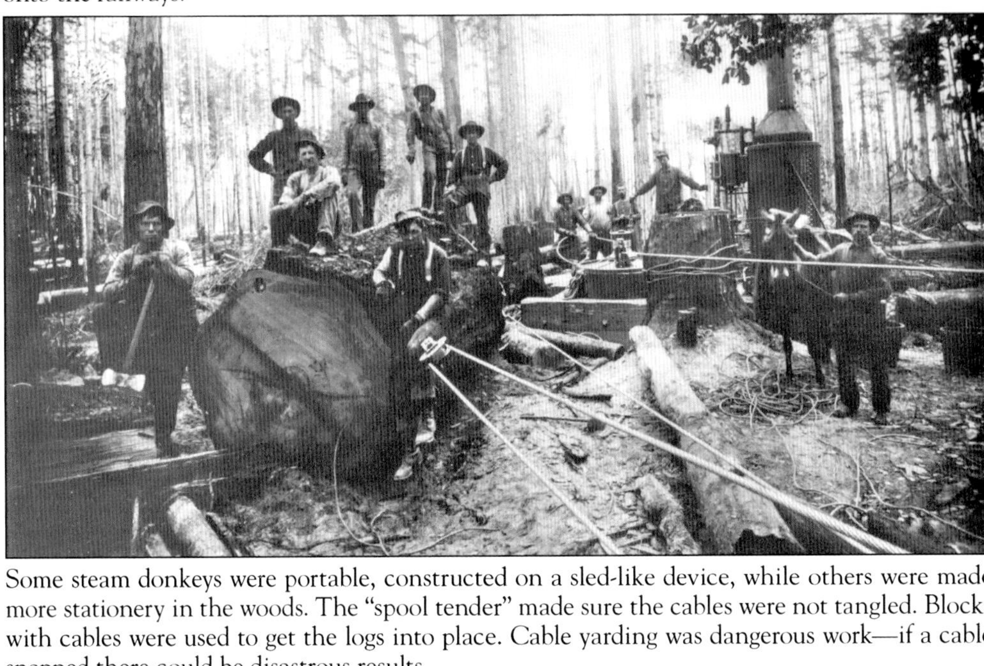

Some steam donkeys were portable, constructed on a sled-like device, while others were made more stationery in the woods. The "spool tender" made sure the cables were not tangled. Blocks with cables were used to get the logs into place. Cable yarding was dangerous work—if a cable snapped there could be disastrous results.

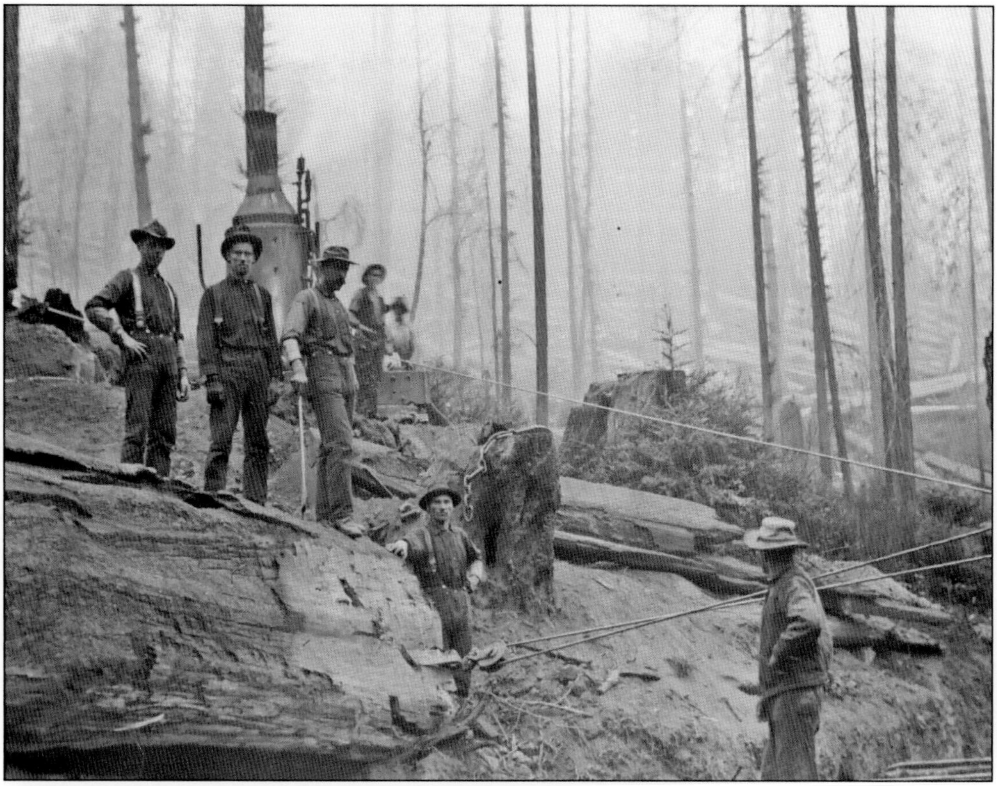

Choke setters had the dangerous job of securing cables on the log before it was winced by the steam donkey. The engineer (or donkey puncher) tended the steam engine, and the spool tender wound the capstan.

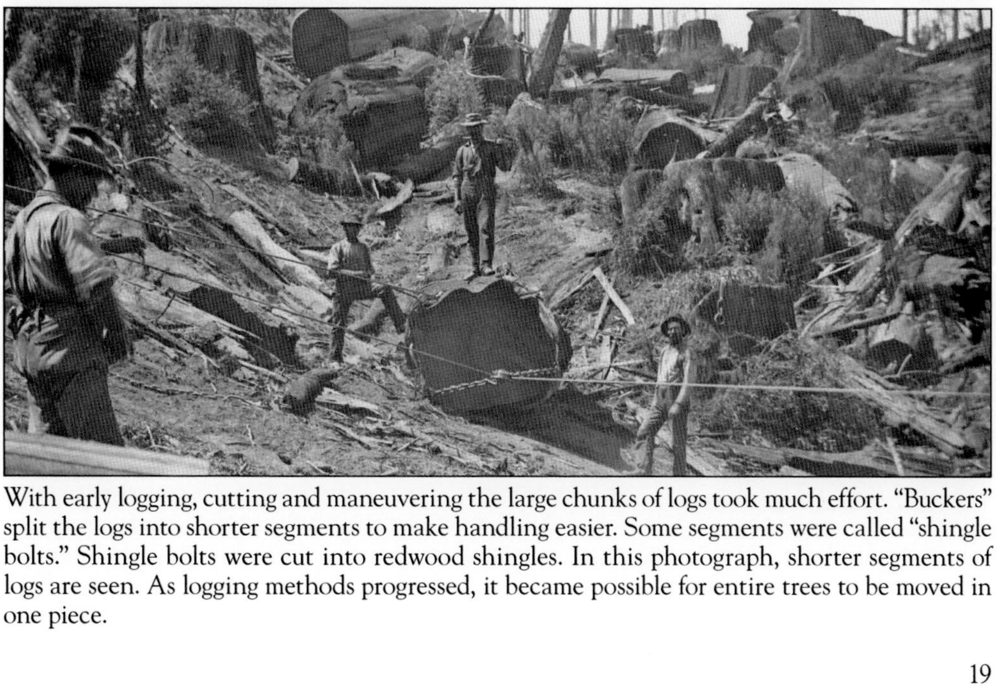

With early logging, cutting and maneuvering the large chunks of logs took much effort. "Buckers" split the logs into shorter segments to make handling easier. Some segments were called "shingle bolts." Shingle bolts were cut into redwood shingles. In this photograph, shorter segments of logs are seen. As logging methods progressed, it became possible for entire trees to be moved in one piece.

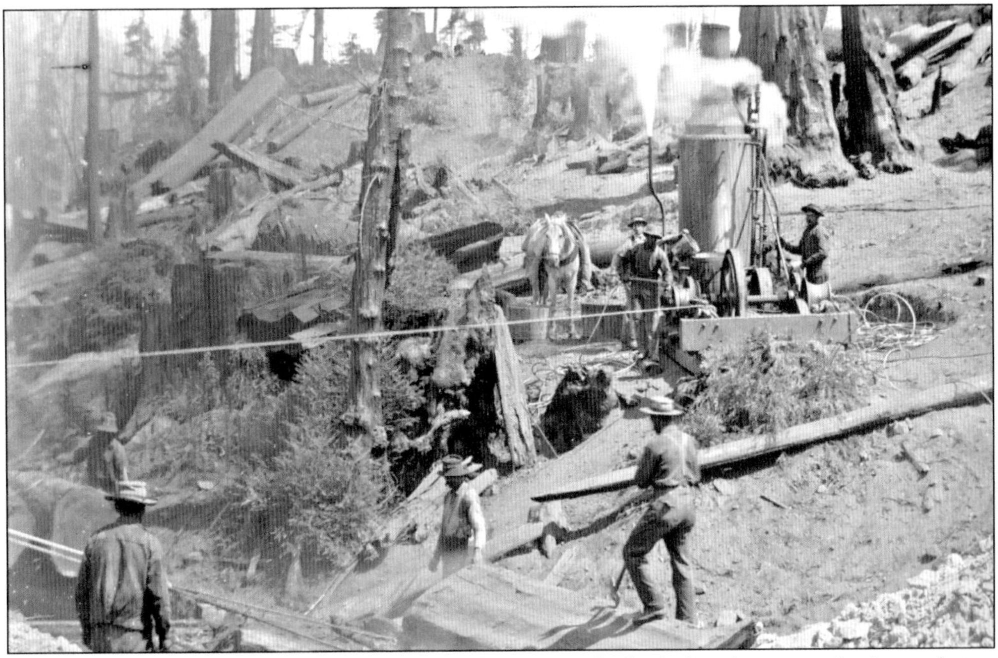

In this early-19th-century photograph, more logging with the help of a steam donkey is being conducted near the river. At first, rope was used for winching the logs, but it was realized that cables were better. After the easy trees along the river were logged, woodsmen had to venture farther and farther into the woods into more and more inaccessible ground.

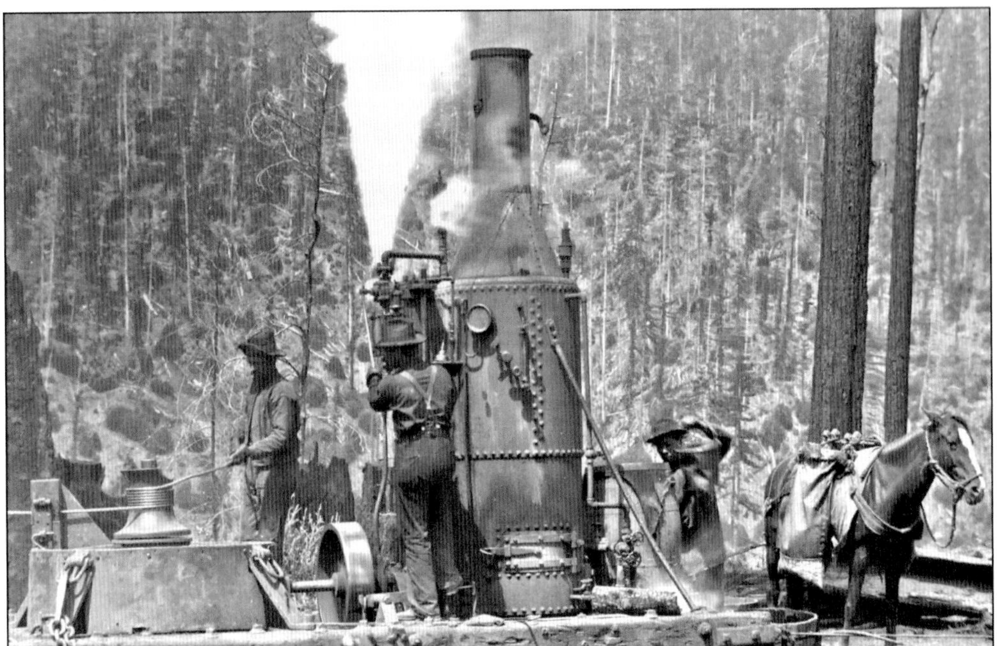

This steam donkey is set in place by the Gualala River. The spool tender is winding the cable on the capstan, which is mounted on a block for stability. The engineer is managing the boiler engine. Keeping the fire going kept the logger busy. A horse was always kept close by, as it carried water for the boiler. Notice the water bag on the side of the horse.

This is another close-up view of the steam donkey. Firewood to feed the boiler is stacked up, ready to burn. A large spool of cable is visible. It took great lengths of cable sometimes to get the logs where they needed to go. This steam donkey setup appears to be well established due to the large piles of firewood stacked up almost like a shelter.

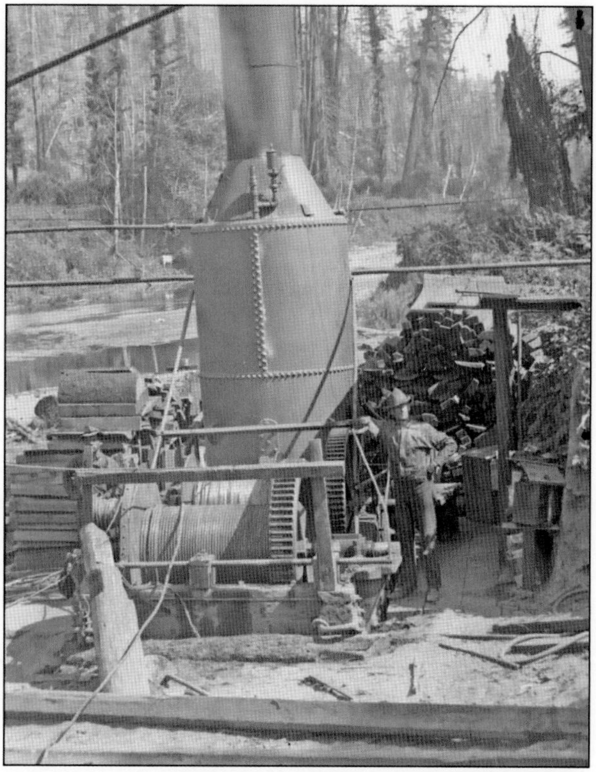

Large logs, cut into segments, are cabled. The Gualala River is seen in the background. To get the logs out of the woods, they had to be either floated down the river or hauled out by teams of oxen on skid roads. In the dry season, logs were piled in the riverbed. Then when the river rose with the rain, a freshet (rush of water) would drive the logs downstream.

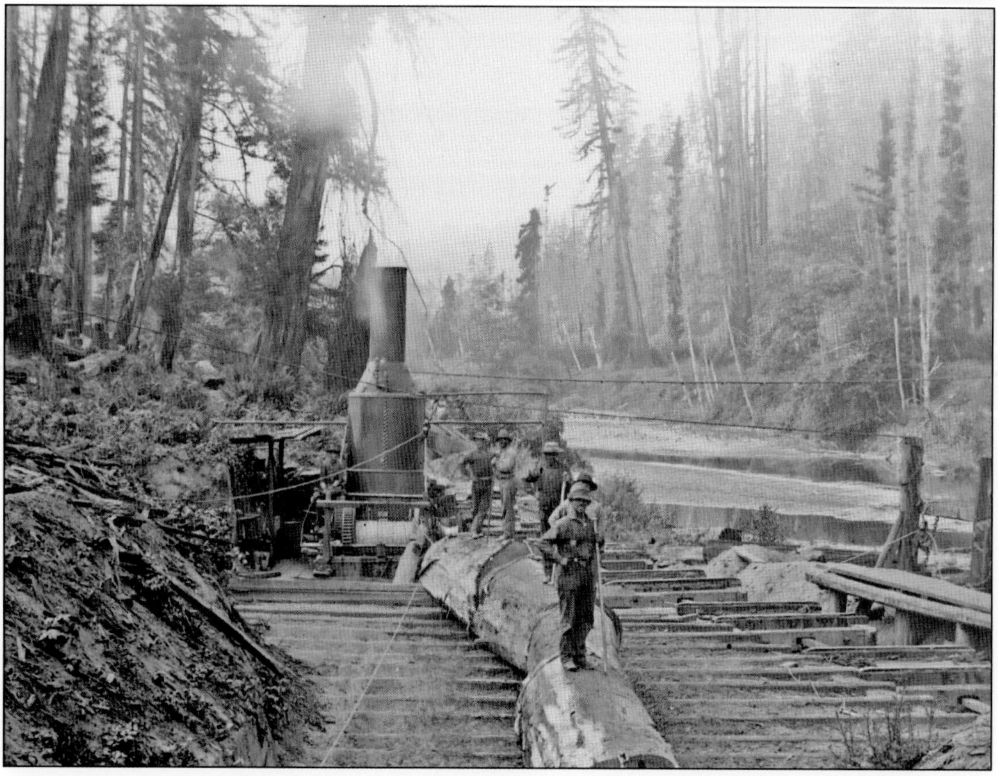

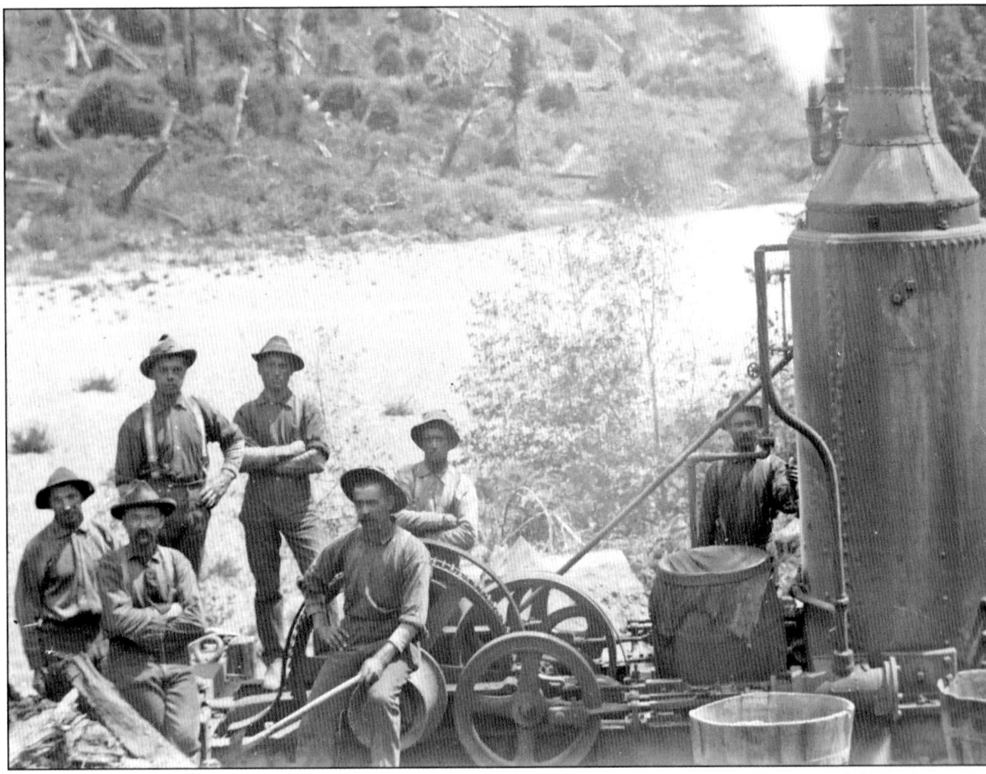

These loggers stand posing for the photograph. One man has on a tie and is most likely from the mill. To work in the woods, men came from all over and traveled with the logging crew. Logging camps were set up all over the backwoods of the Gualala River area.

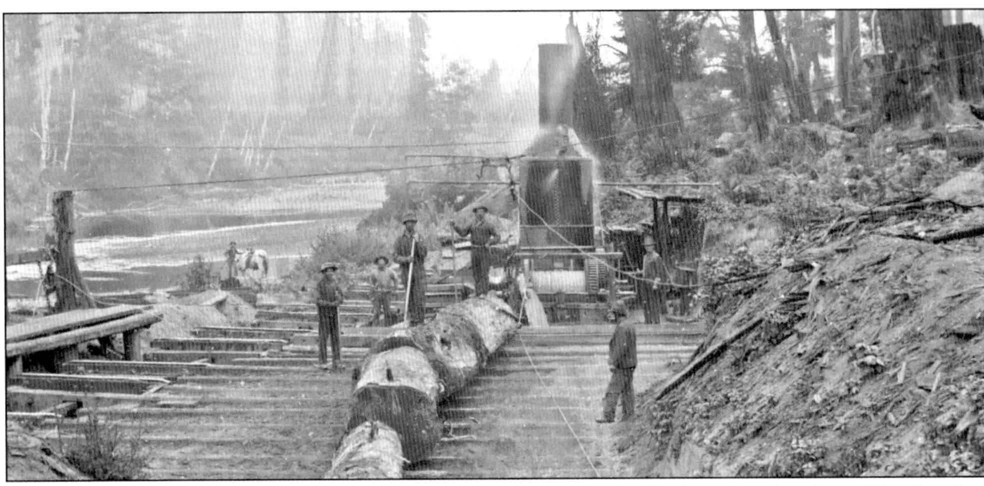

This photograph shows the steam donkey and winch moving the logs on a landing. The landing was a key point on the river. Because the Gualala River is fed by so many tributary creeks, loggers ventured up each one seeking more timber. Logging areas and camps were named after these areas, such as Rockpile and Switchville (where the river splits), all the way to Valley Crossing.

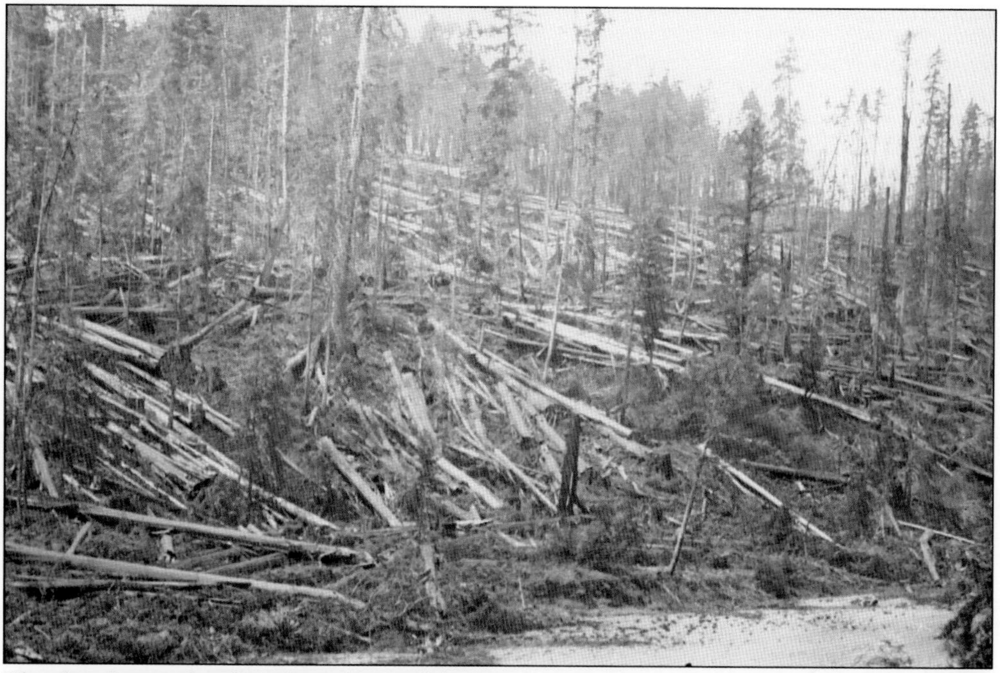

The abundance of timber along the Gualala River was immense. George Batt, in a 1914 column for the *Point Arena Record* wrote, "Let me take you up the North Fork and show you the millions upon millions of feet of the finest timber . . . Follow me for more than twenty-five miles up the main river called on the map 'the Wheatfield' and there we find over a billion feet. . . . Then we go up the Buckeye . . . then there is Rockpile, the South Fork . . . all with abundance of timber to last for years and years."

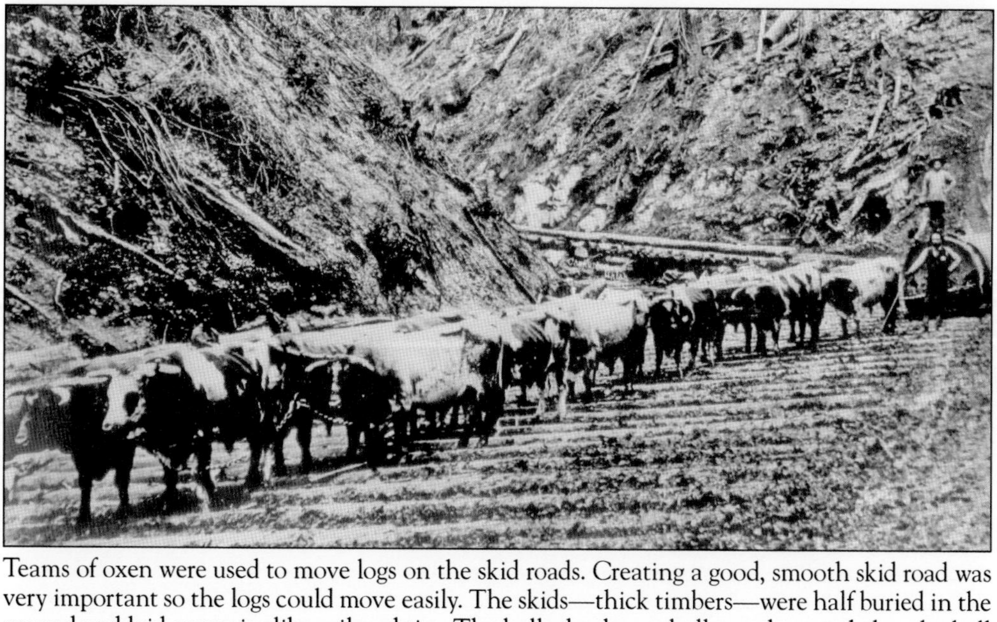

Teams of oxen were used to move logs on the skid roads. Creating a good, smooth skid road was very important so the logs could move easily. The skids—thick timbers—were half buried in the ground and laid crosswise like railroad ties. The bull whacker or bull puncher tended to the bull teams. The skid greaser made sure the skid road was slick enough. It was important for the skid road to have the proper grade for the oxen—not too steep or too long.

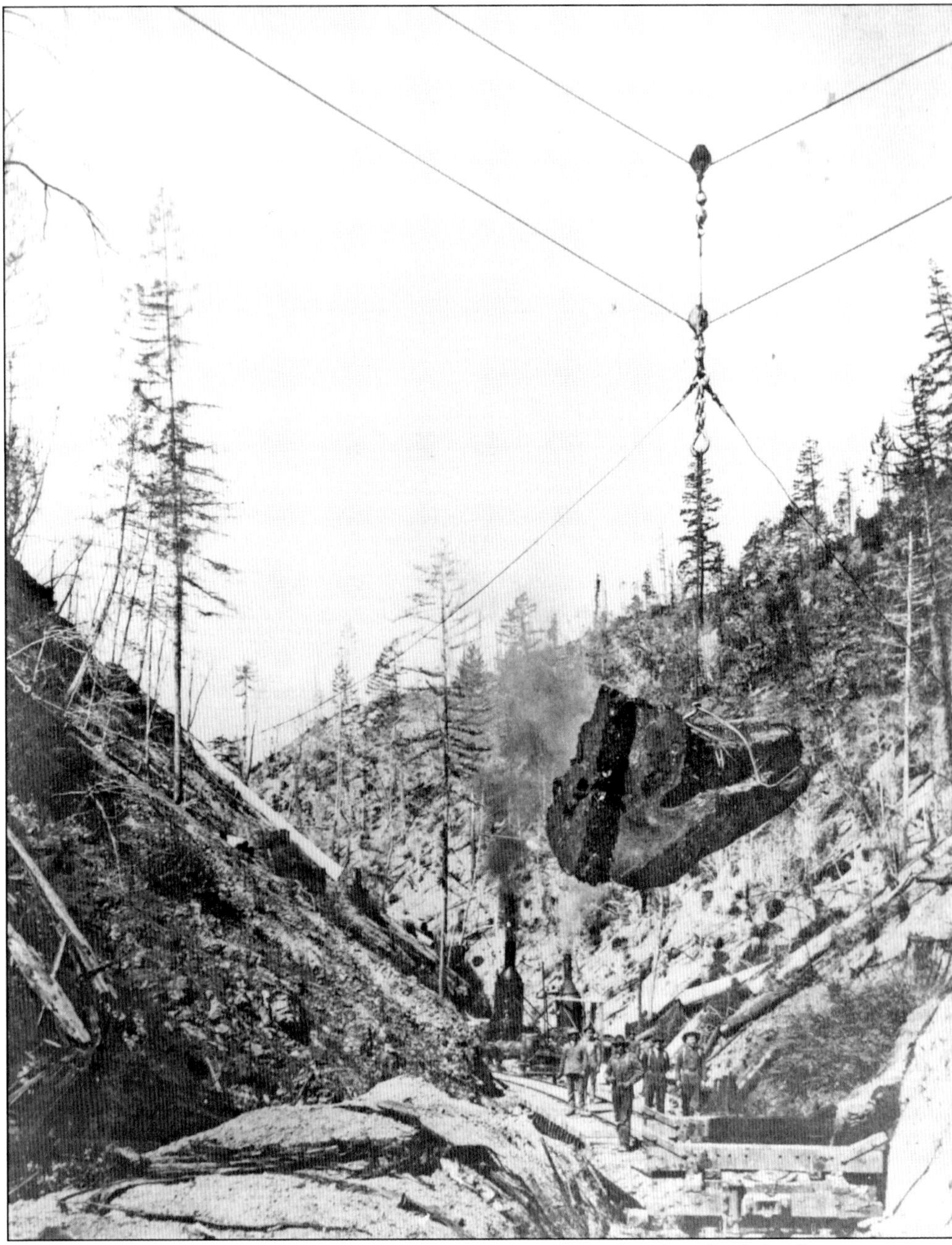

This photograph shows a large log being loaded onto the railcar by a high lead. In some cases, several lengths of cables had to be used, along with blocks, to move logs of this size. As seen in the photograph, the hillsides have been extensively logged. Since many of the early loggers in this area came from the East, the size of the coast redwood trees often became a perplexing problem. They were not used to trees of this size. The coast redwood can grow up to an inch in diameter each year as well as 2 feet in height.

Three

The Mills and Railway

The Gualala Mill was the closest transport spot for much of the timber near the Gualala River and surrounding area. To get logs more easily to the mill, the Gualala Mill Company built the railway in 1872. It ran from the woods to the mill, then north 4 miles to Bourne's Landing, which was the shipping point out to sea. Engine No. 4 is loaded with huge logs, having pulled into the Gualala Mill.

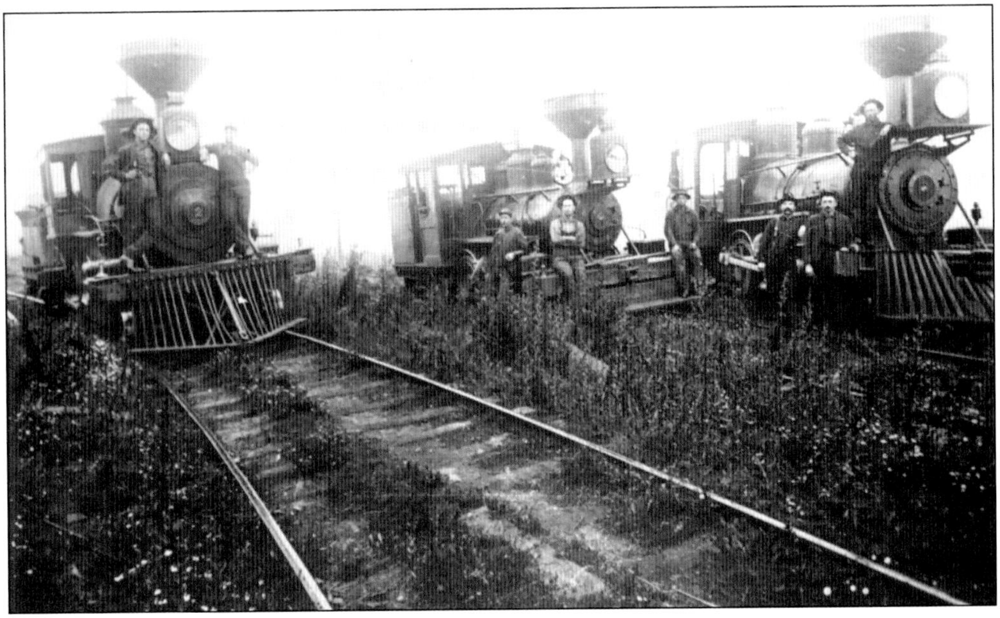

Unusually wide-gauge tracks were used for the railway. This was mainly because of the existing track laid for the skid roads. Because the track was so wide, special engines had to be built. The railway first had 5 miles of tracks in 1889, then increased the track to 10 miles in 1891, and gradually extended to 15 miles in 1901. The railroad was not in operation from 1907 to 1911. From 1912 to 1921, it was operational off-and-on and the track was extended again. After the Heywoods sold the Gualala Mill Company, the railway operated until 1922. It was abandoned and scrapped in approximately 1942. (Below, courtesy of Arline Hamilton.)

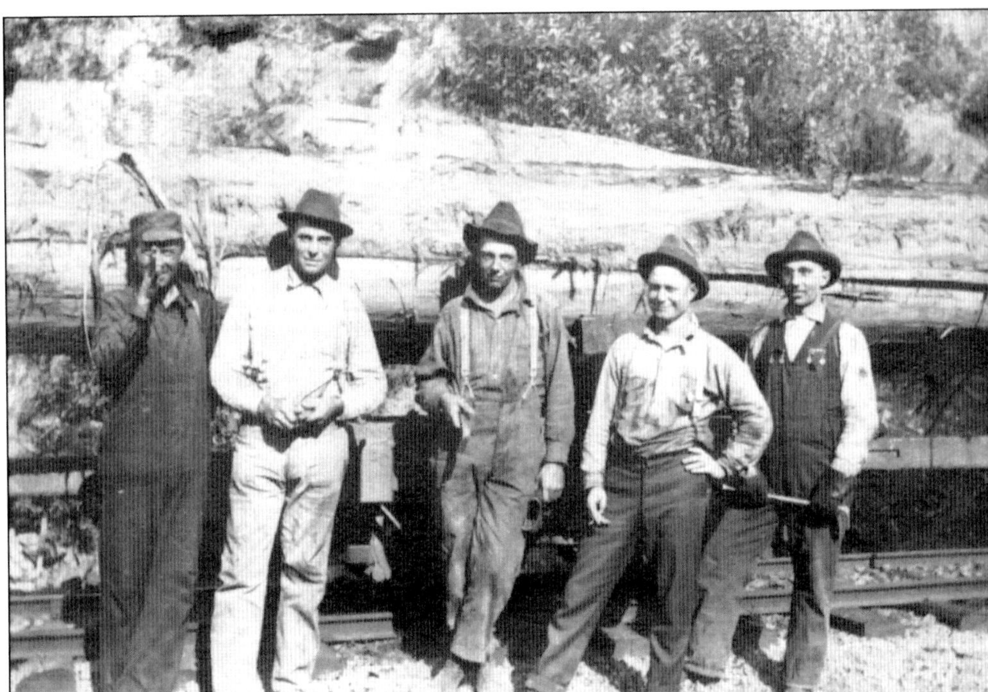

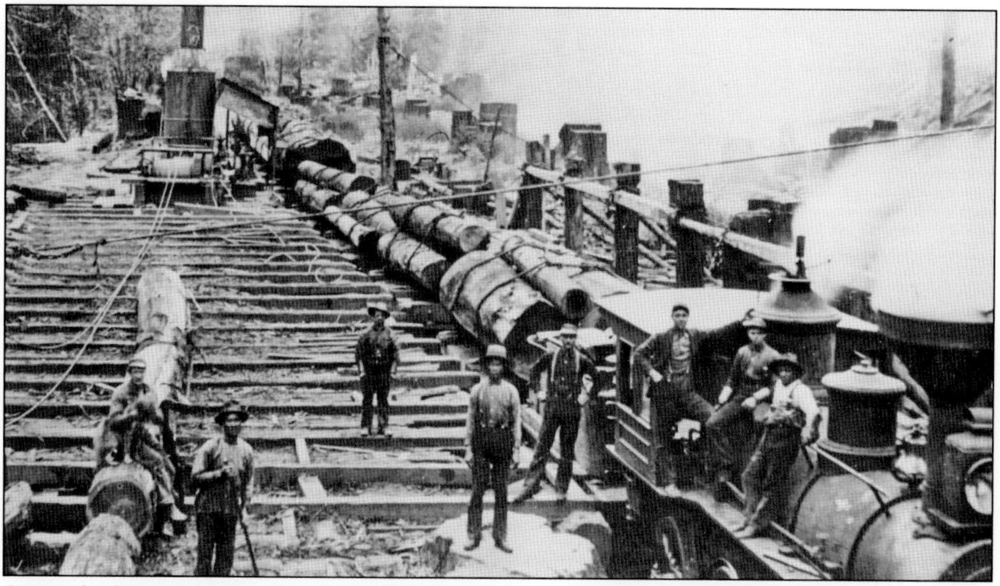

Steam donkeys also assisted with loading the logs onto the trains. In this photograph, the timber is set crosswise on the loading area. Logs are roped together to keep them steady. The first two engines of the Gualala railway were built in San Francisco. No. 1 was called "W. B. Heywood" and No. 2 was called "S. H. Harmon" after the mill owners.

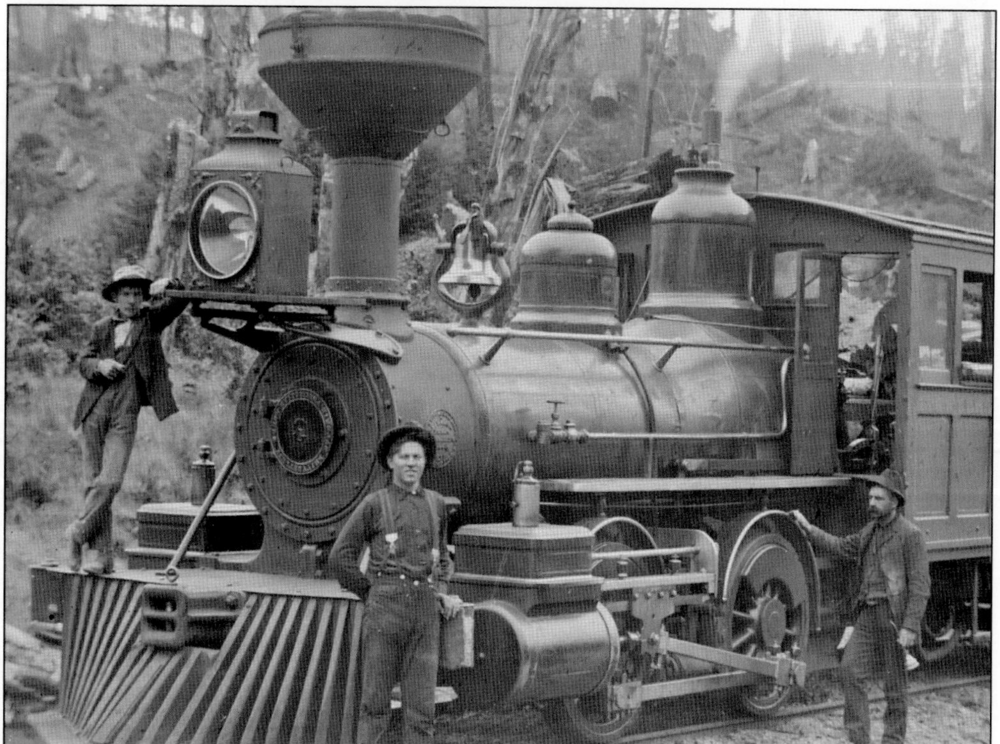

Gualala Mill Company Engine No. 3 was an engine built by the Baldwin Company. This engine was added in the late 1800s. A roundhouse was constructed at Mill Bend to house the engines. Engine No. 1 was retired in 1908 and Engine No. 2 was retired in 1912.

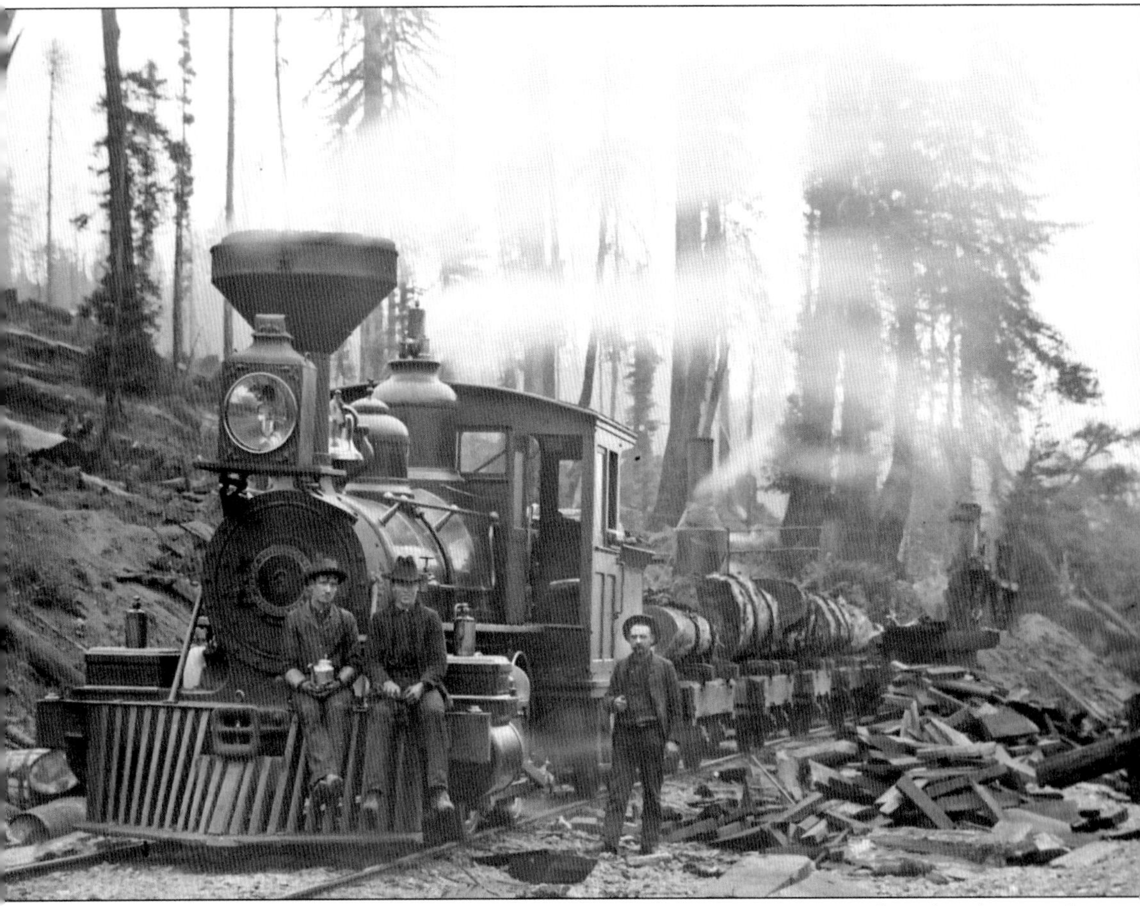

Gualala Mill Railway Engine No. 3 was added as logging momentum increased. In this photograph, the wide tracks are clearly visible. The Gualala railway did not operate at night, so the engineer would often remove the headlight.

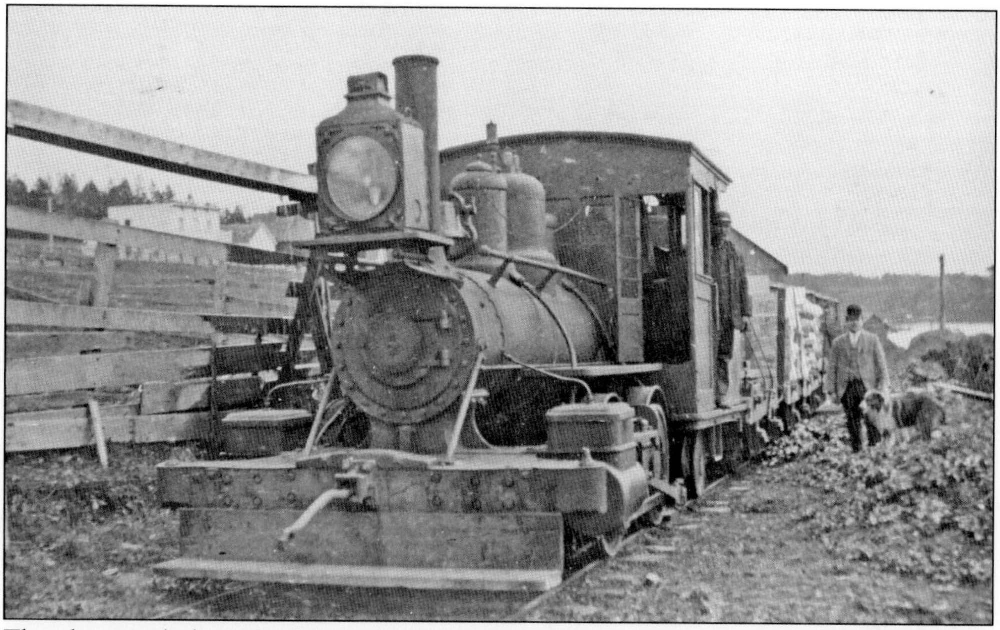

This photograph shows Gualala Mill Railway Engine No. 1 with the engineer. The railway sped up the logging process. In addition to the four engines, the railway also had 32 logging flatcars and a bicycle with an outrigger that the trackwalker used to inspect the rails.

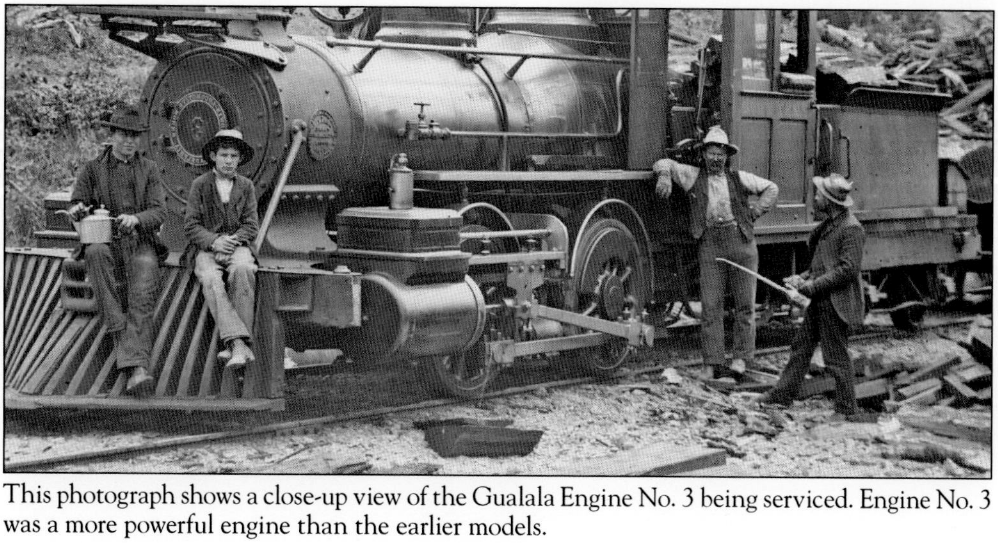

This photograph shows a close-up view of the Gualala Engine No. 3 being serviced. Engine No. 3 was a more powerful engine than the earlier models.

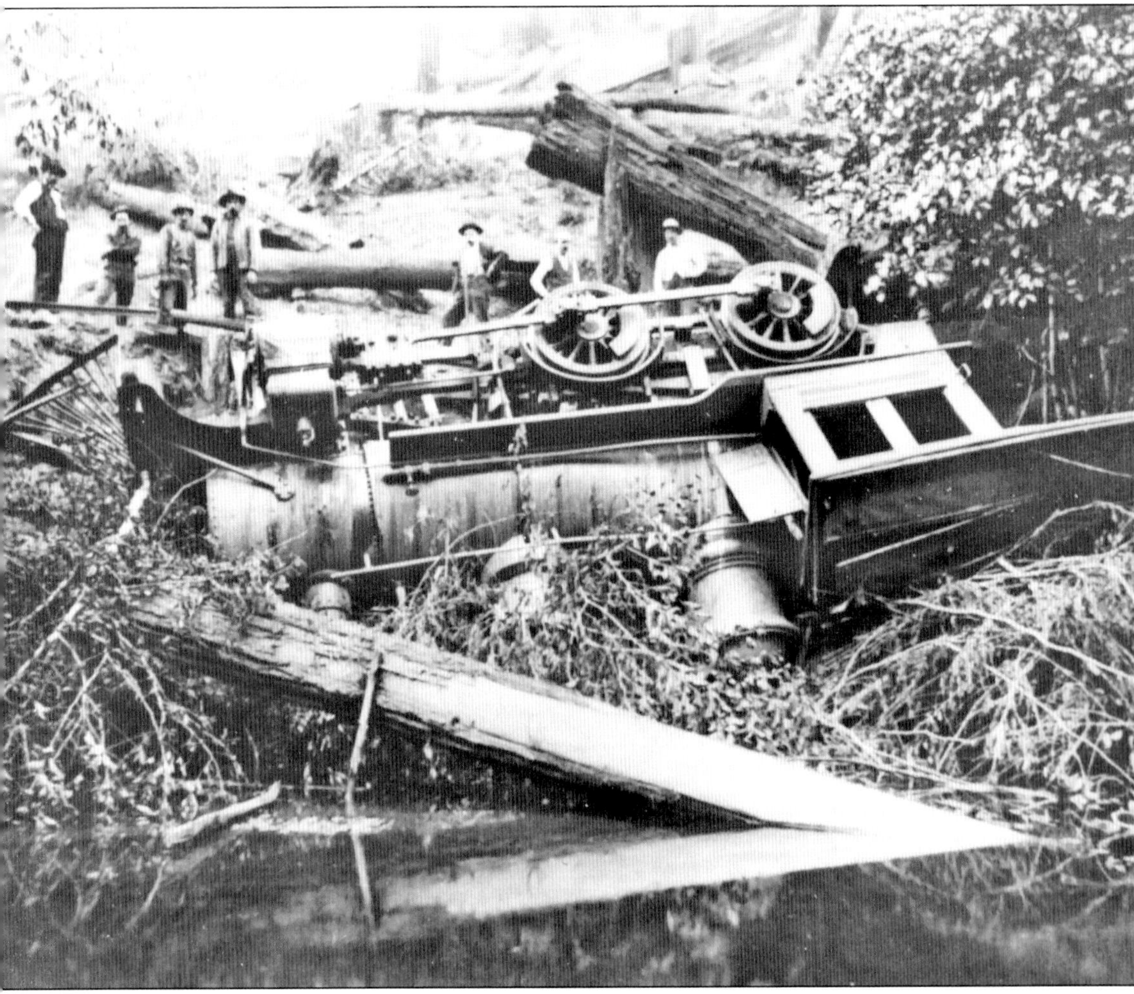

Gualala Mill Company Engine No. 2 wrecked near Rockpile Creek in 1900. The *Point Arena Record* from April 6, 1900, reported, "A train on the Gualala railroad yesterday jumped the track at Rockpile. From the meager particulars at hand we learn that one of the trainmen was badly shaken up if not seriously injured."

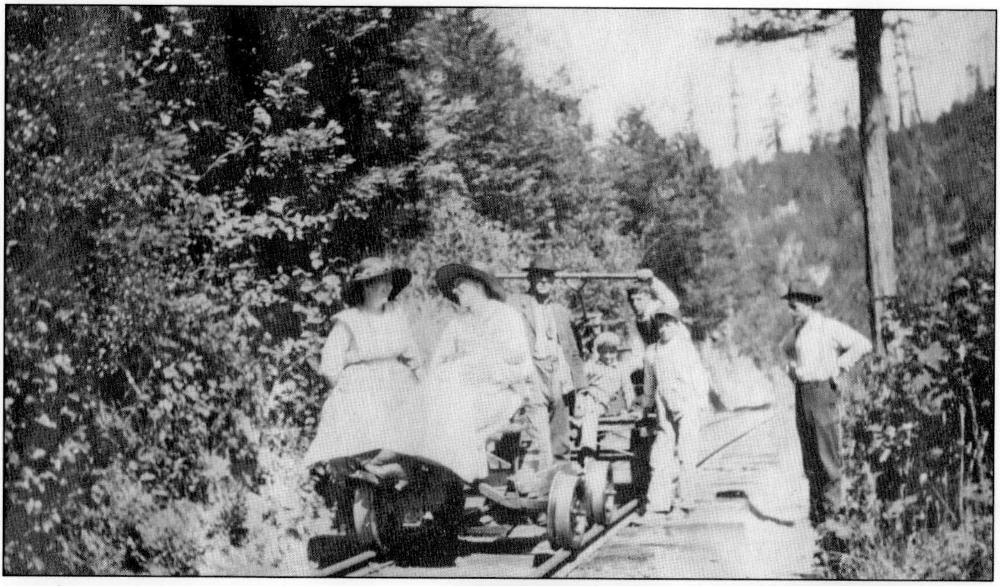

Handcars were constructed to travel on the railway by the use of human pumping power. They were used occasionally to transport people for fun. In order to get to some remote picnicking areas, the handcar made travel easier. (Courtesy of William McMillen Kramer.)

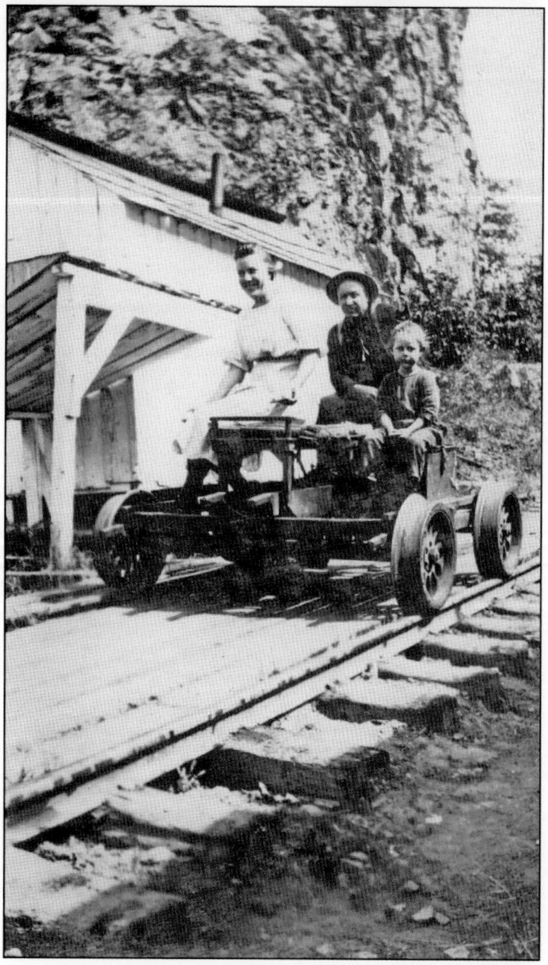

Shown in the photograph is a railway "speeder" transporting two logging camp employees and Arline Hamilton (far right). Arline grew up in the Gualala area logging camps, as her father was a train engineer and woodsman. When she was only a year old, she fell off a speeder and narrowly escaped injury. (Courtesy of William McMillen Kramer.)

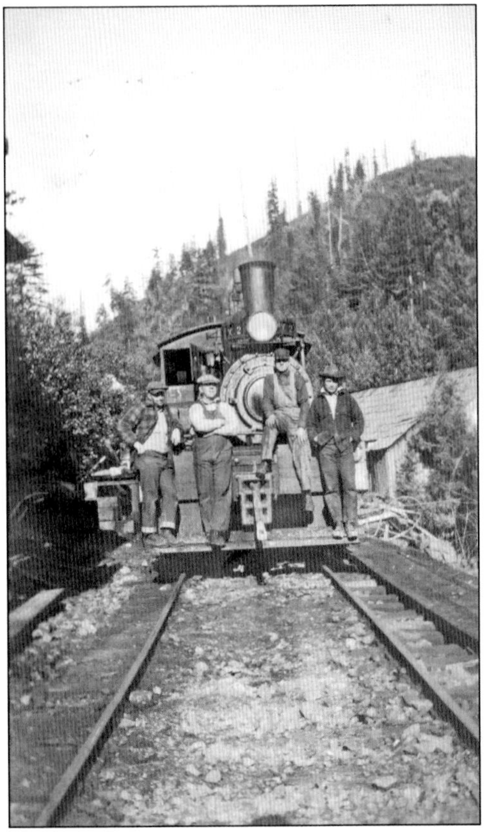

The train crew is taking a break. With the advent of the railway, timber could be accessed more easily and transported to the mill more quickly. Logged hillsides can be seen in the distance. (Courtesy of William McMillen Kramer.)

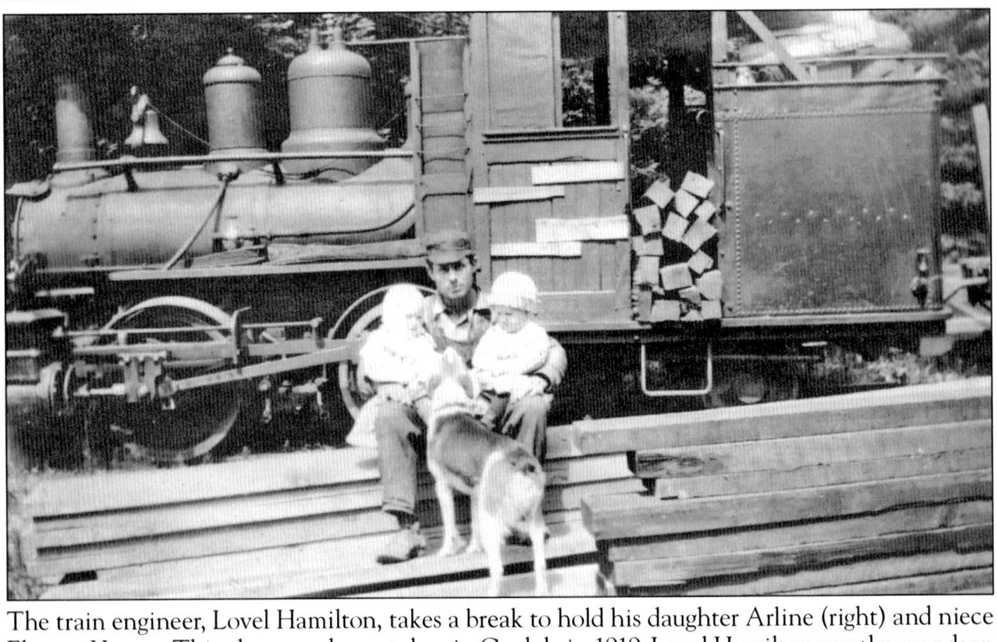

The train engineer, Lovel Hamilton, takes a break to hold his daughter Arline (right) and niece Eleanor Hunter. This photograph was taken in Gualala in 1919. Lovel Hamilton was the grandson of John Archibald Hamilton, one of the original settlers of Point Arena. (Courtesy of William McMillen Kramer.)

Pile drivers, powered by a portable steam donkey on a rail, were used to help construct the railroad bridges. Railroad bridges were sometimes washed out due to heavy rains. The steam donkey is mounted onto a railcar so it can be moved easily. This photograph was taken in the early 1900s. As documented in the *Point Arena Record*, June 23, 1905, "Work on the extension of the railroad up the north fork of the Gualala River is progressing rapidly and soon the company will be logging from that section of good timber."

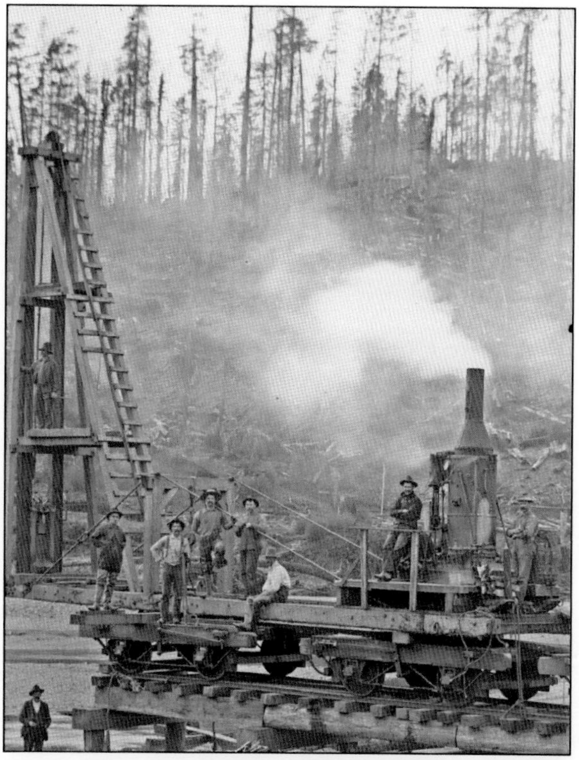

Oxen are skidding logs to the loading ramp. Although the steam donkeys took over some of the functions of the ox teams, the oxen were still used. The steam donkeys freed up the oxen for tasks that were better suited for them, and the steam donkeys were good in tight, inaccessible areas.

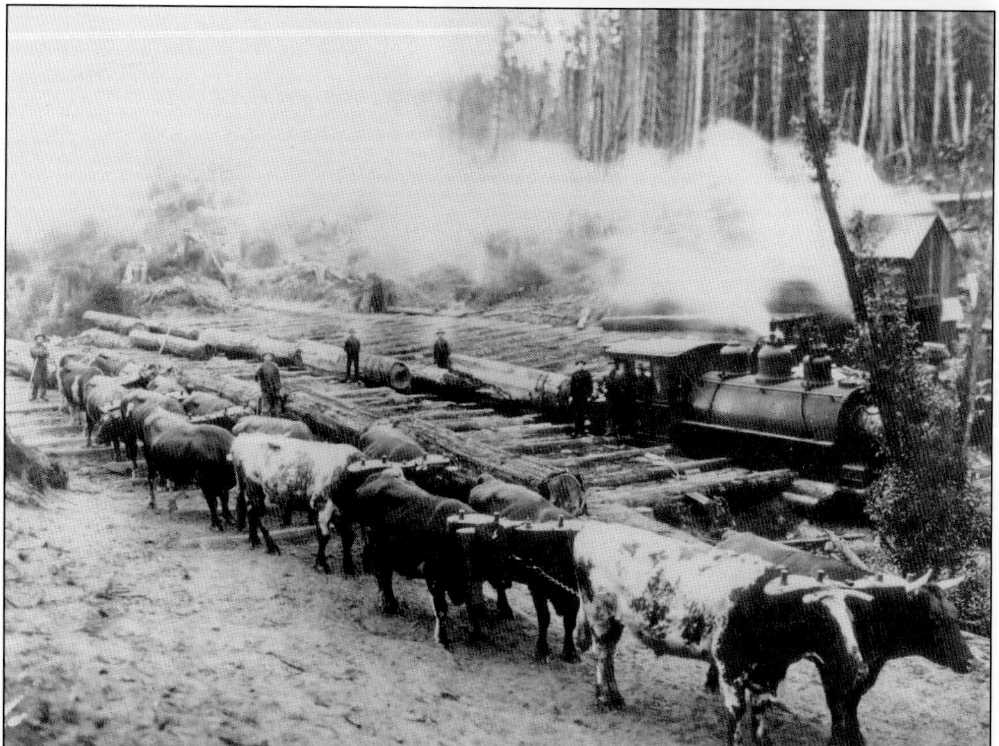

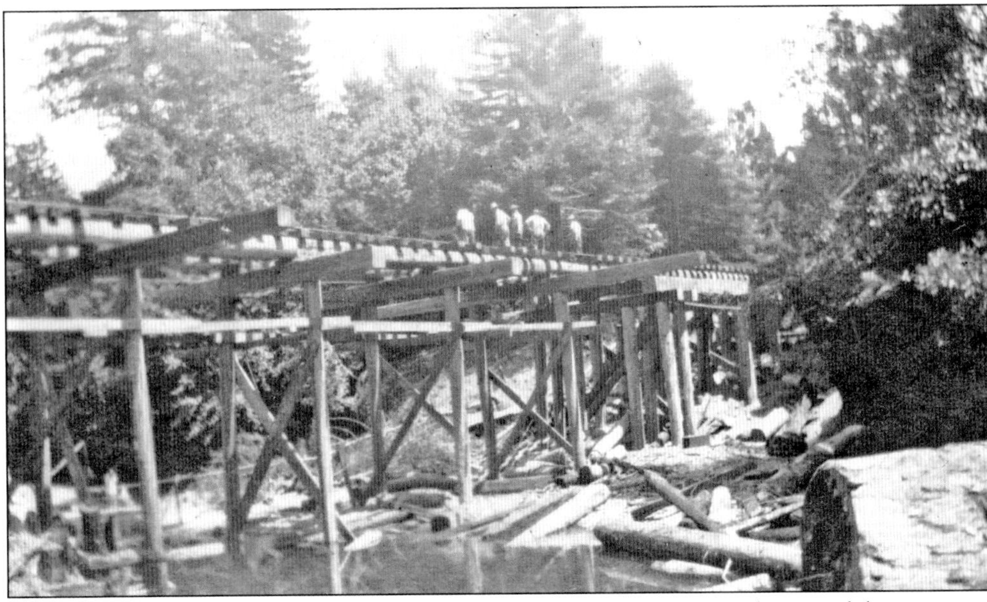

The Rockpile Creek area contained some very large trees. In 1906, a tree was harvested that measured 17 feet in diameter. To get to the trees, railroad bridges had to be constructed. This photograph shows the new railroad bridge nearing completion. (Courtesy of William McMillen Kramer.)

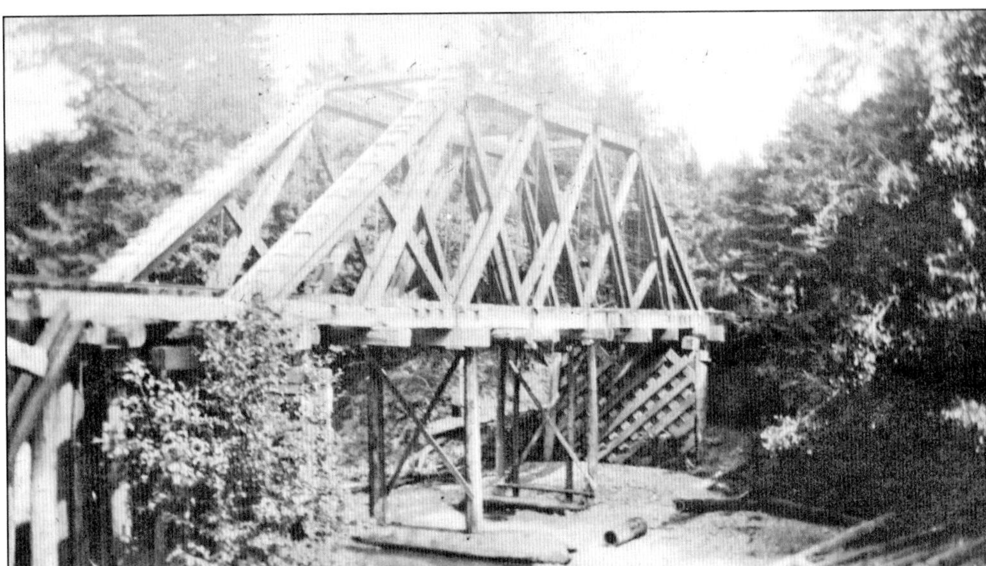

Rockpile Creek is a tributary to the South Fork of the Gualala River, stemming from the east. Timber was logged up Rockpile Creek for many miles. Eventually it became necessary for the railroad to have access to the logging efforts. (Courtesy of William McMillen Kramer.)

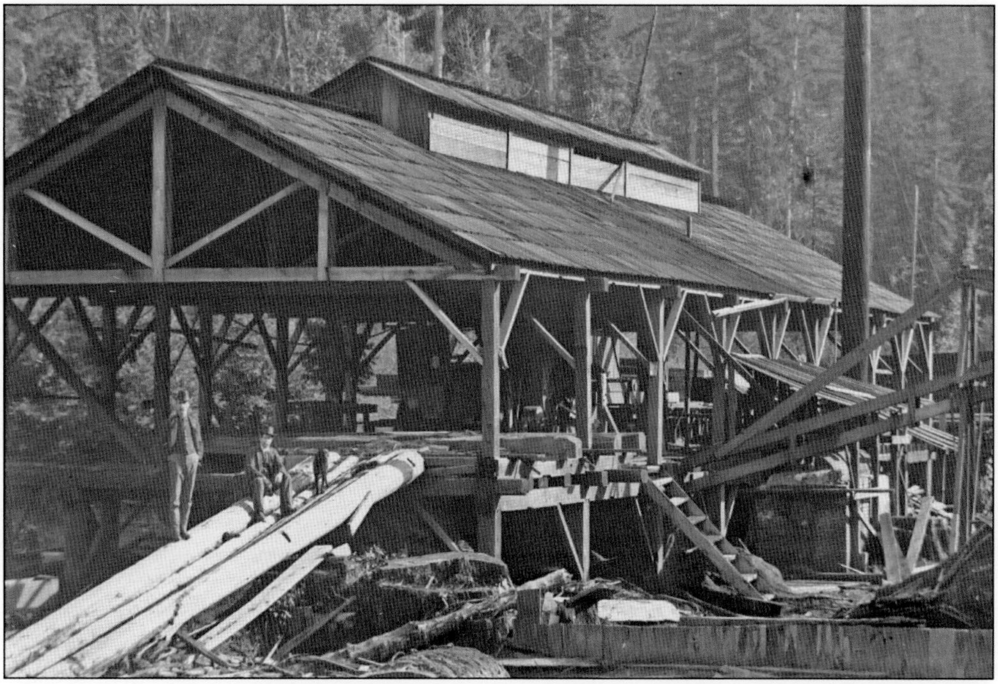

The Hickman Mill was built in 1896 by John E. Hickman. Hickman's nephew George Fiscus, who took most of the photographs in this book, began his career as a bark peeler for his uncle. The Gualala Mill burned in 1906 and for a while the Hickman Mill was the only mill between Greenwood (Elk) and Duncan's Mills. Shown below are employees of the mill.

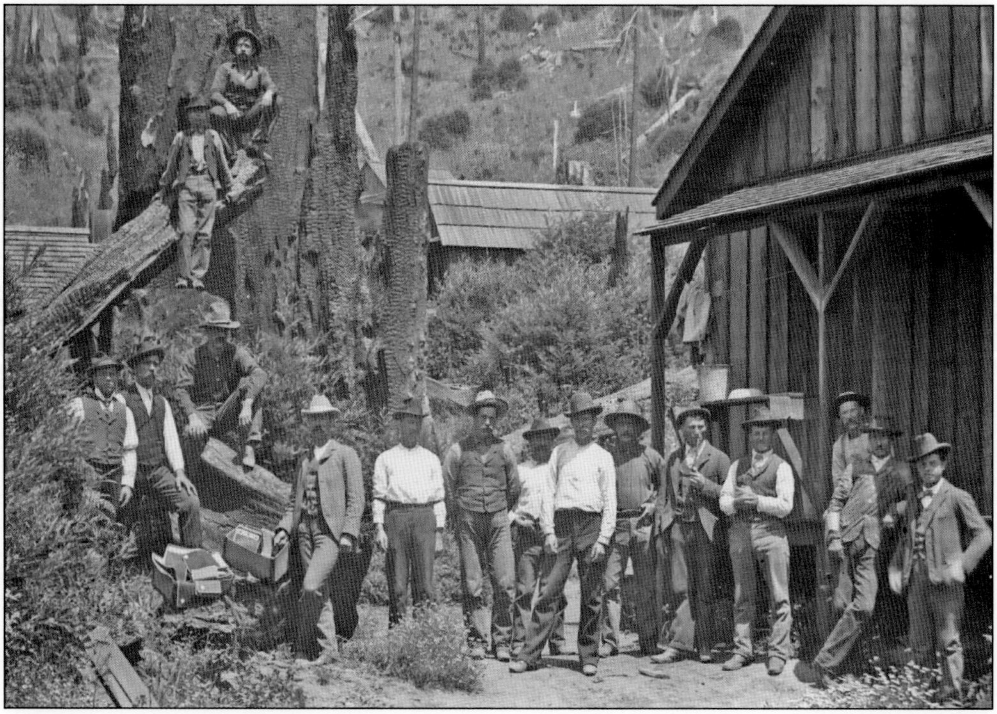

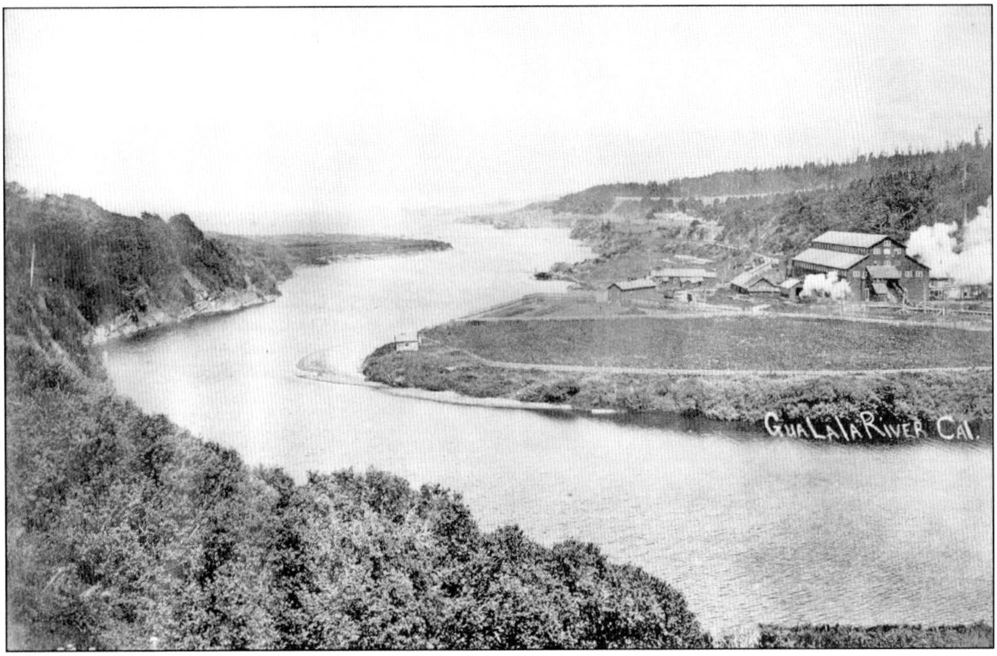

This photograph shows the river flat view of the Gualala River as it meets the ocean. The Gualala Mill is shown in the foreground. The first mill built on the Gualala River, by Rutherford and Webber, was taken over by the William Heywood and S. H. Harmon in 1872.

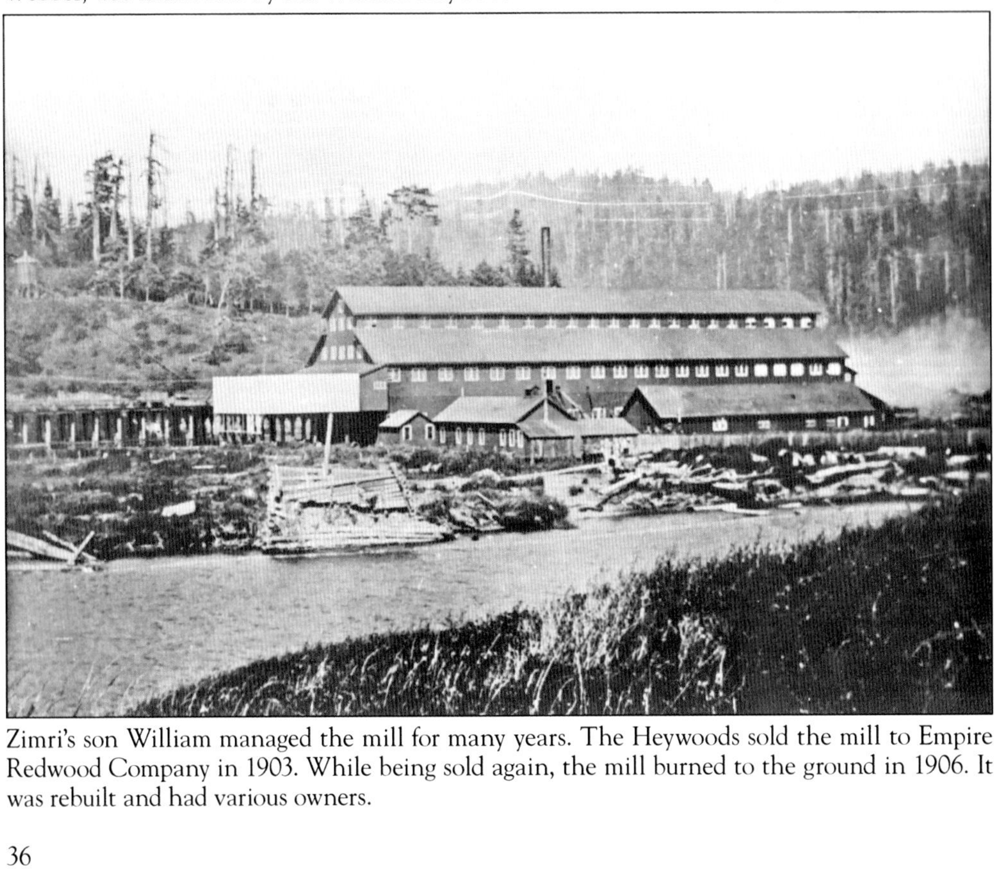

Zimri's son William managed the mill for many years. The Heywoods sold the mill to Empire Redwood Company in 1903. While being sold again, the mill burned to the ground in 1906. It was rebuilt and had various owners.

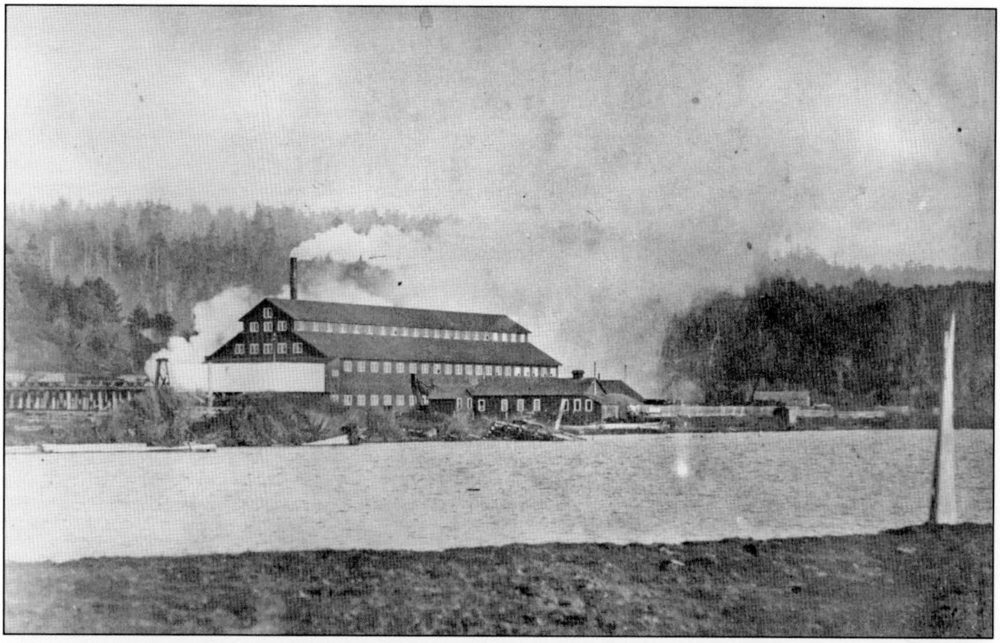

This view of the mill around 1900 is from the ferry landing. The mill had the capacity of 30,000 board feet of lumber per day.

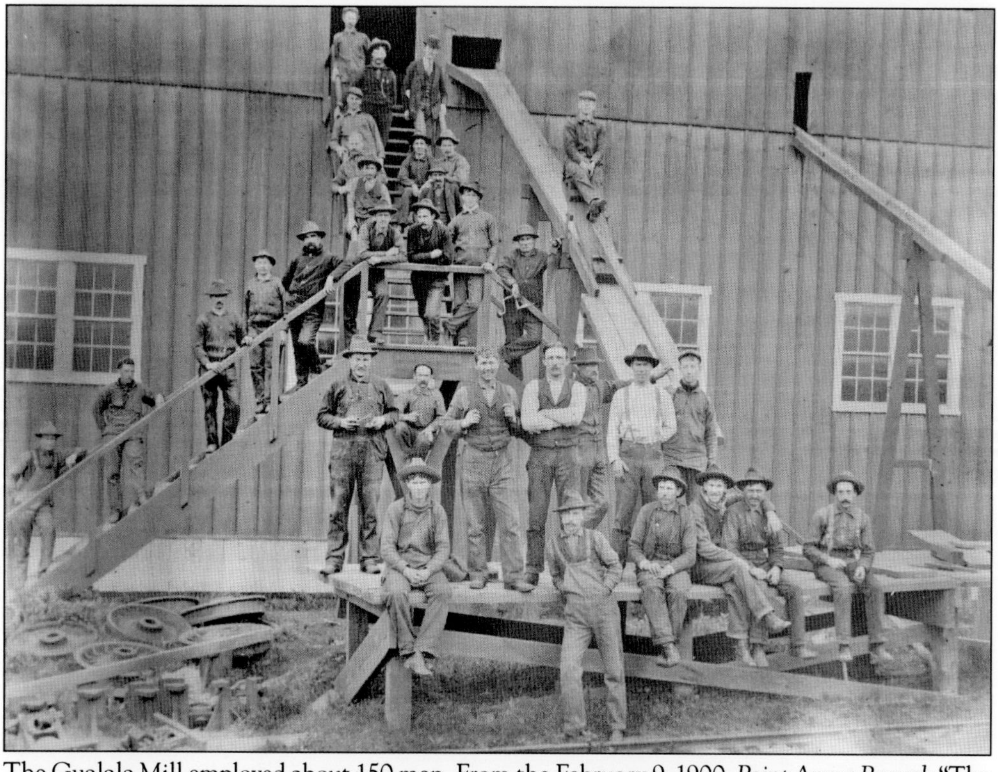

The Gualala Mill employed about 150 men. From the February 9, 1900, *Point Arena Record*: "The Gualala Mill is again running at full blast and a large number of working men are consequently made happy."

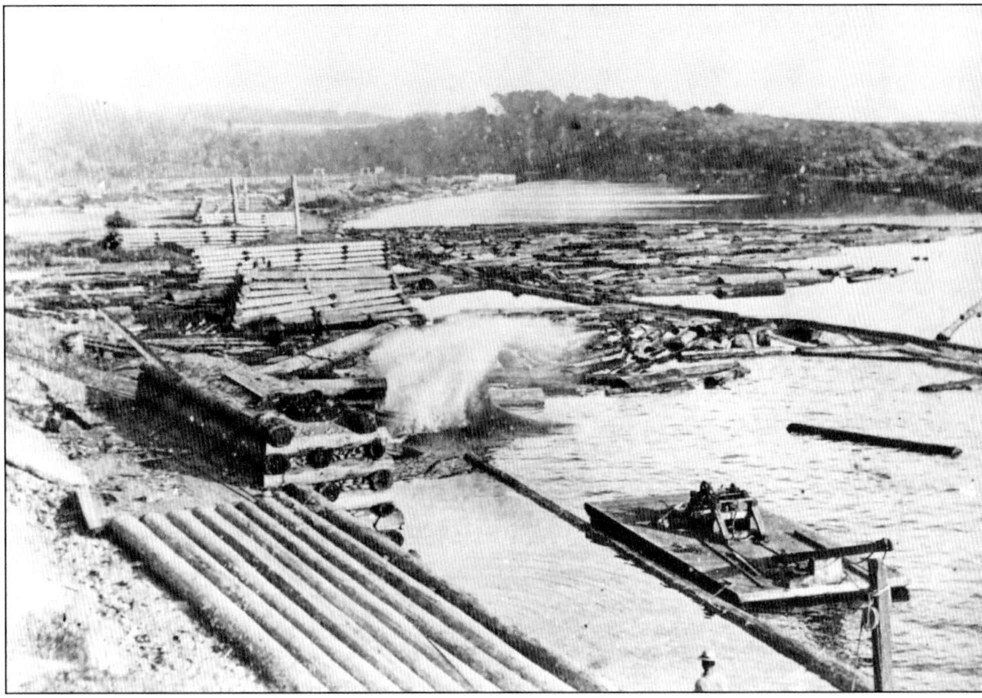

This photograph shows the Gualala Mill looking south toward Mill Bend. The log crib structures were built by the Chinese to hold the logs.

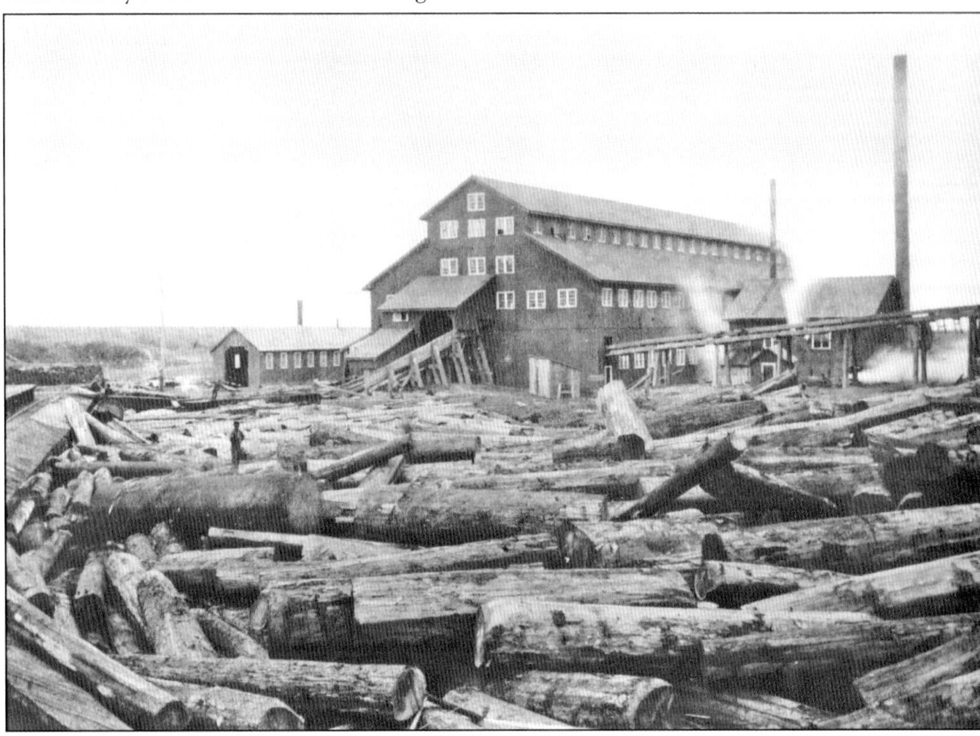

This *c.* 1900 view of the mill shows the logs ready to go. The mill burned shortly after 1906, which drastically affected the town.

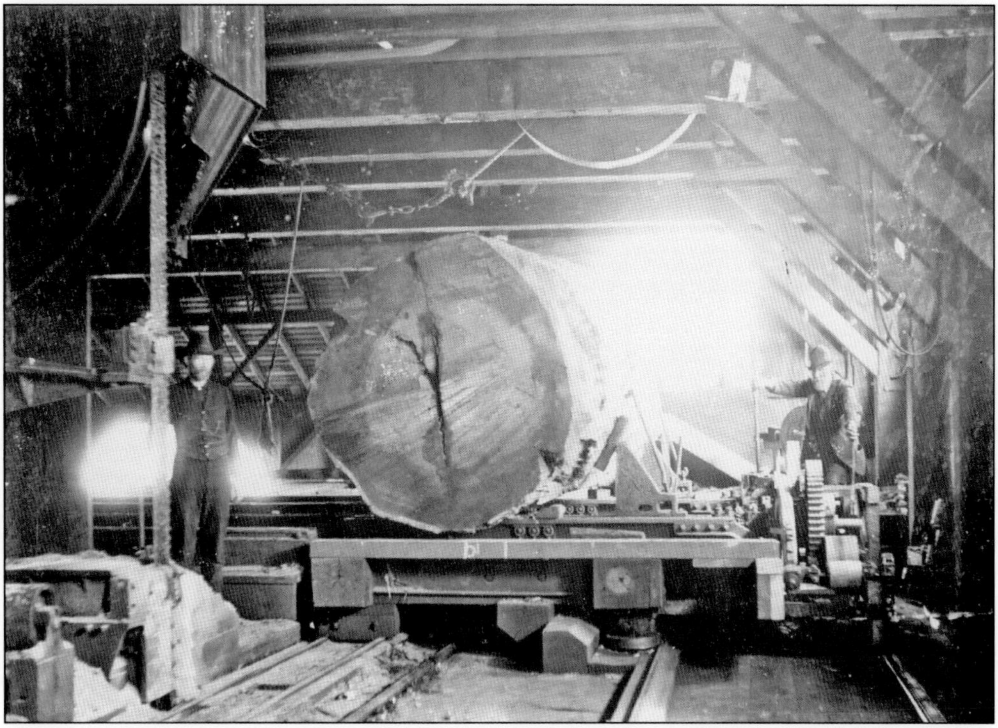

The Gualala Mill was very modern for its time and equipped with a bandsaw. This photograph is a rare view of the inside of the mill, showing the log carriage and saw. (Courtesy of Mendocino Historical Society.)

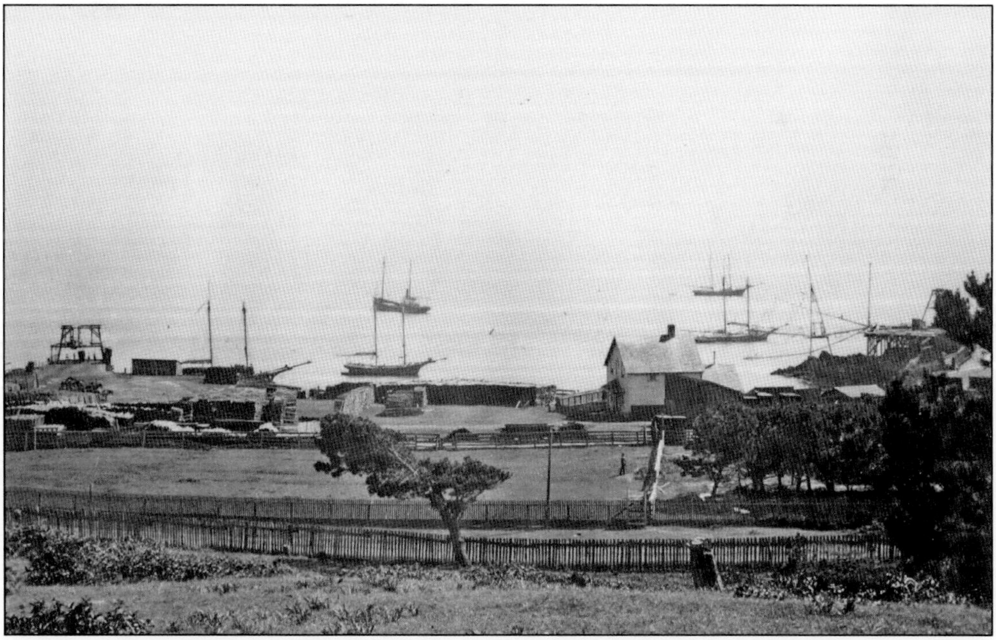

Lumber from the Gualala Mill was hauled 3 miles north to Bourn's Landing, where schooners waited. Wagons of tan oak bark and redwood ties were also loaded here. This landing was better protected than other landings. (Courtesy of Mendocino Historical Society.)

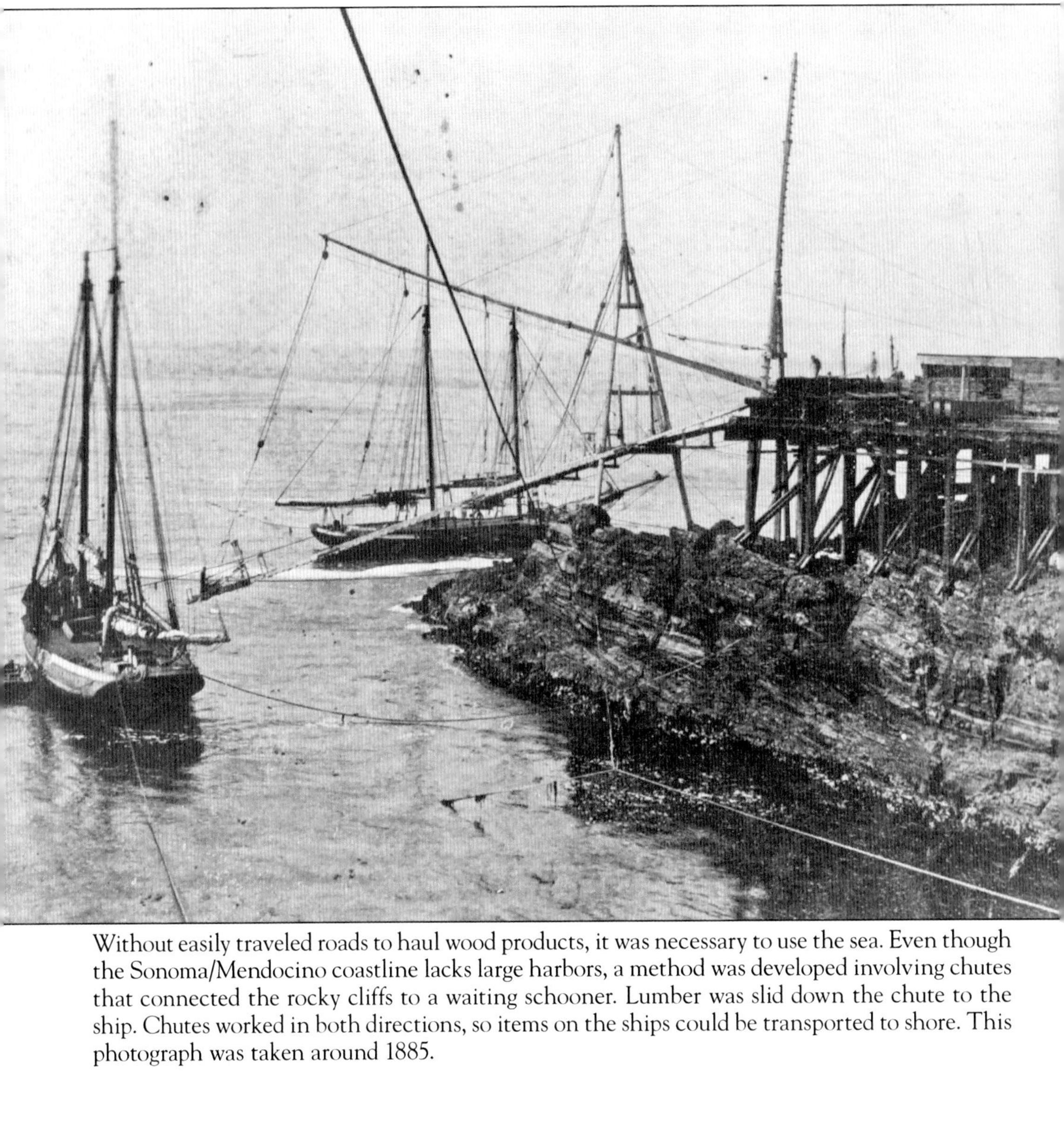

Without easily traveled roads to haul wood products, it was necessary to use the sea. Even though the Sonoma/Mendocino coastline lacks large harbors, a method was developed involving chutes that connected the rocky cliffs to a waiting schooner. Lumber was slid down the chute to the ship. Chutes worked in both directions, so items on the ships could be transported to shore. This photograph was taken around 1885.

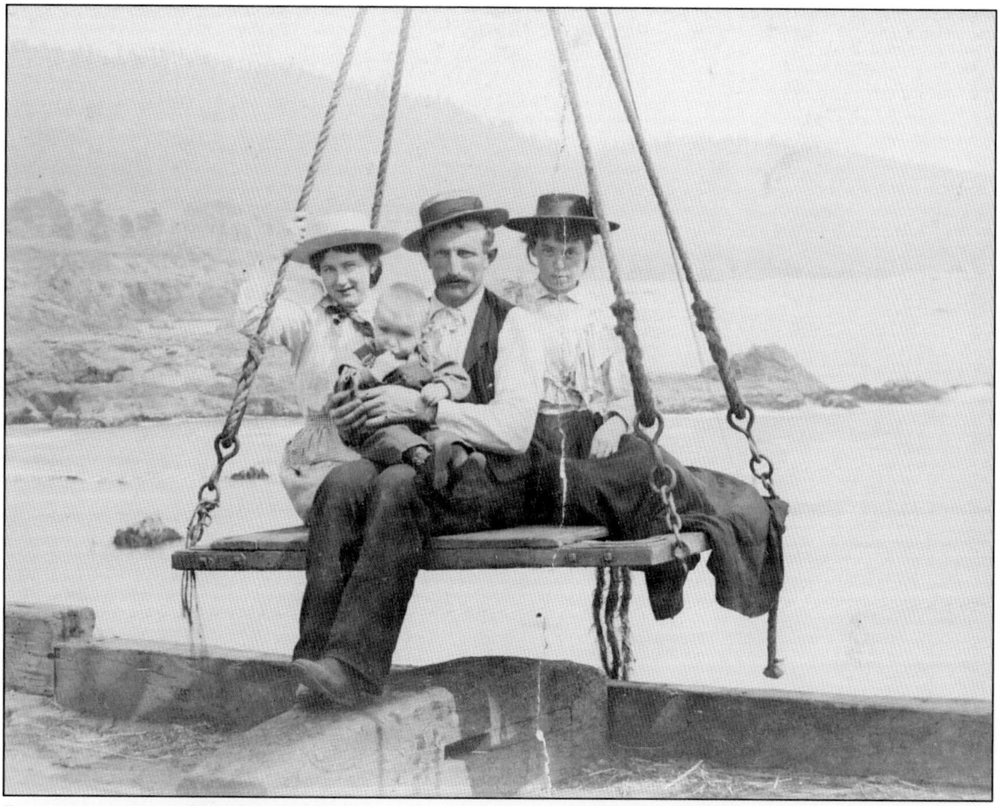

Passengers were also transported to schooners by wire chutes, called trapeze chutes. Pictured around 1900 are James and Viola Christensen with their children.

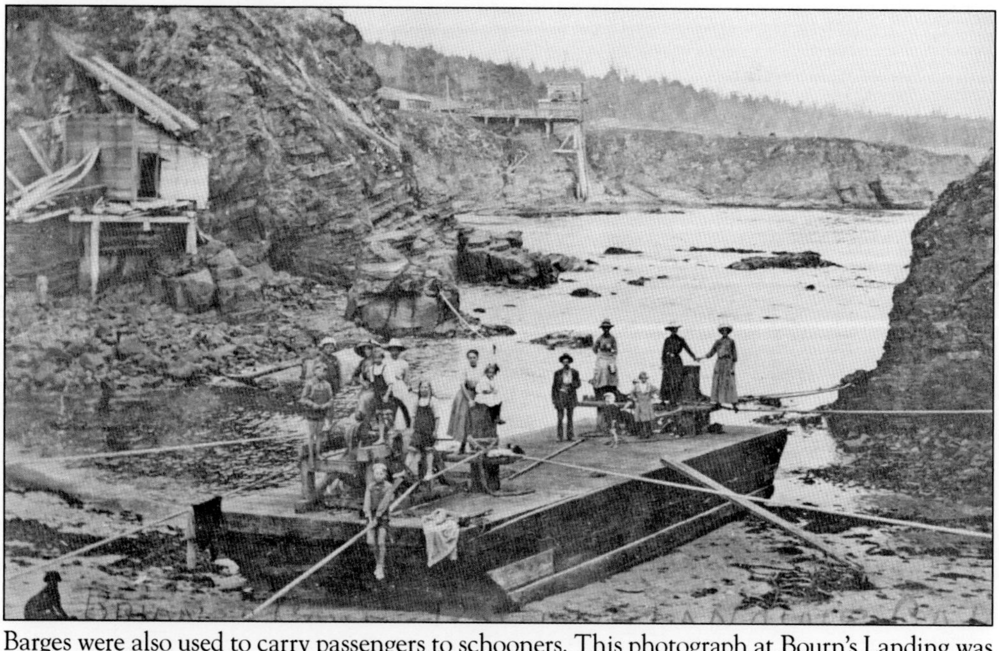

Barges were also used to carry passengers to schooners. This photograph at Bourn's Landing was taken around 1890. (Courtesy Mendocino County Historical Society.)

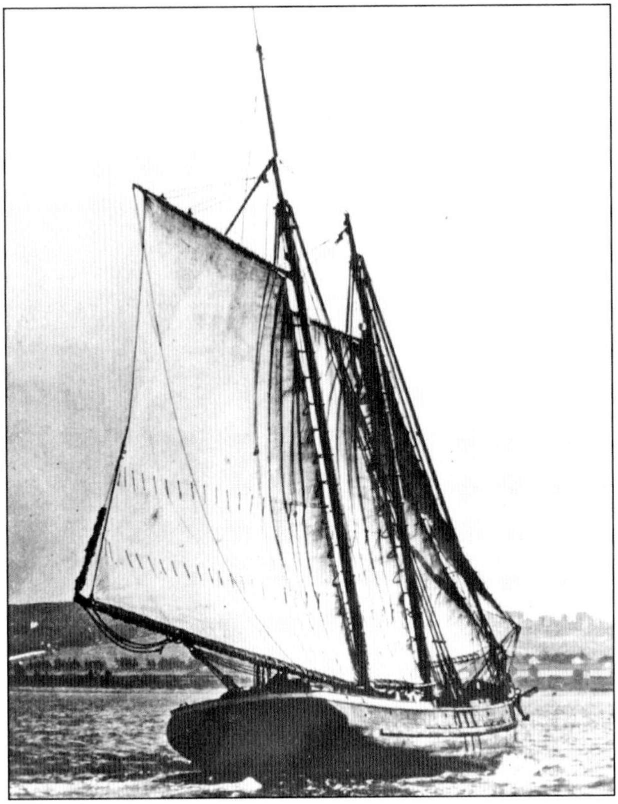

This photograph, taken by George Fiscus, is of a typical schooner in this time period. The schooners were small and able to slide into narrow openings, thus earning the nickname "dog hole" schooners—for openings so small a dog could not turn around.

This is a rare photograph of a ship being built, possibly at Black Point. Some of the schooners used in the lumber trade were made locally.

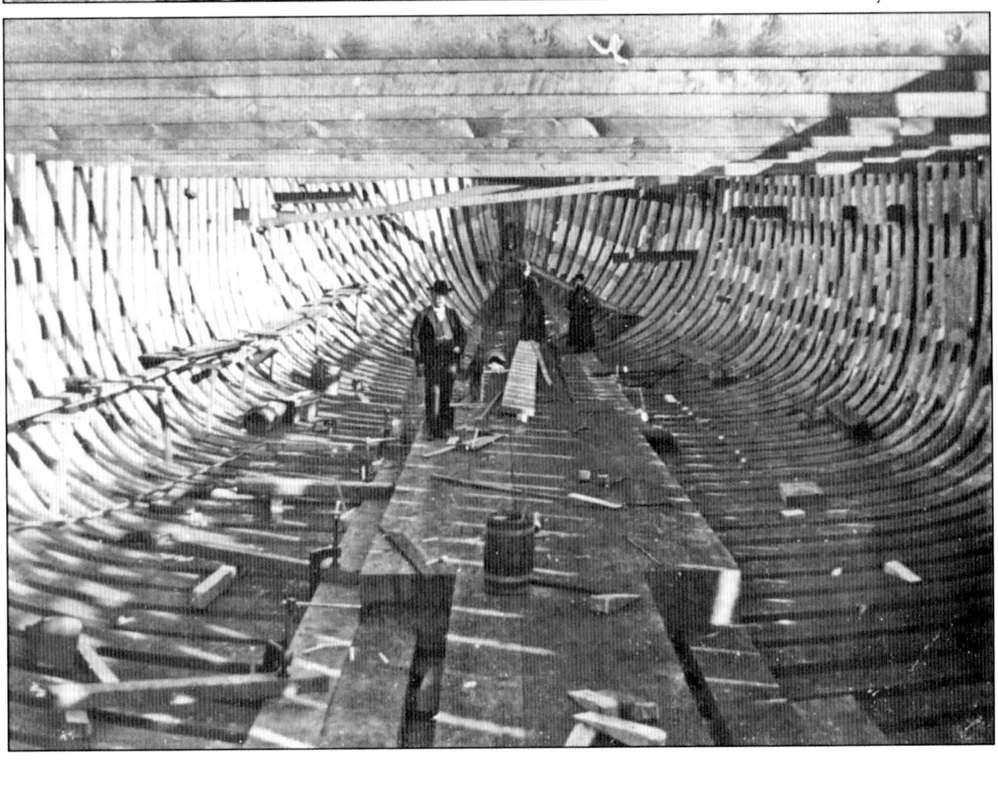

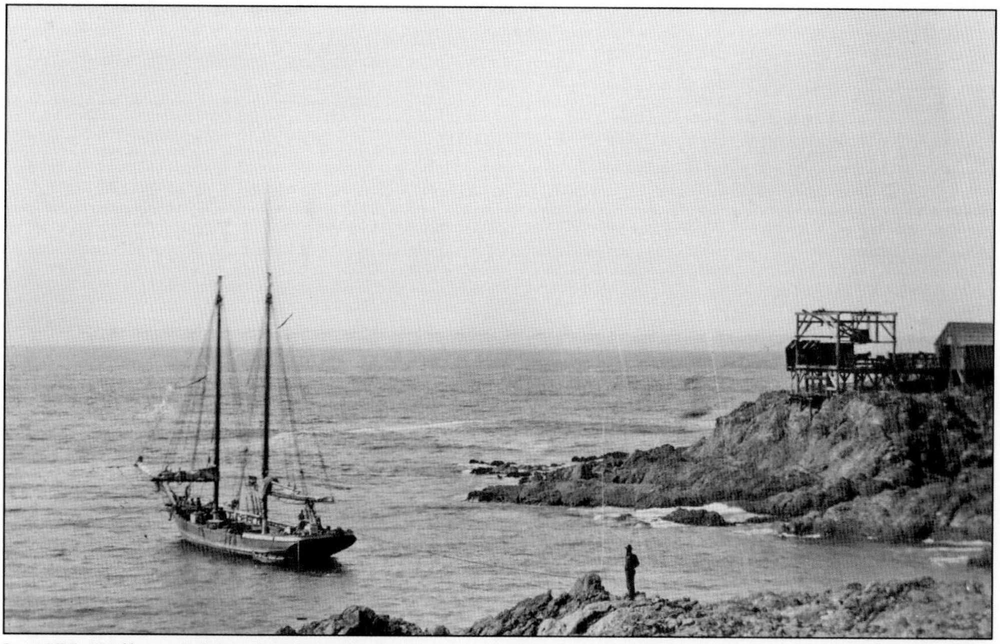

In 1875, William Bihler developed a landing and chutes at Black Point, now a part of Sea Ranch. It was a somewhat dangerous landing and only used in the summer months.

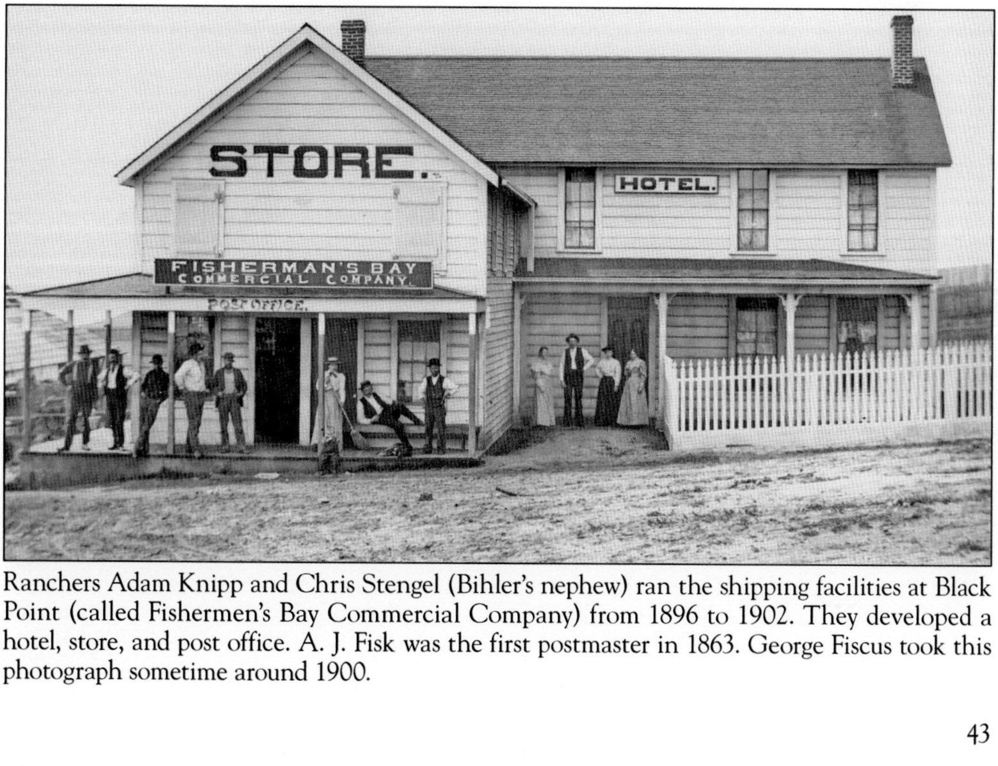

Ranchers Adam Knipp and Chris Stengel (Bihler's nephew) ran the shipping facilities at Black Point (called Fishermen's Bay Commercial Company) from 1896 to 1902. They developed a hotel, store, and post office. A. J. Fisk was the first postmaster in 1863. George Fiscus took this photograph sometime around 1900.

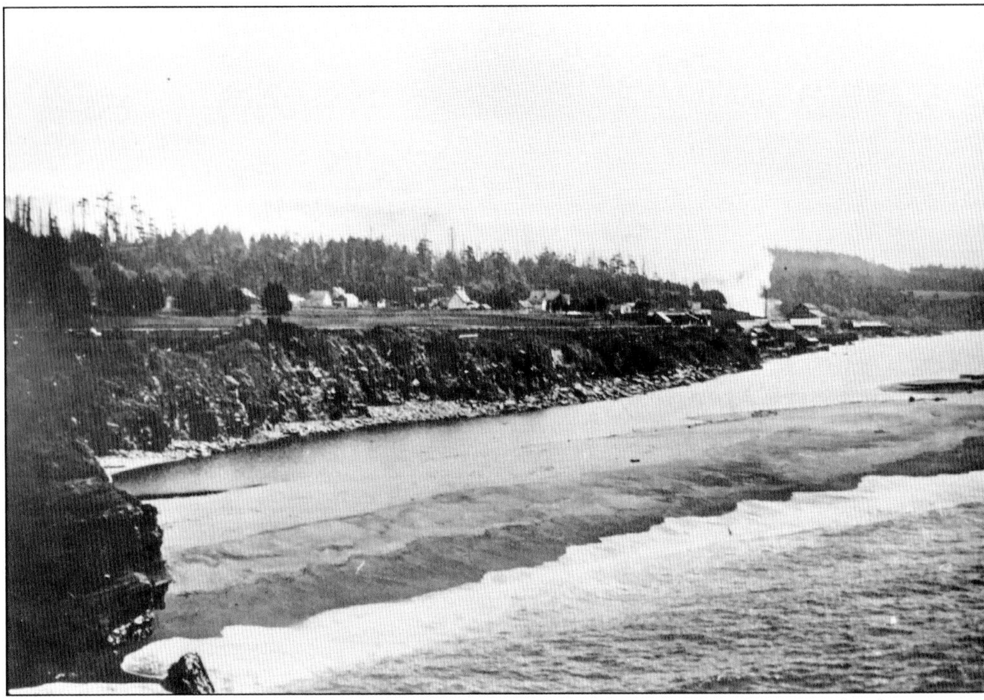

Gualala in the turn of the century looks different than today. In this photograph, the ocean is in the foreground with the estuary in the back and Gualala in the distance. The Gualala River is spilling to the south at the far right of the photograph.

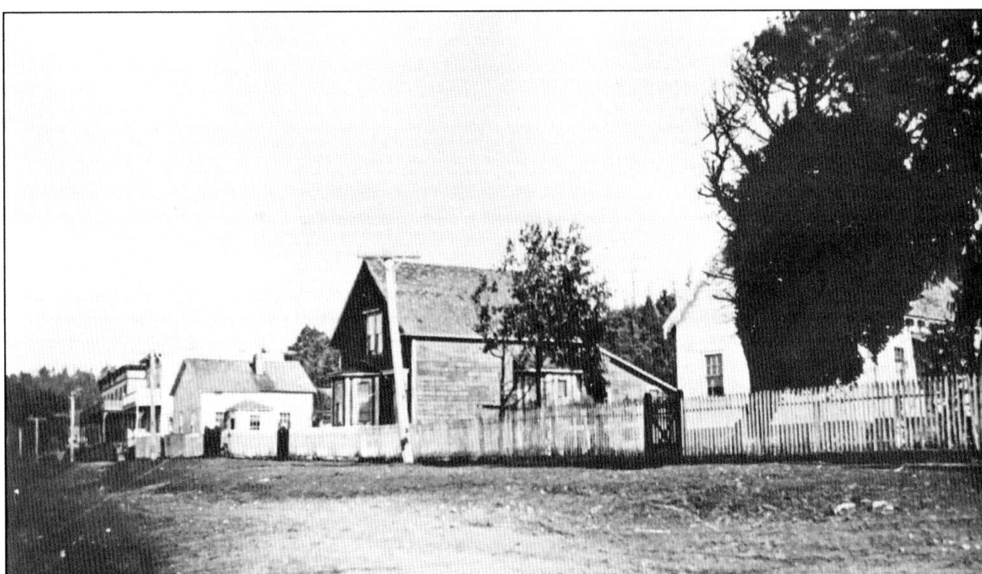

Cyrus D. Robinson is credited with founding the town of Gualala. Downtown Gualala in the early 1900s was somewhat like a typical western town in that most activity was centered around the mill. The mill owners owned almost everything in the town. Gualala was a bustling town in this era, with a stage stop, post office, opera house, dancing school, and a brass band.

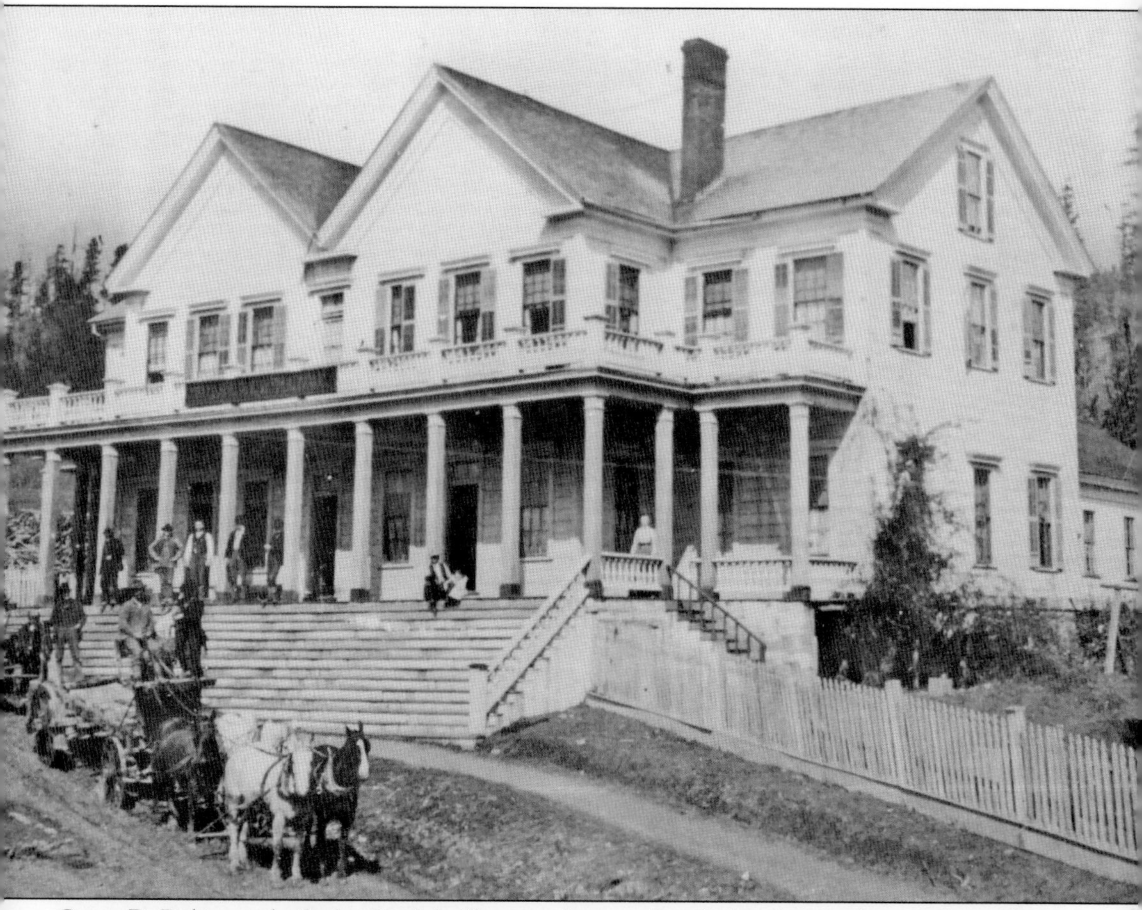

Cyrus D. Robinson built the Gualala House—the town's only hotel and saloon. It burned in 1903. Gualala was a vacation spot even in this time period. After the railroad was put in from Sausalito to Duncan's Mills, travel to Gualala was made easier. Even so, it took a long day to travel to Gualala from San Francisco by stage and railroad. The entire stage route from Duncan's Mills to Gualala (before going on to Point Arena) was through Plantation, Fisk's Mill, Stewarts Point, Black Point, then Gualala. It was $5 to ride the stage.

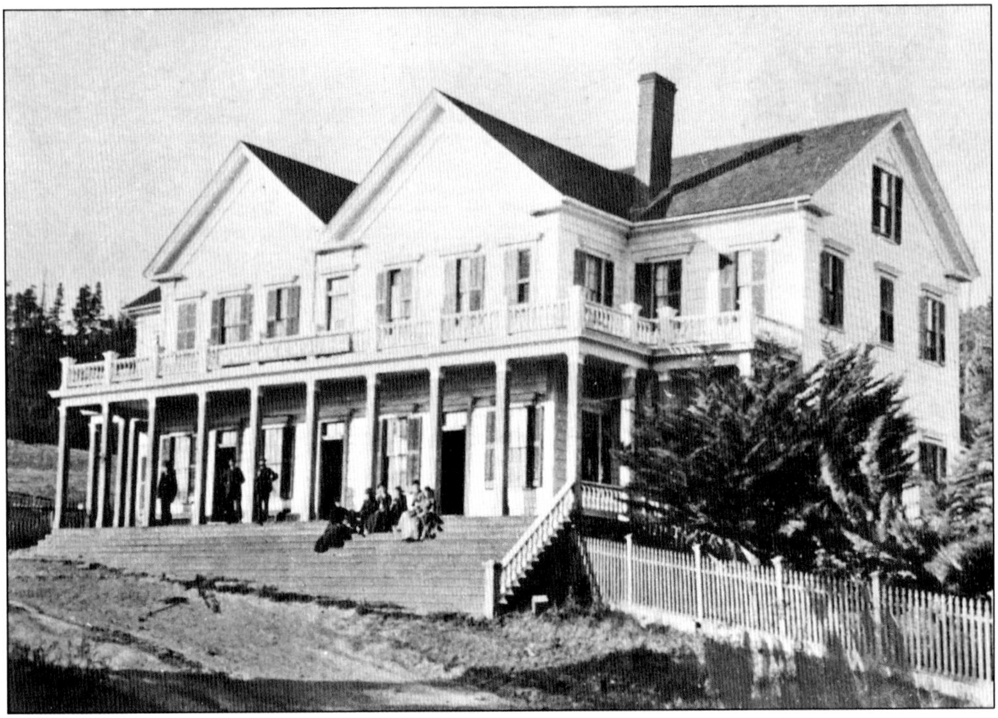

After the Gualala House burned in 1903, the present day Gualala Hotel (seen below) was built. Many lumbermen used the Gualala Hotel as their home while they worked in the woods.

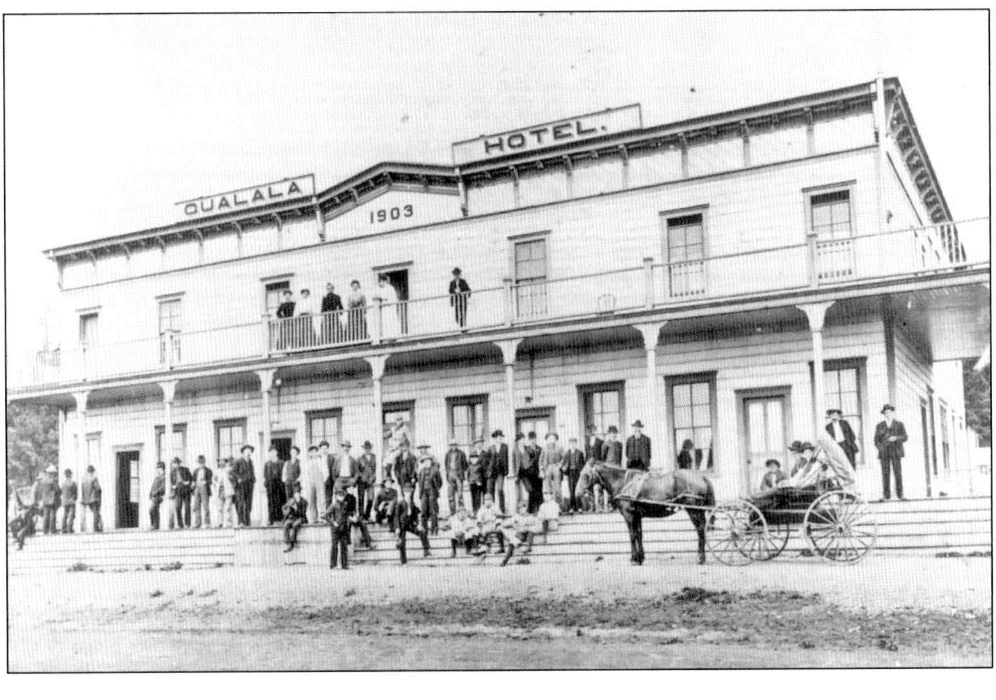

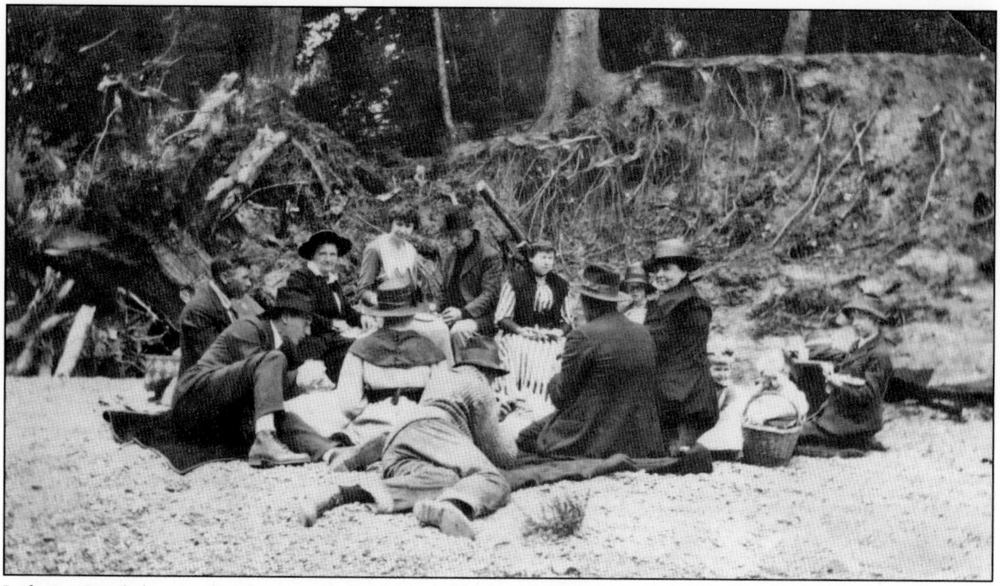

Life in Gualala revolved around the river. Photographed in July 1919, the Hamilton and Hunter families enjoy the sandy beach area. This might be a picnic on the Fourth of July, which was celebrated with much enthusiasm in the area. (Courtesy of William McMillen Kramer.)

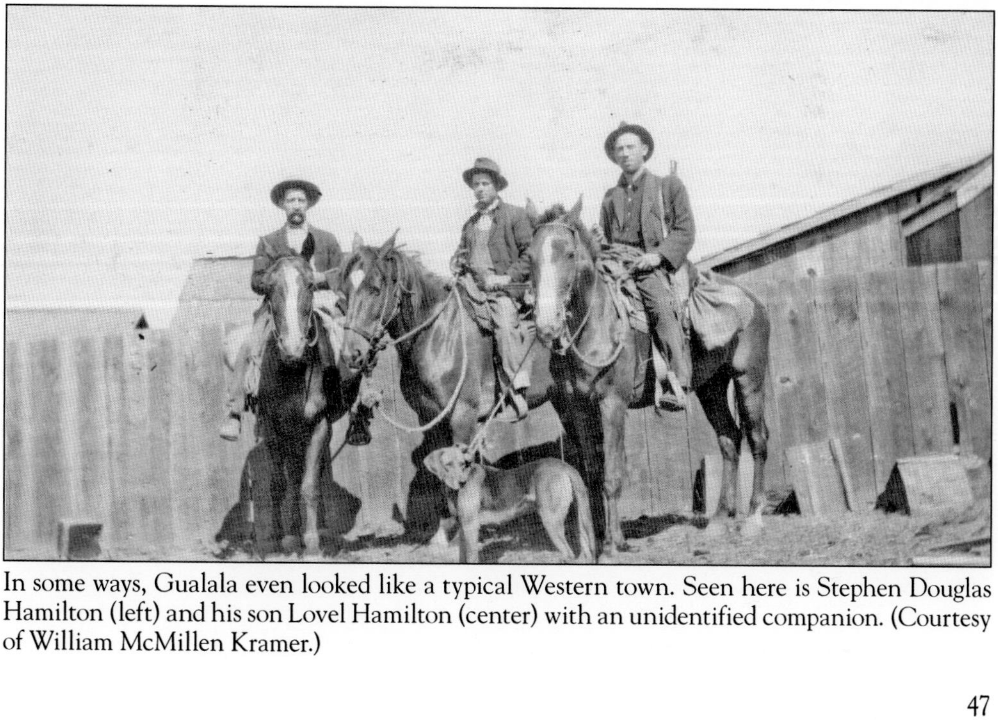

In some ways, Gualala even looked like a typical Western town. Seen here is Stephen Douglas Hamilton (left) and his son Lovel Hamilton (center) with an unidentified companion. (Courtesy of William McMillen Kramer.)

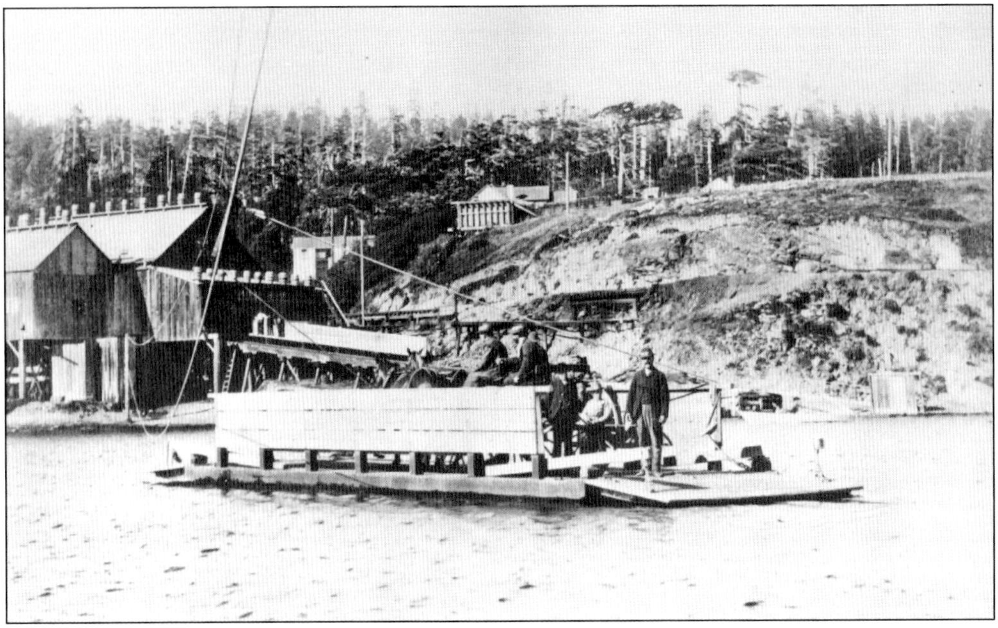

A bridge crossing the Gualala River was not constructed until 1892. Before that time, a ferry transported people over the river. Rufus Niles was the ferryman. The ferry was not without problems. According to legend, the ferryman was not always timely, and prices for crossing were quite steep. Residents in both Sonoma and Mendocino counties joined together to argue that a bridge should be built.

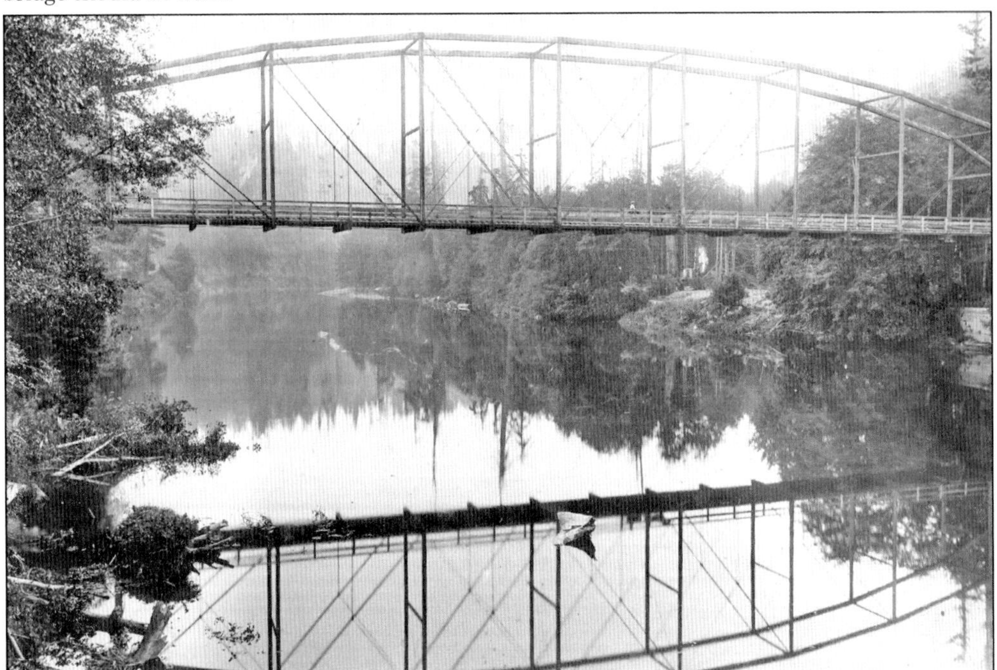

The first bridge over the river was located upstream from the current Gualala Bridge. Local residents assisted with both constructing and inspecting the bridge. (Courtesy of the Mendocino County Historical Society.)

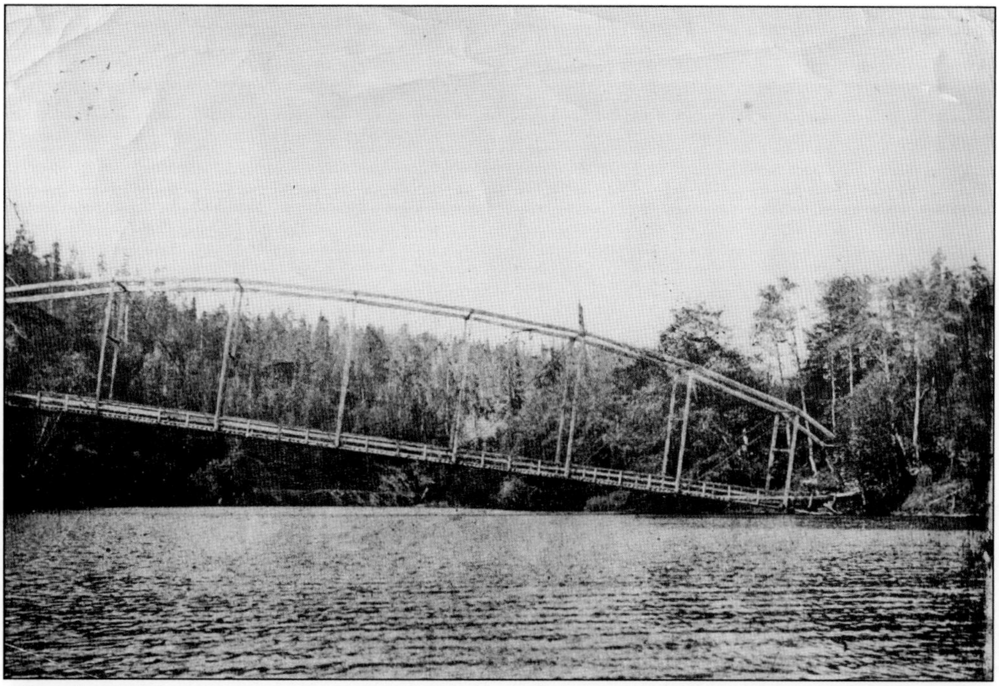

After the 1906 earthquake, the Gualala Bridge was damaged. It had to be raised about 12 feet on one side, which took several months to complete. (Courtesy of the Mendocino County Historical Society.)

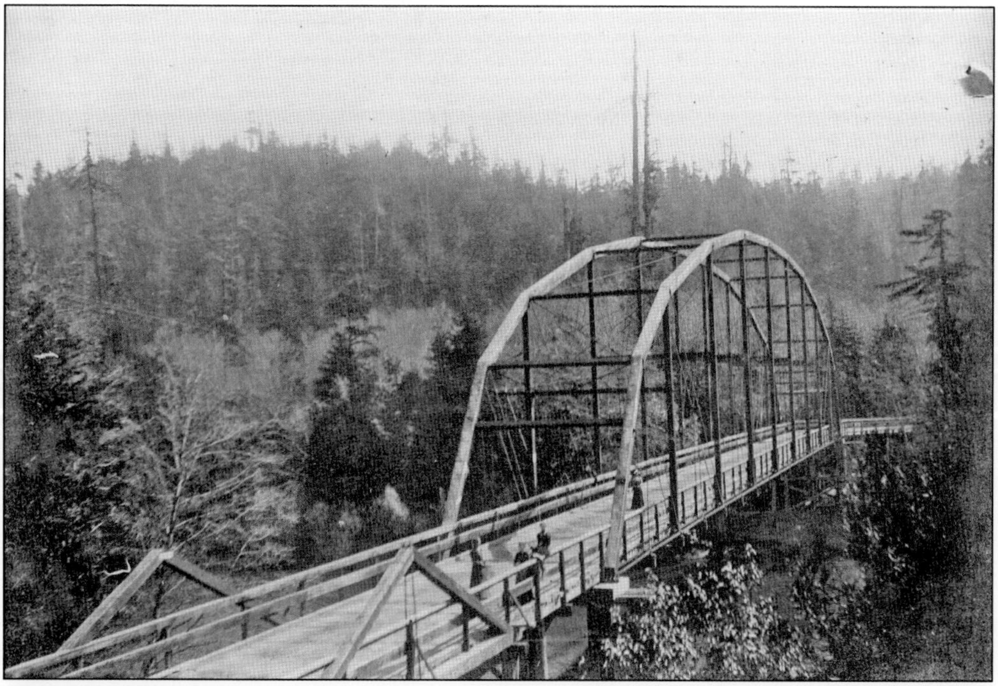

This view of the Gualala Bridge is looking upstream. The ridges around the bridge are filled with timber. Several people are seen on the bridge. (Courtesy of the Mendocino County Historical Society.)

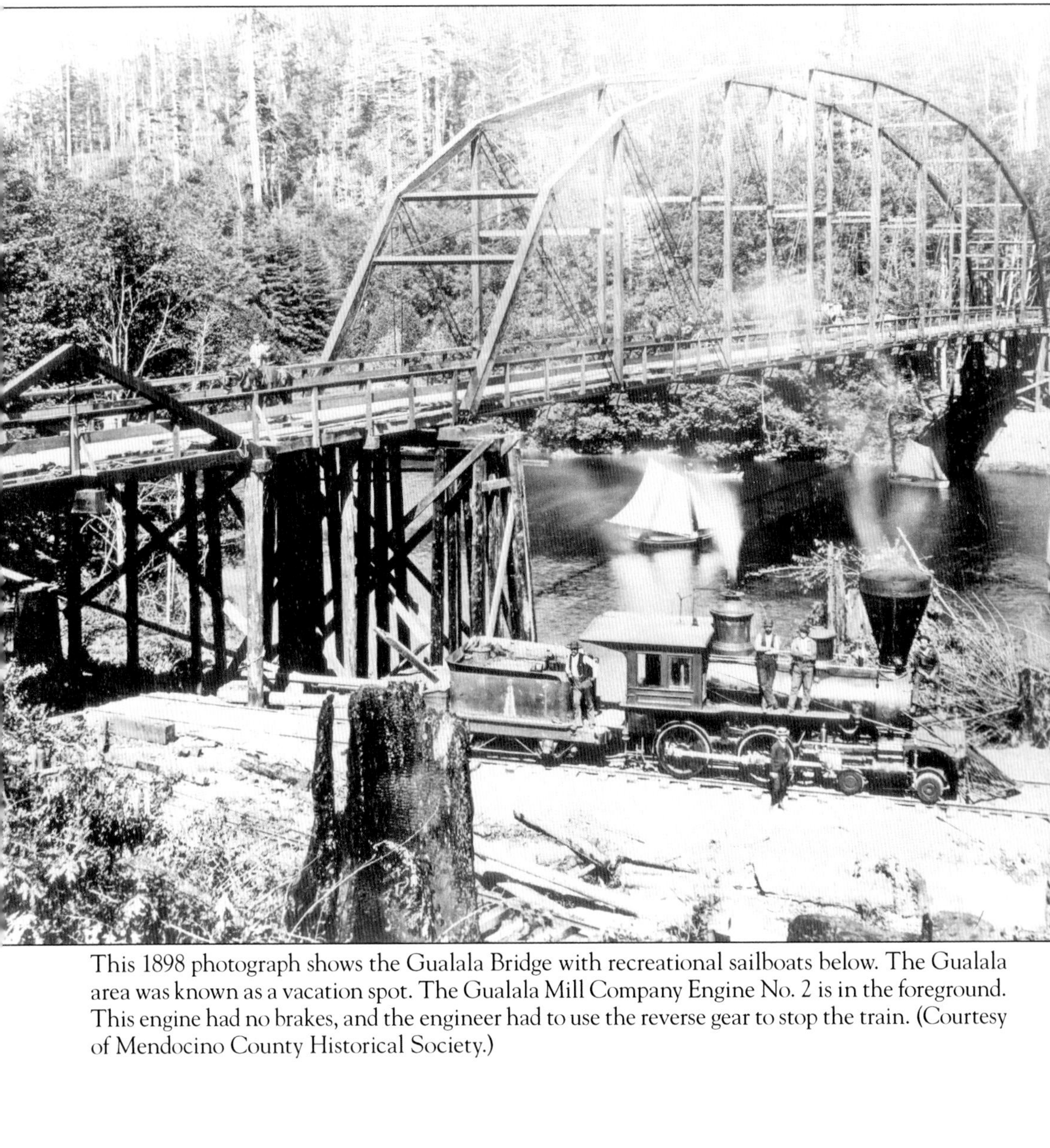

This 1898 photograph shows the Gualala Bridge with recreational sailboats below. The Gualala area was known as a vacation spot. The Gualala Mill Company Engine No. 2 is in the foreground. This engine had no brakes, and the engineer had to use the reverse gear to stop the train. (Courtesy of Mendocino County Historical Society.)

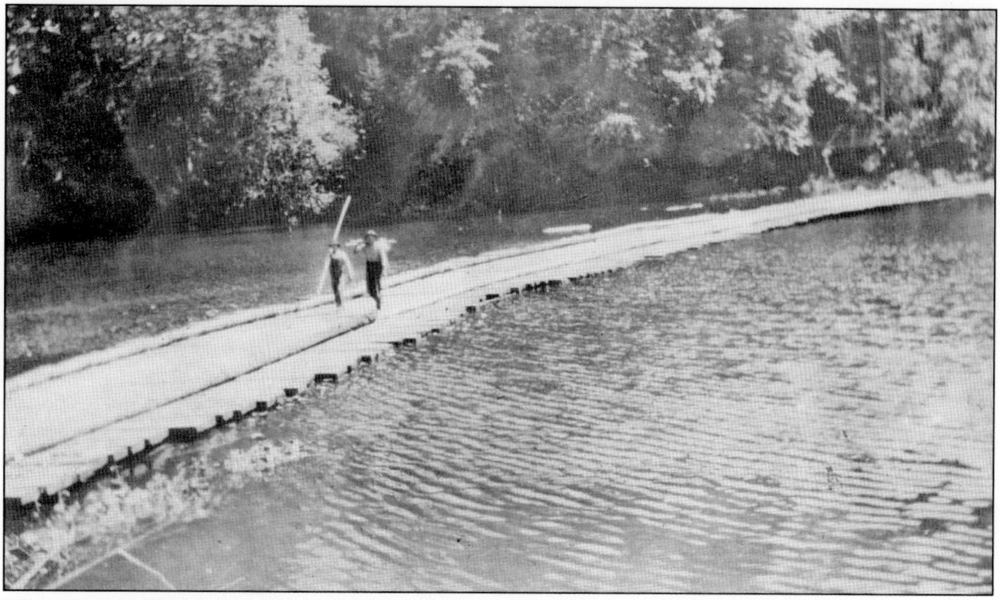

The Gualala Bridge lasted until 1919, when it collapsed. Until a new bridge could be built, a temporary bridge of planks was built. This photograph, taken in May 1919, shows two local residents crossing the temporary bridge. (Courtesy of William McMillen Kramer.)

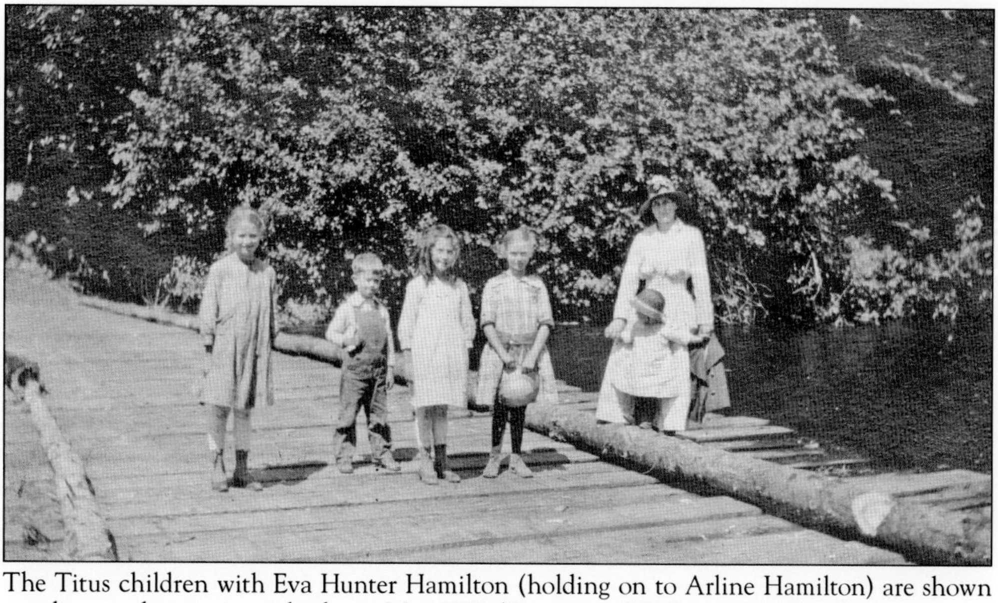

The Titus children with Eva Hunter Hamilton (holding on to Arline Hamilton) are shown standing on the temporary bridge in May 1919. (Courtesy of William McMillen Kramer.)

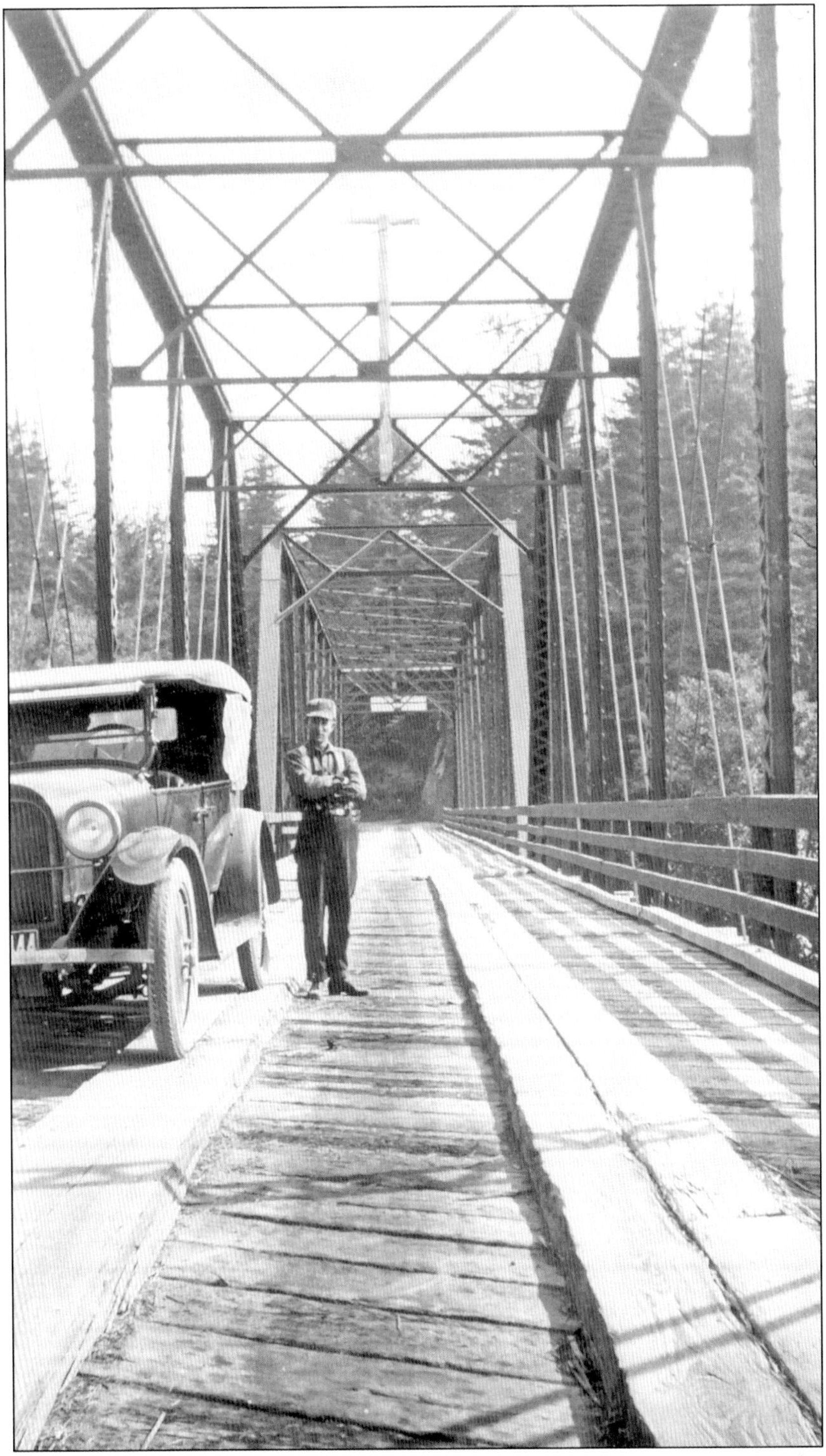

A new steel bridge was constructed that lasted for approximately 40 more years. The current Gualala bridge was built downriver about a mile closer to the mouth of the river. (Courtesy of Mendocino County Historical Society.)

Four

Settling In

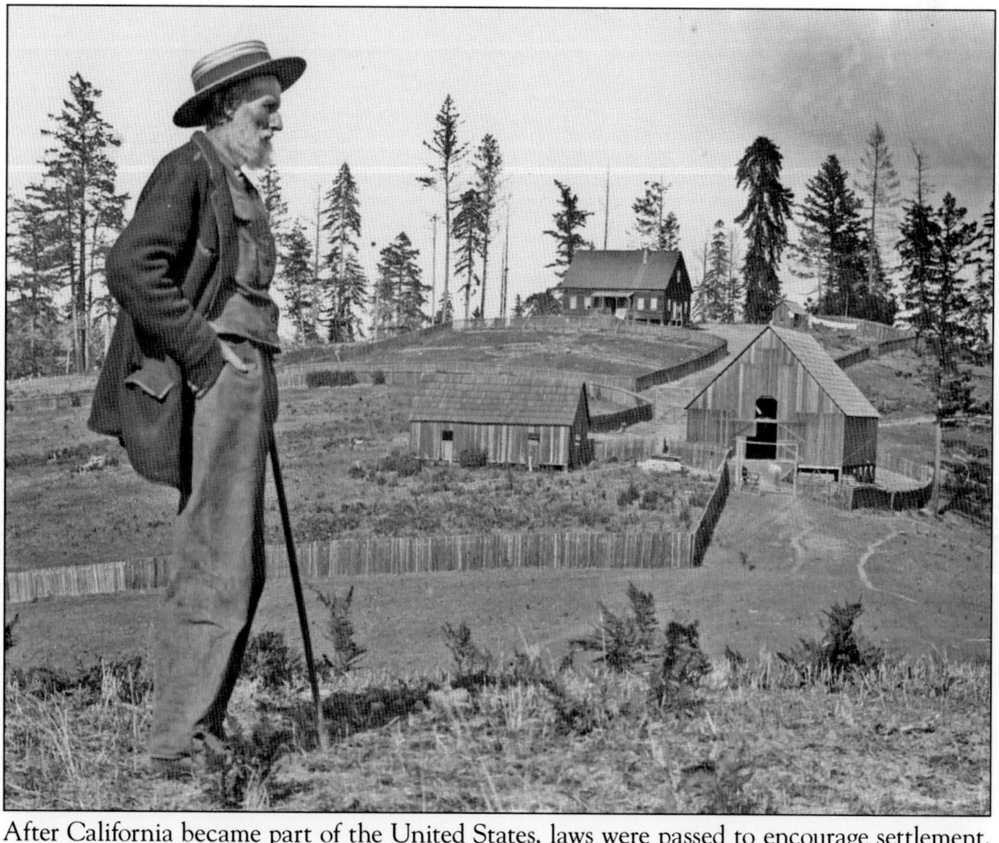

After California became part of the United States, laws were passed to encourage settlement. The Homestead Act of 1862 allowed settlers to claim 160 acres of land. Often times, early settlers bought land that the timber companies later purchased. This resulted in some timber companies ending up with very large lots of land.

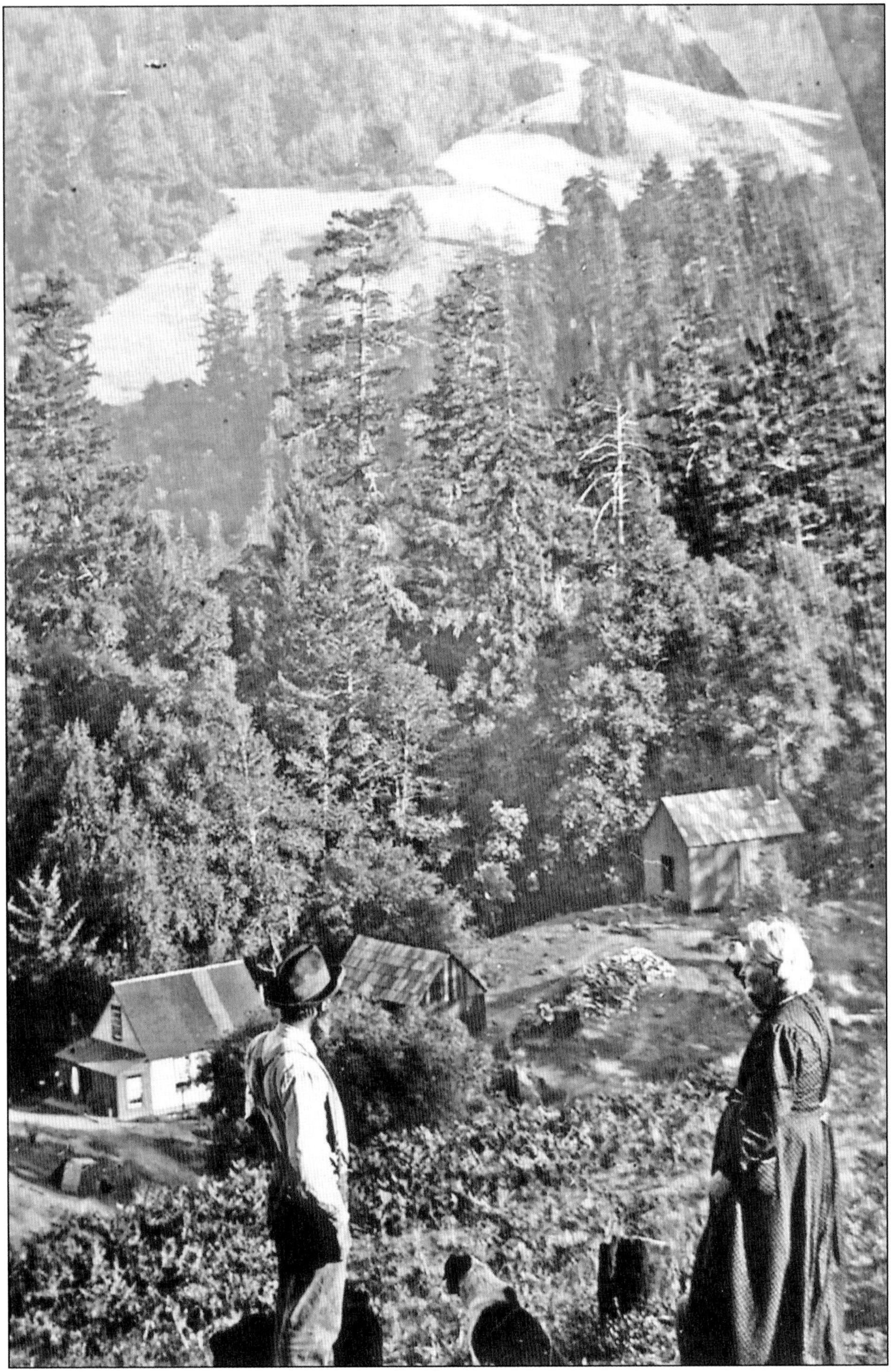

Early settlers of Annapolis were resilient people who worked hard. George Batt wrote in his August 1912 *Press Democrat* newspaper column, "Laziness is not known in Annapolis under any circumstances. Every man, woman, and child was born to be busy here, and busy with delight."

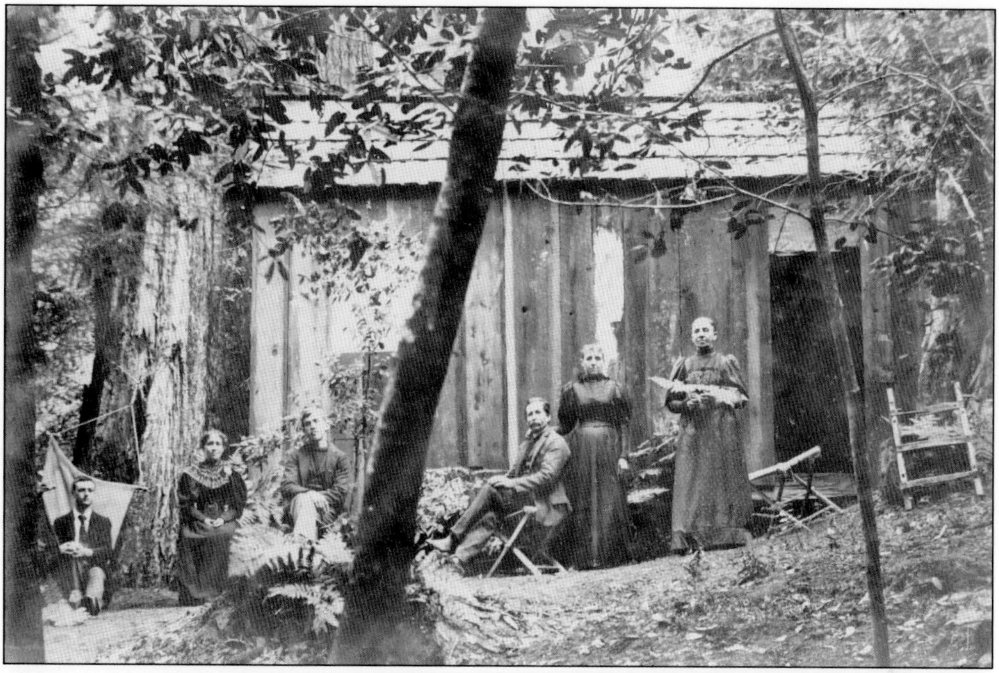

This is a photograph of the home of John E. Hickman. He and his family settled in the area in the late 1800s. Hickman built Hickman Mill in Annapolis in 1896.

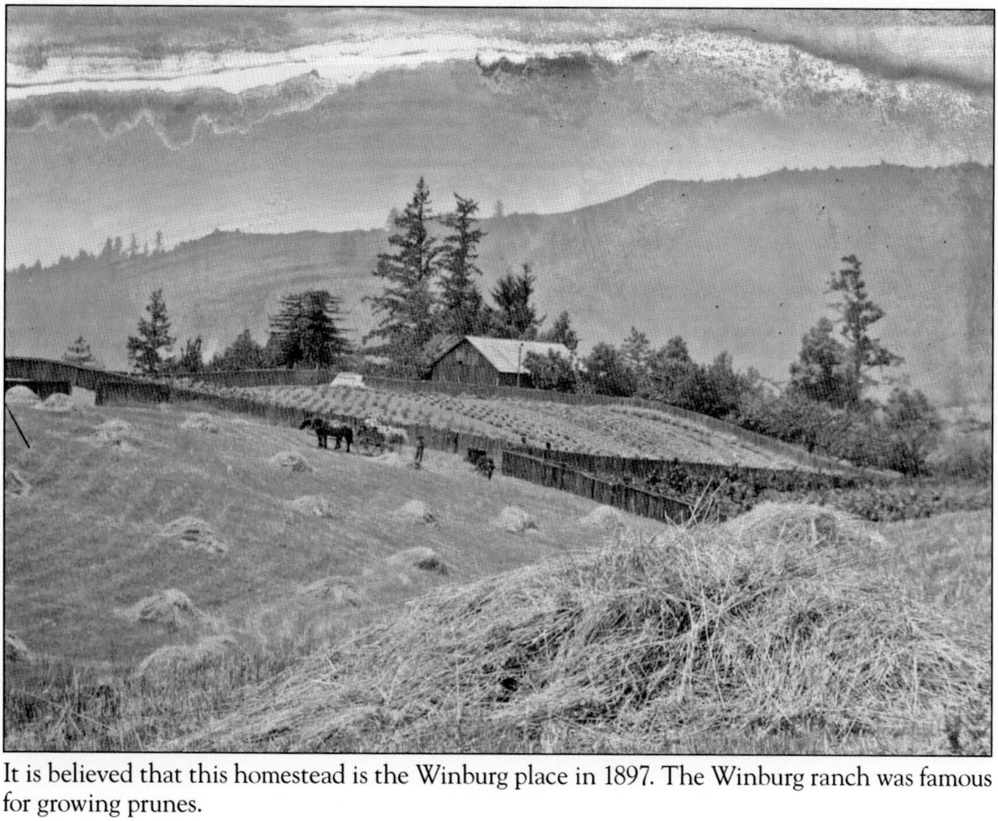

It is believed that this homestead is the Winburg place in 1897. The Winburg ranch was famous for growing prunes.

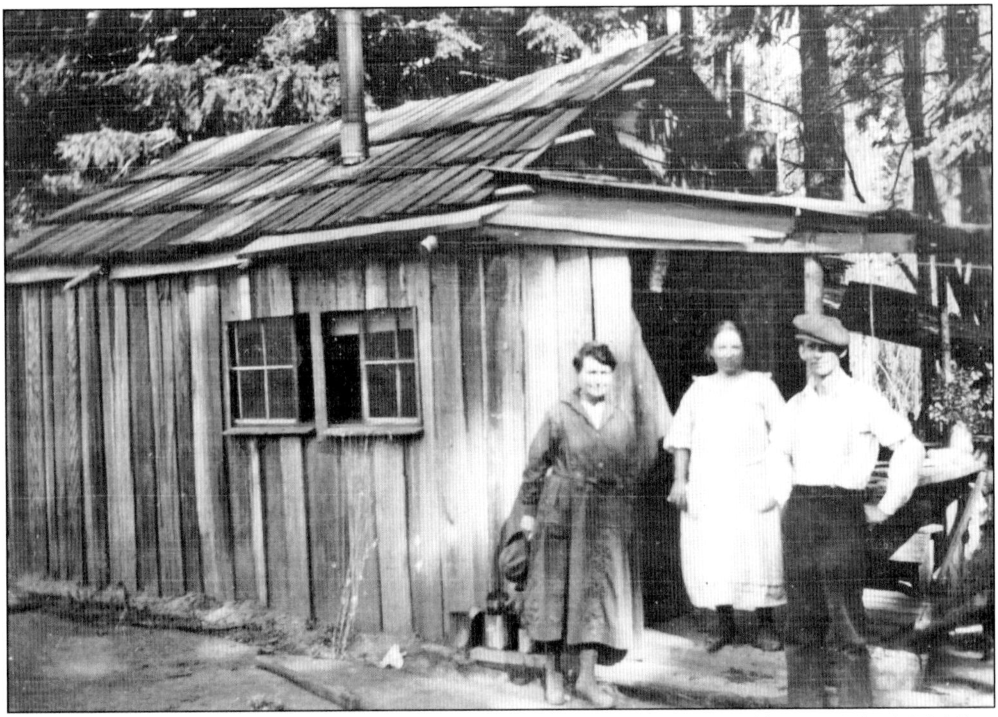

The McMillens were one of the founding families of Annapolis. Pictured here is Silas McMillen (right) with his wife, Irina Parkins McMillen (center), and an unidentified woman. The Parks and McMillen families traveled to California from Indiana.

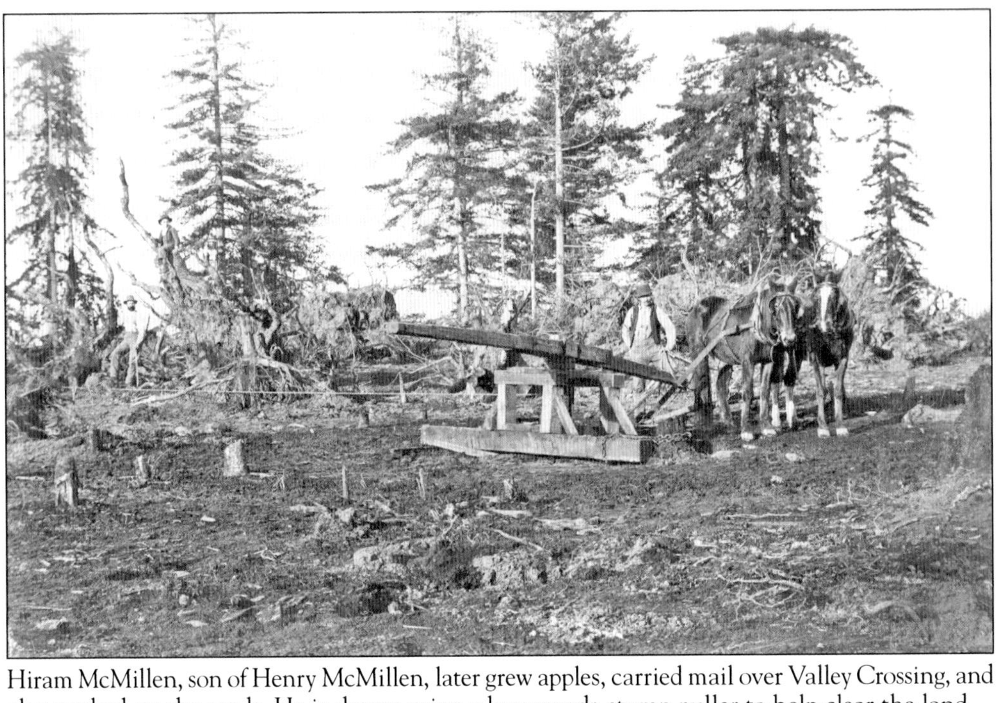

Hiram McMillen, son of Henry McMillen, later grew apples, carried mail over Valley Crossing, and also worked on the roads. He is shown using a homemade stump puller to help clear the land.

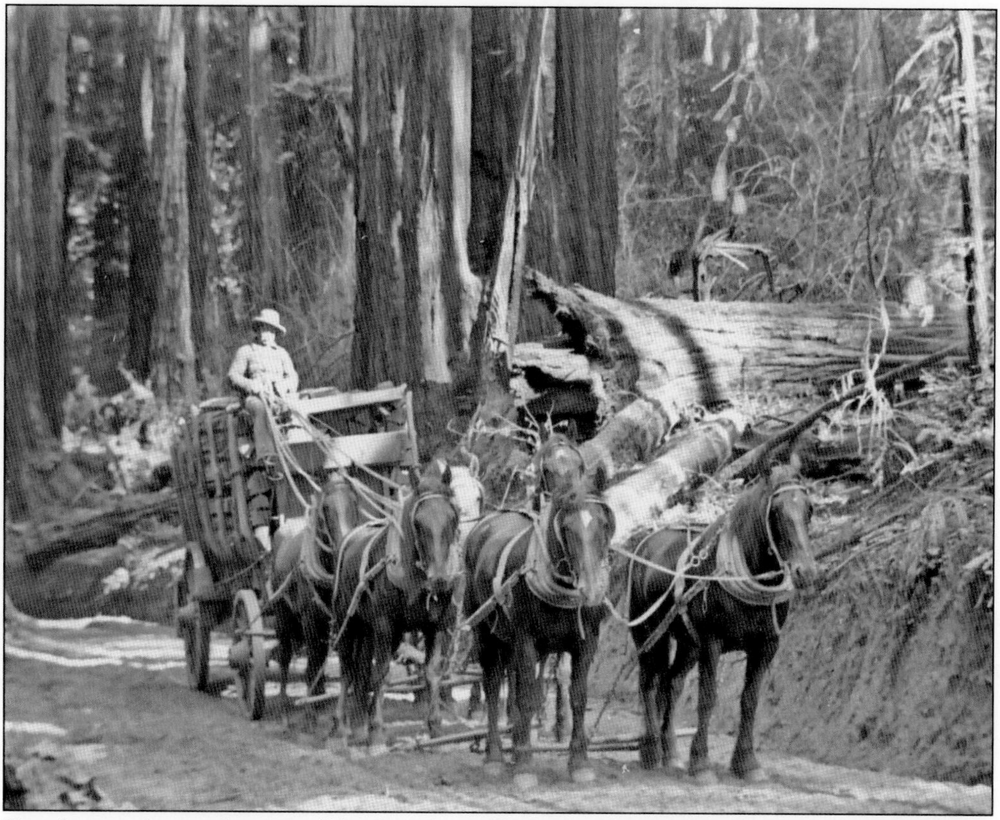

Traveling in Annapolis was still hard work, as the roads were rough, narrow, and windy. Hauling firewood was a common task.

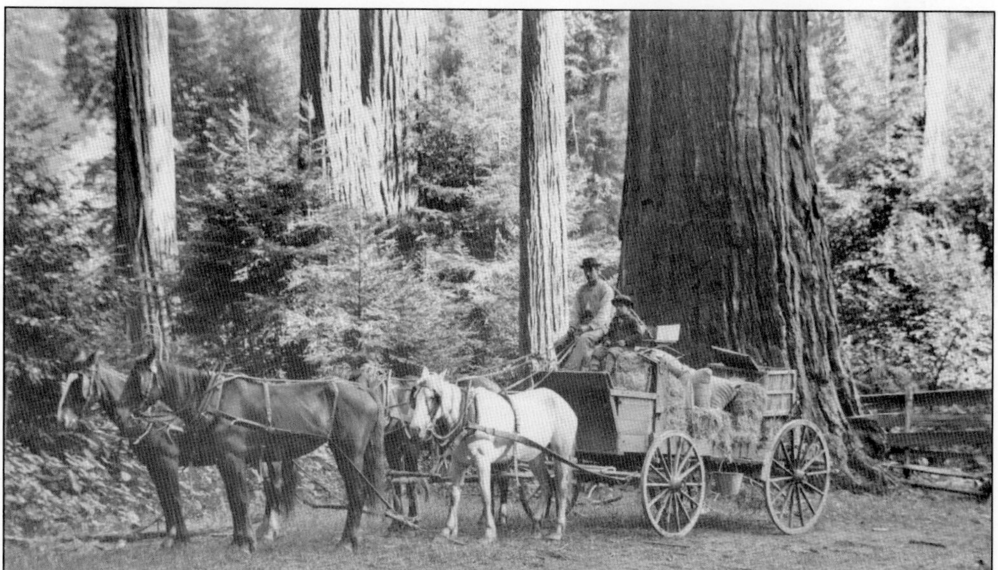

This photograph shows the team of horses hauling hay over Annapolis road. Notice the size of the tree bordering the road. Fences and gates divided properties and often had to be opened and closed while traveling the roads.

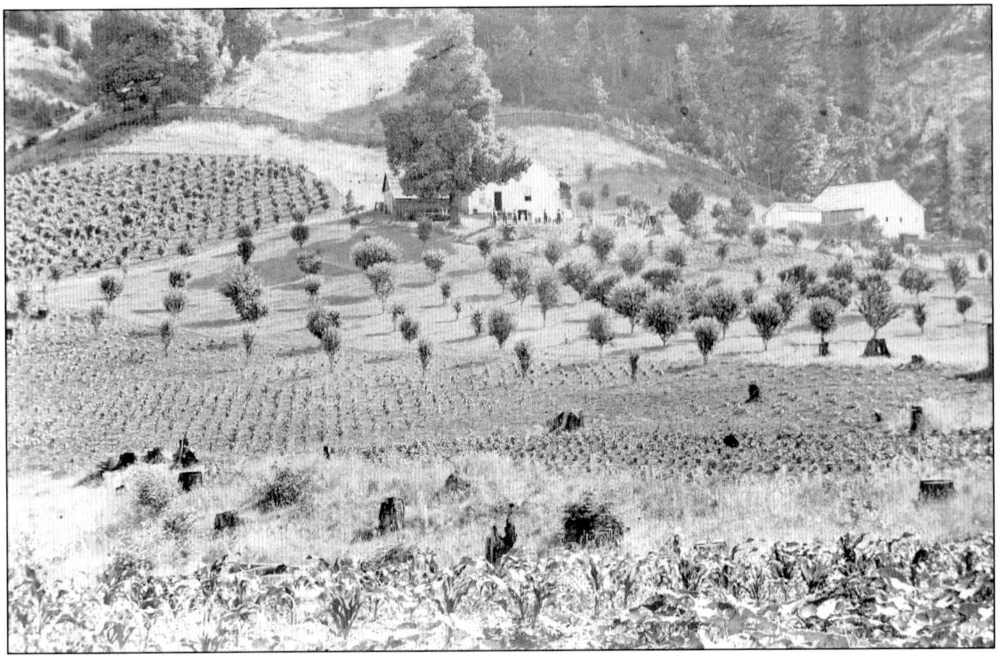

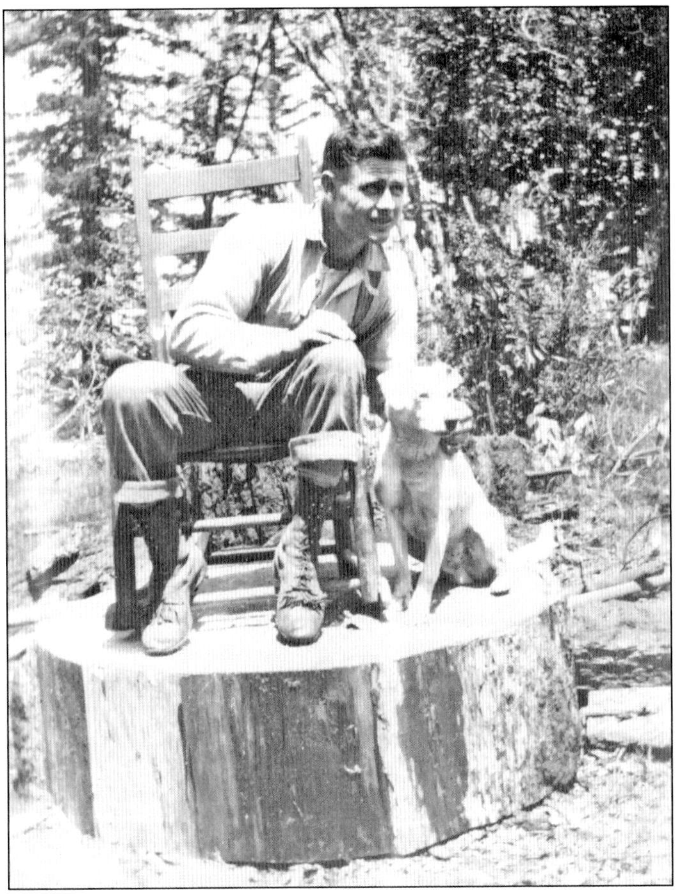

Annapolis residents began to realize the climate was ideal for growing fruit. The combination of plentiful rain but warm spring and summers coupled with the coastal fog created great growing conditions. Soon orchards started being planted. This is a photograph of the Ben Franchini ranch. Ben Franchini came to the United States in 1882 from Italy.

Lovel Hamilton, a Gualala Railway engineer, relaxes in his outdoor living room in 1919. (Courtesy of Arline Hamilton.)

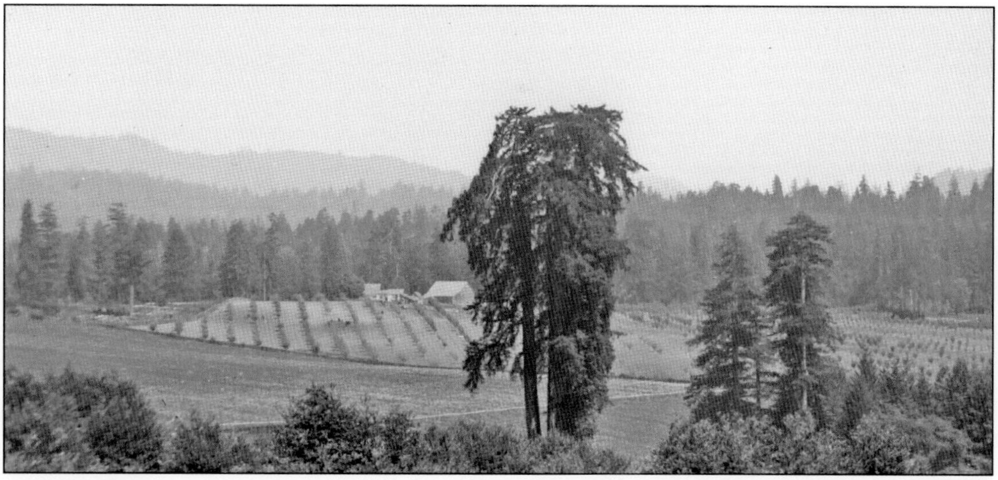

Some of the earliest settlers of Annapolis chose land in the flat valley area of Annapolis where the post office and school are now located. Looking from the Fiscus Ranch to the Wetmore Orchards, hese photographs show the valley views of this land and the ridges of timber toward the west from two different views. The orchards, which later became famous for apples, are clearly visible in this 1900 photograph.

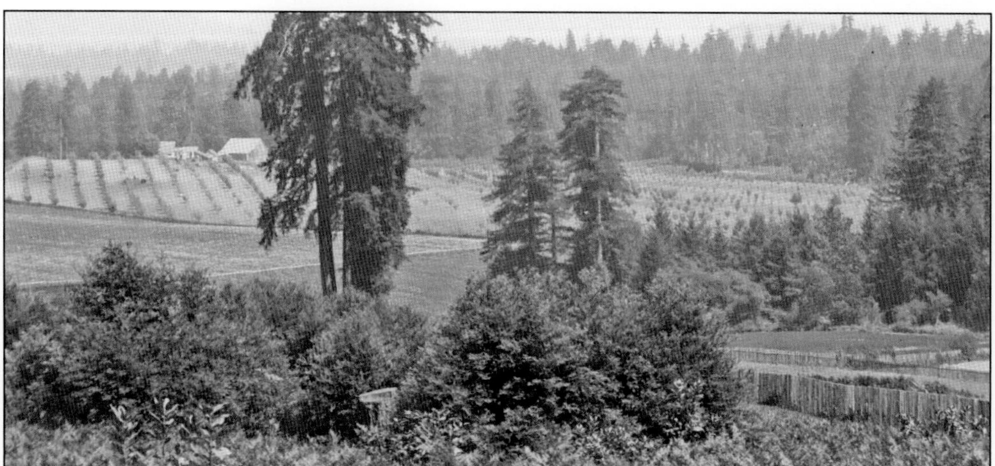

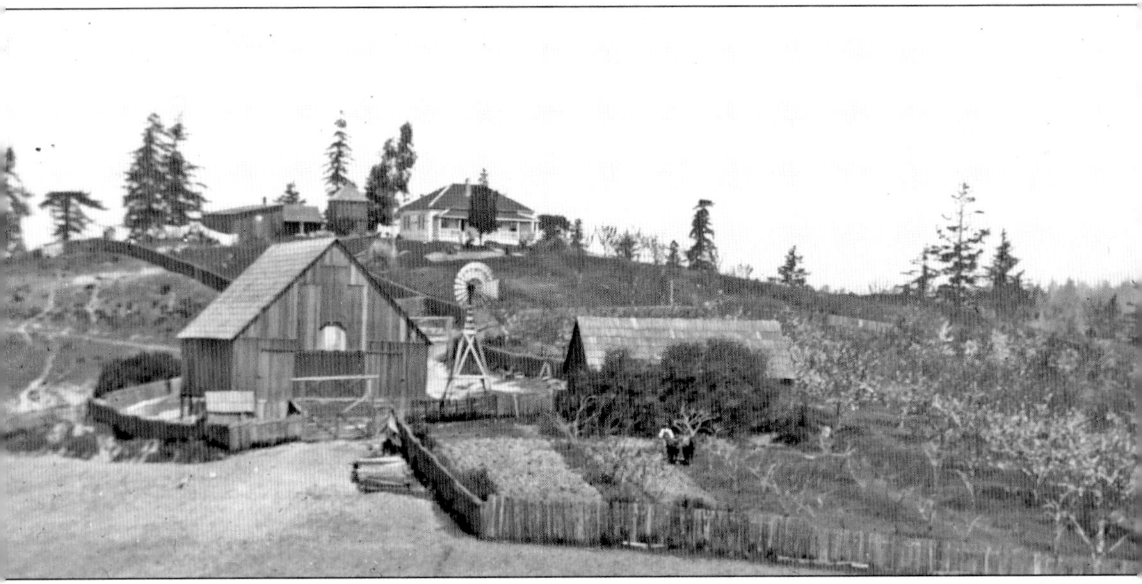

This is an early photograph of the Petersen family's Nob Hill Ranch. The house was built by George Fiscus for a sea captain named Sunberg near the turn of the century. Captain Sunberg, who was probably a schooner captain, then sold the ranch to Claus Petersen. Claus later died at the ranch in 1911. The ranch remained in the family for many years. It is now the home of Peay Vineyards.

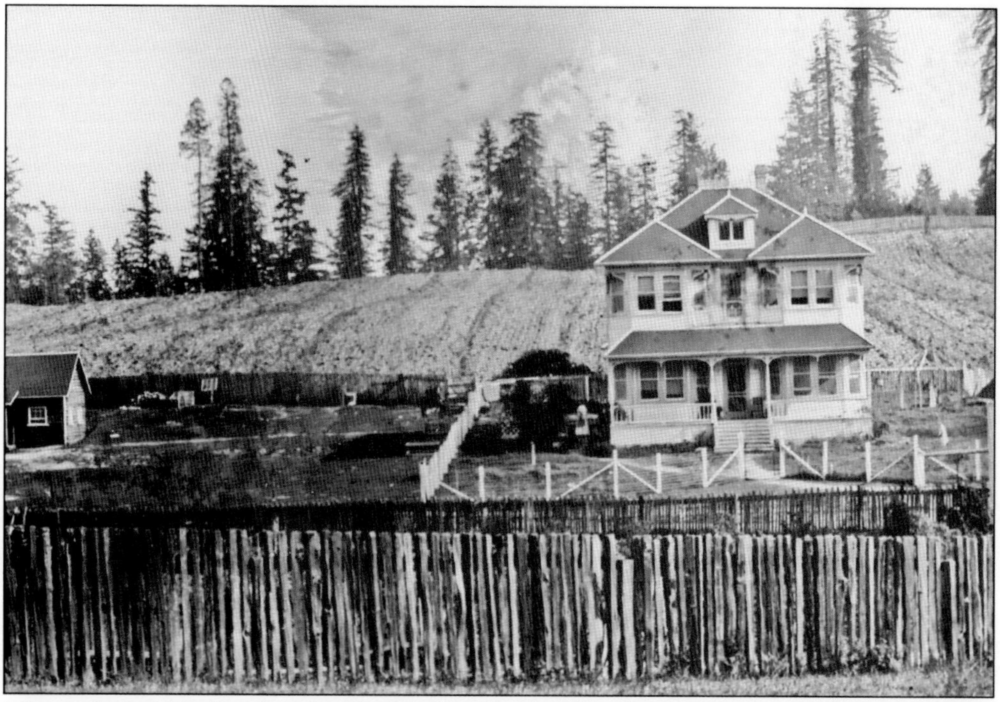

John and Mary Patchett lived in Annapolis with their family. They had 10 children. John kept an accounting book of their farm that is available for review in the Sonoma County Library. The Patchett home is now the Starcross Monastery.

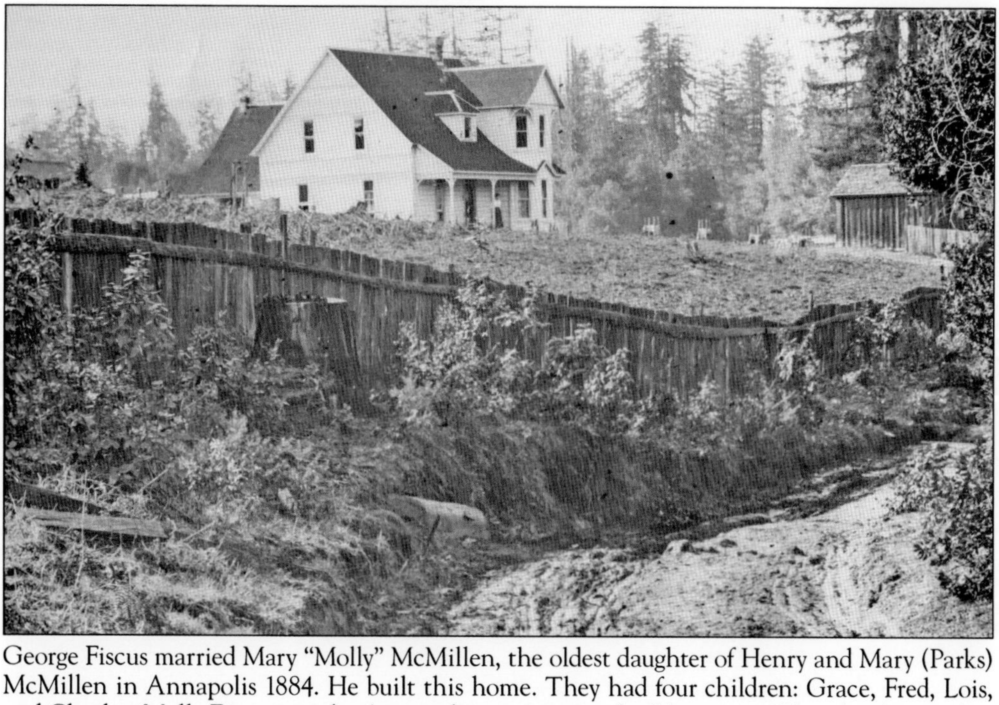

George Fiscus married Mary "Molly" McMillen, the oldest daughter of Henry and Mary (Parks) McMillen in Annapolis 1884. He built this home. They had four children: Grace, Fred, Lois, and Charley. Molly Fiscus was the Annapolis postmistress for 46 years until her daughter-in-law Alice took over.

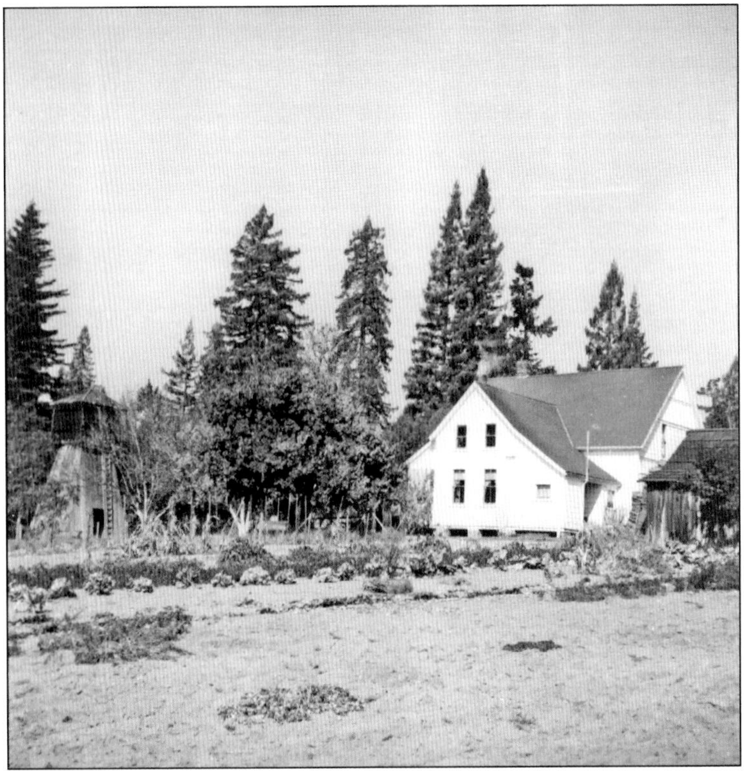

This home, built by George Fiscus, still stands behind the Annapolis Post Office.

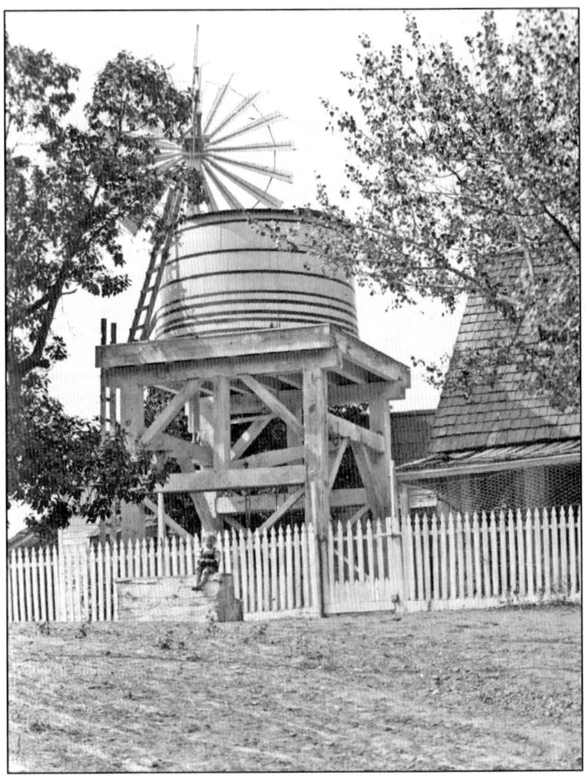

Residents made good use of the local building materials, including constructing such elaborate structures as the water tower and windmill.

Local residents often banded together to work in the woods or on building projects. These two loggers are seen taking a rest in their homemade bench in the tree.

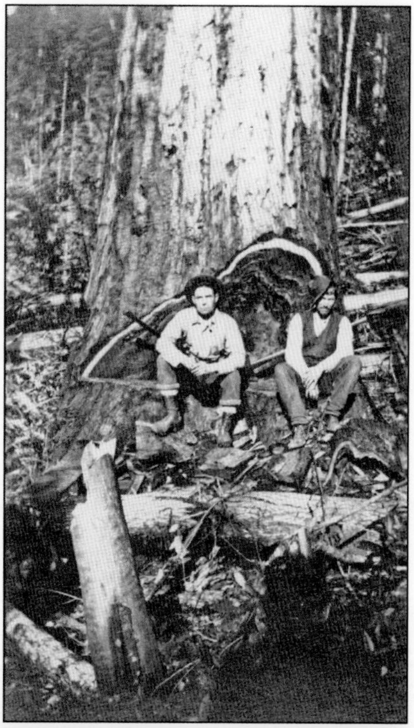

J. R. "Jim" Christensen had a ranch near Valley Crossing. George Batt wrote, "Jim cannot be beaten for kindheartedness." Christensen was known for raising hogs and potatoes.

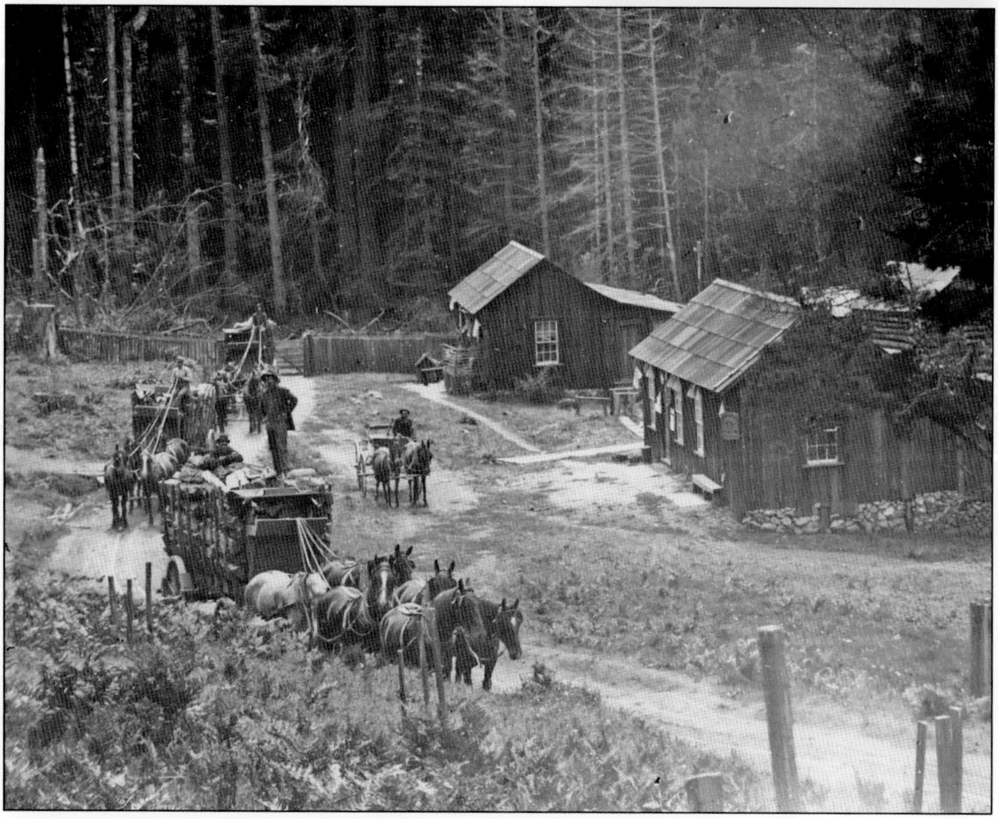

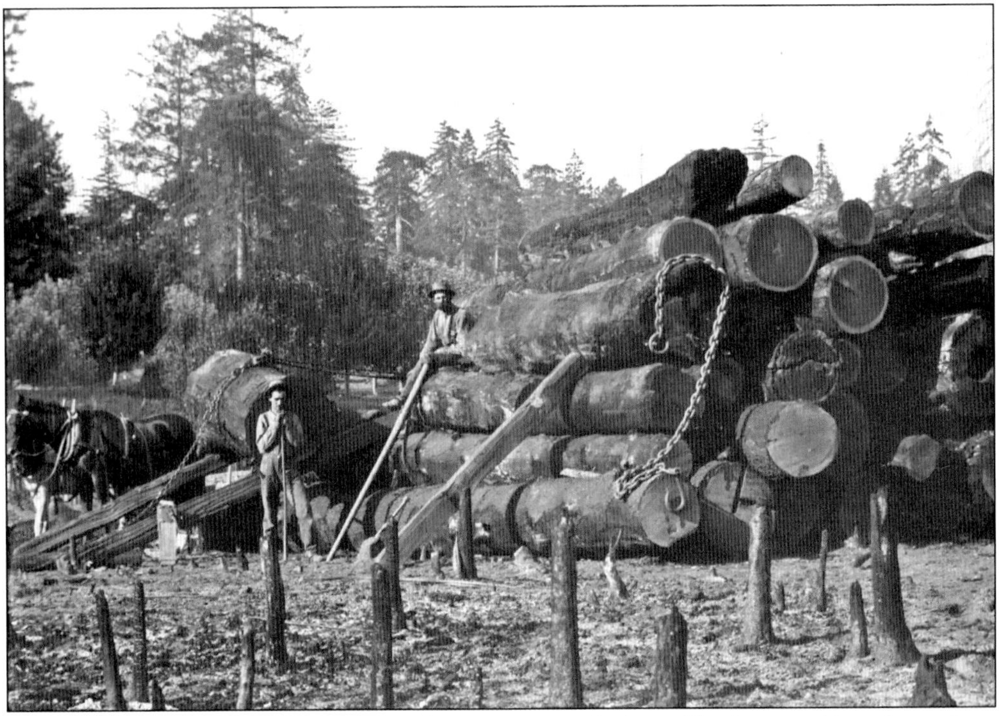

George Ross was an early settler who made quite a name for himself in logging. He is shown here clearing his land in the early 1900s.

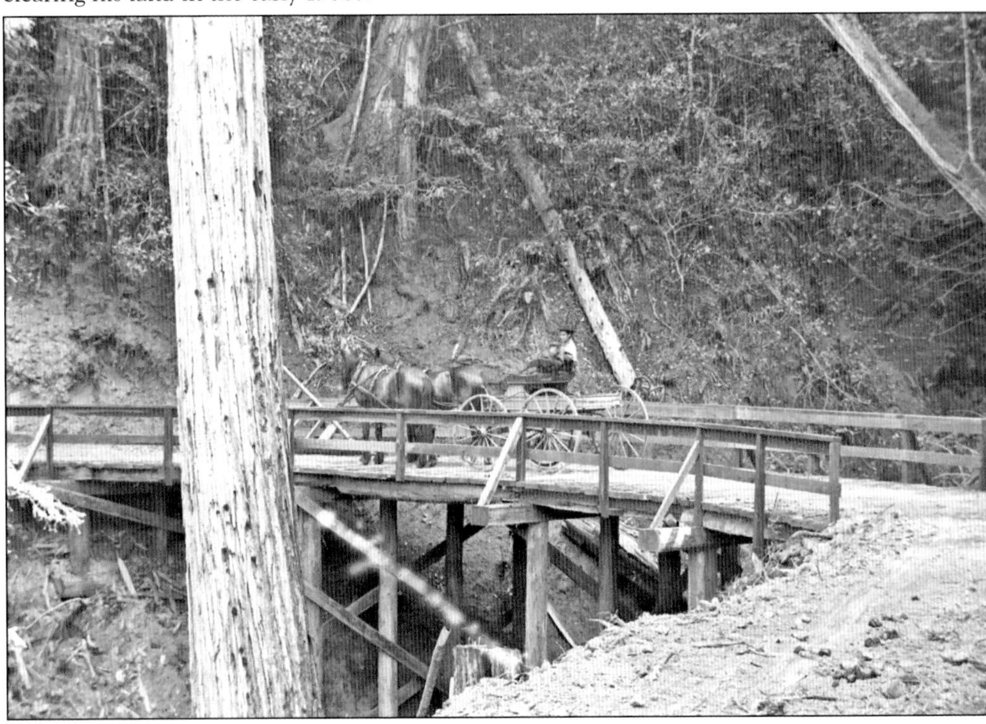

Travelling around Annapolis was challenging at times. Early residents learned to value the caretakers of the roads. This is a photograph of Molly Fiscus and her son Charley.

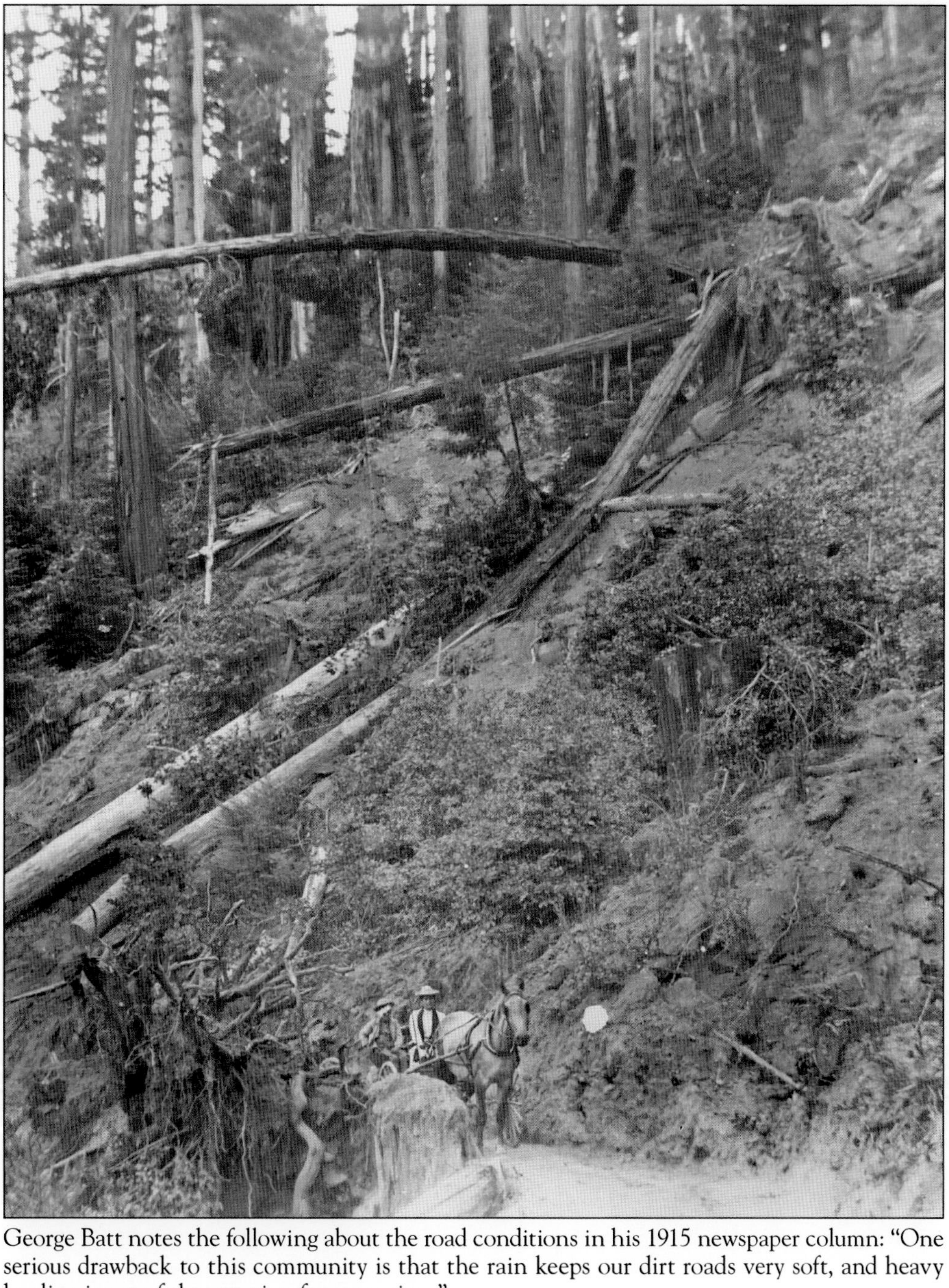

George Batt notes the following about the road conditions in his 1915 newspaper column: "One serious drawback to this community is that the rain keeps our dirt roads very soft, and heavy hauling is out of the question for some time."

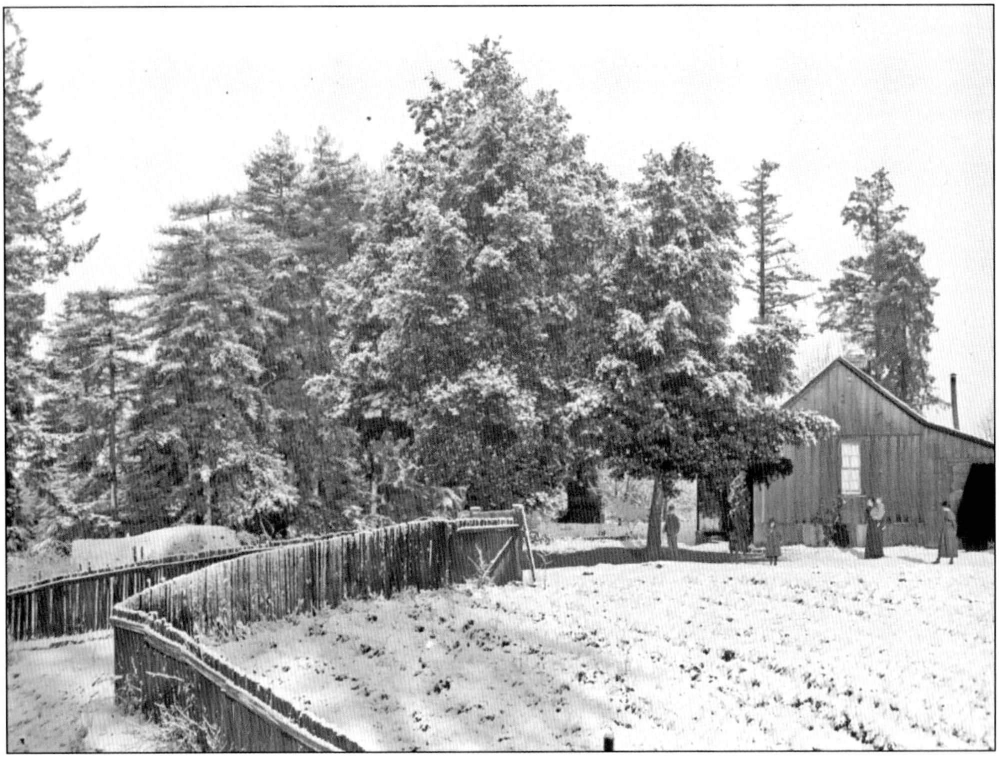

Since Annapolis is situated at an elevation of about 700 feet above sea level, it does snow on occasion. Seen here is an unusual amount of snow for the area on Hoover Ridge.

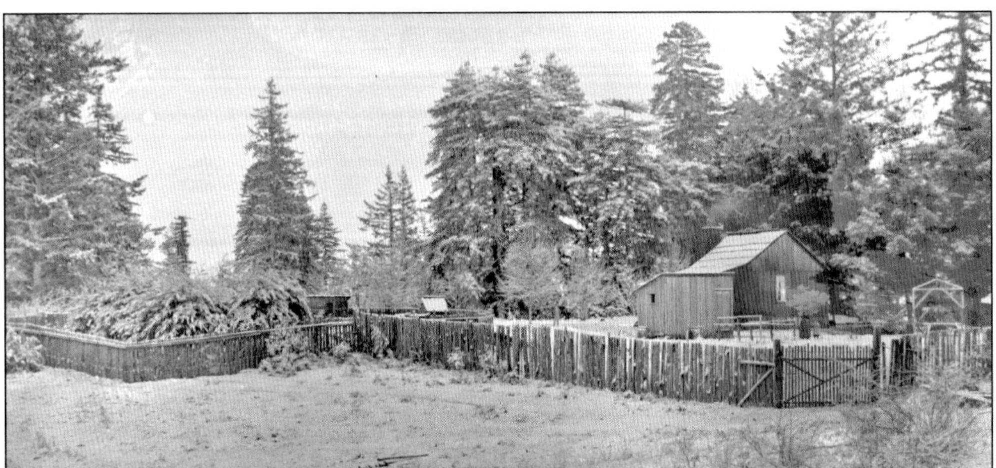

This is another view of a snowy scene in Annapolis, taken in 1900.

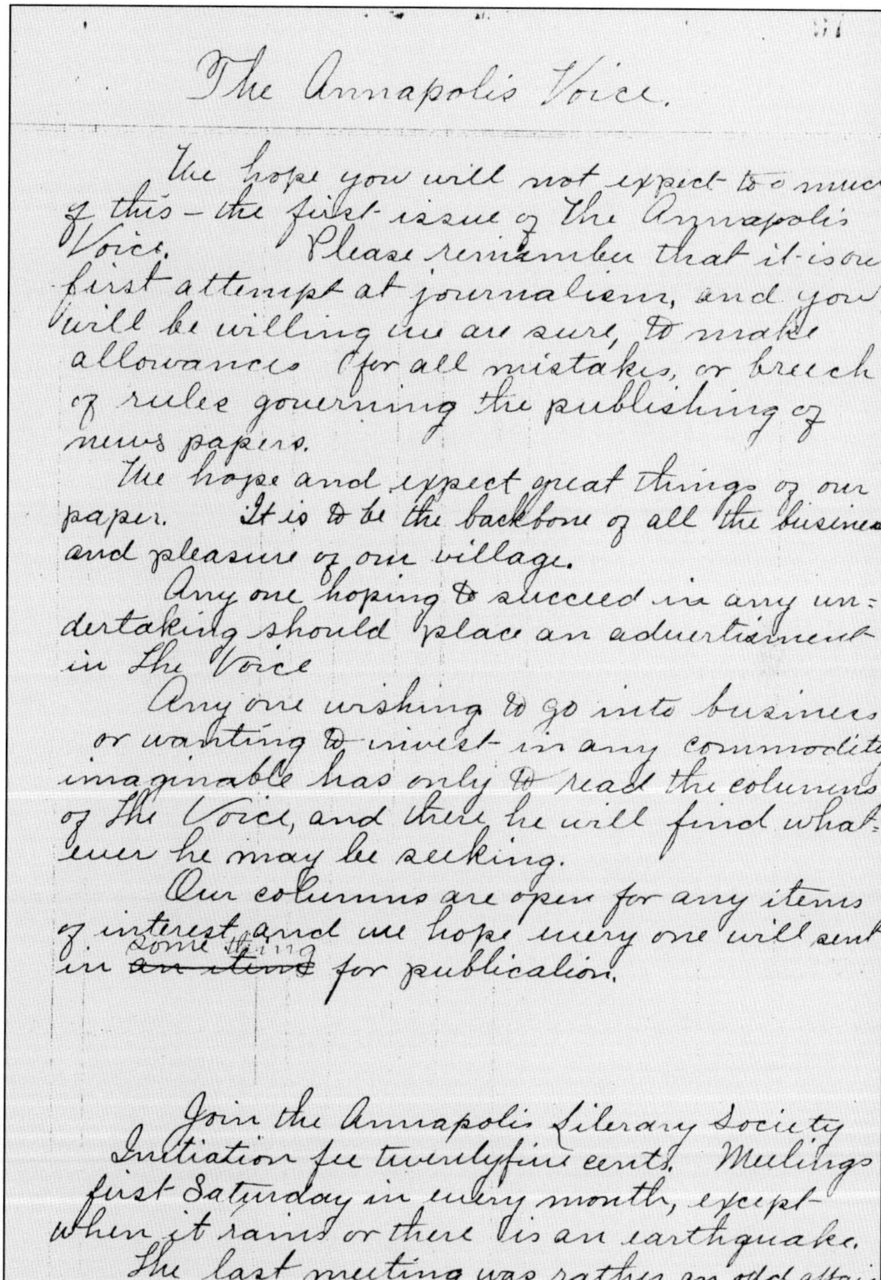

The Annapolis Voice.

We hope you will not expect to much of this – the first issue of the Annapolis Voice. Please remember that it is our first attempt at journalism, and you will be willing we are sure, to make allowances for all mistakes, or breech of rules governing the publishing of news papers.

We hope and expect great things of our paper. It is to be the backbone of all the business and pleasure of our village.

Any one hoping to succeed in any undertaking should place an advertisement in The Voice

Any one wishing to go into business or wanting to invest in any commodity imaginable has only to read the columns of the Voice, and there he will find whatever he may be seeking.

Our columns are open for any items of interest and we hope every one will send in ~~an item~~ some thing for publication.

Join the Annapolis Literary Society Initiation fee twentyfive cents. Meetings first Saturday in every month, except when it rains or there is an earthquake.

The last meeting was rather an odd affair inasmuch as there was only one officer (the Secretary) present. Guess the President forgot all about it. We will have to send some of the girls to remind him the next time.

In the early 1900s, a group of Annapolis residents decided to write their own literary magazine. The *Annapolis Voice* was born. Primarily written by members of the Patchett family, the newsletter documented life in Annapolis. (Courtesy of Sonoma County Library.)

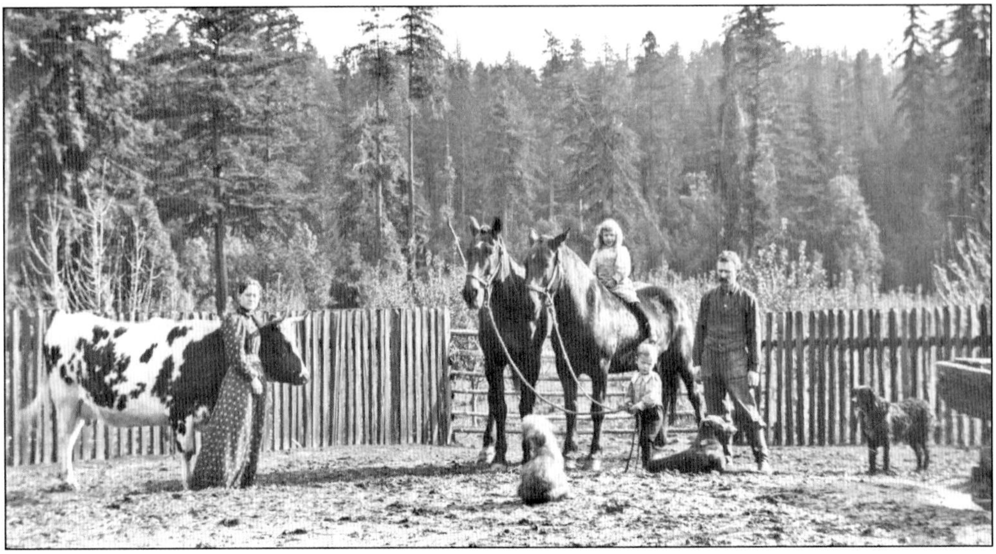

Charley Wetmore, who is credited for naming Annapolis, is shown with his family in 1900. The Wetmore Orchards became famous for their apples as well as other fruits. Apples were dried and then shipped by schooner to San Francisco.

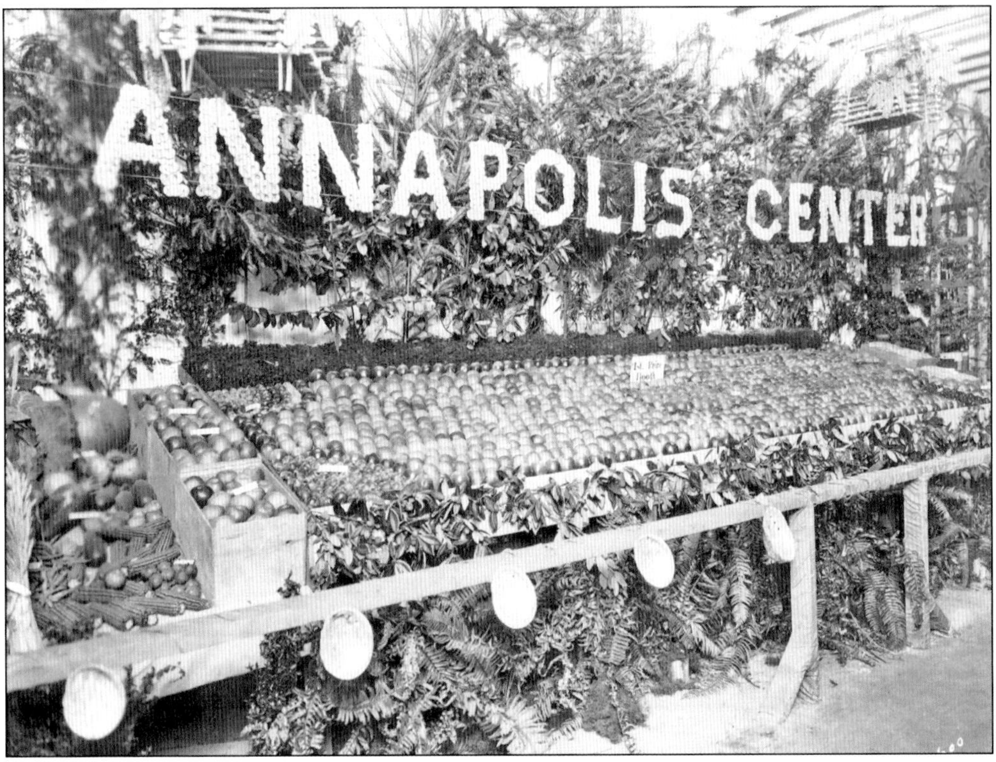

This photograph is most likely from the Sonoma County Fair. Annapolis soon became known all over for its fine fruit. Wrote George Batt in 1911, "We have a berry season of six months, beginning with strawberries and ending with the very valuable huckleberry, which beats them all for pies and shortcakes. Our cherry season lasts three months . . . We have apples nine months of the year and pears nearly as long."

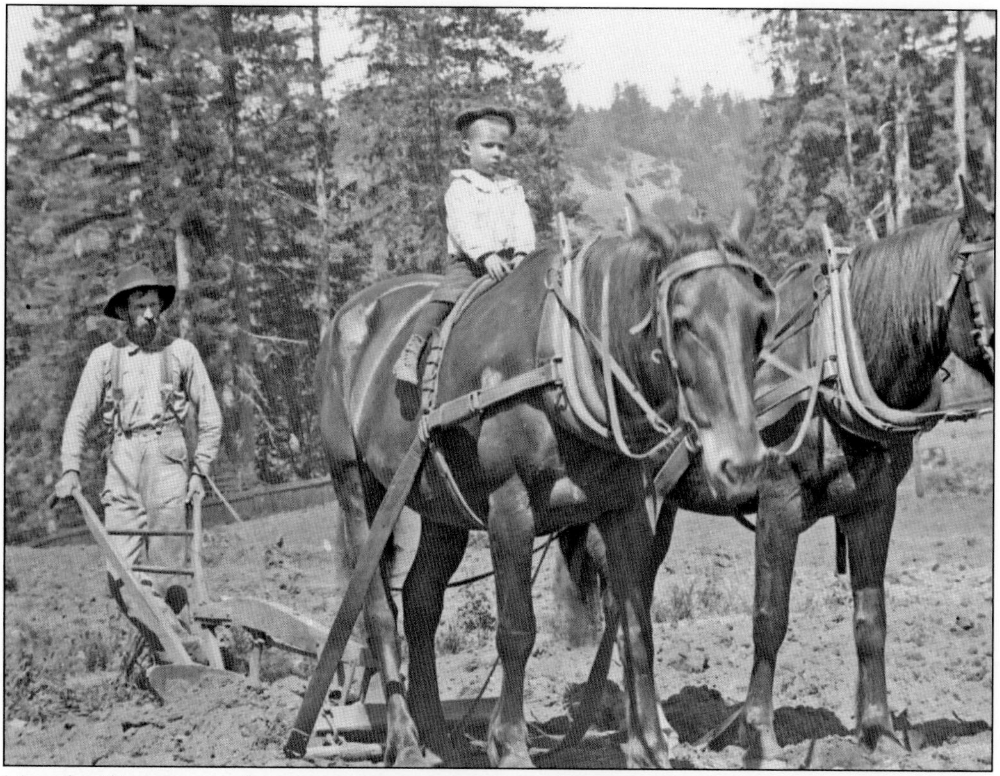

Most families grew apples, prunes, pears, apricots, and many other fruits. George Fiscus is seen plowing with Charley riding on the horse.

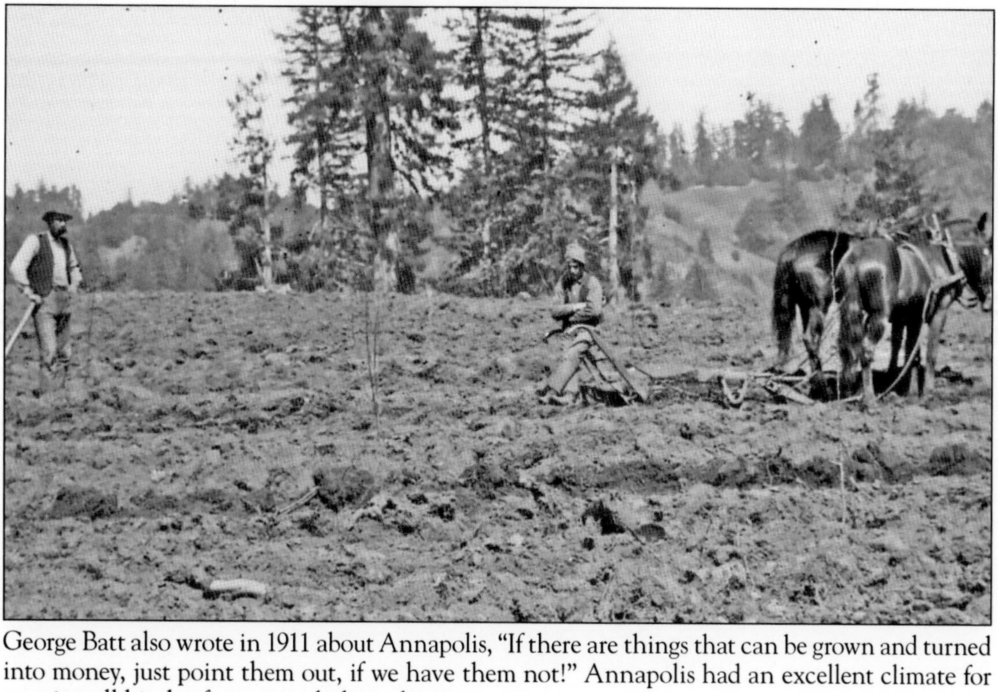

George Batt also wrote in 1911 about Annapolis, "If there are things that can be grown and turned into money, just point them out, if we have them not!" Annapolis had an excellent climate for growing all kinds of crops, including olives.

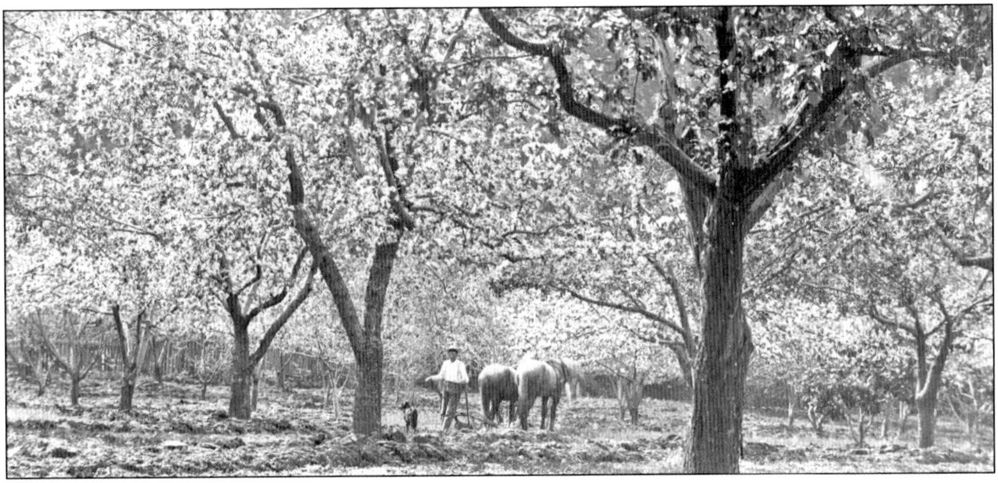

The photograph above shows a prune orchard in full bloom. Besides apples, Annapolis was known for heavy prune production, with several families steadily growing prunes. George Batt wrote in 1915, "All of the orchardists have had a fine fall to finish drying and ship their apples and prunes. There has been a great demand for Annapolis dried apples. Wetmore Bros. alone contracted for 50 tons and could have sold much more. Our Gravensteins were in great demand in the city, and soon this fine apple will be as famous here as on 'Gold Ridge.' Sonoma County will be greatly enriched by her Gravenstein apples."

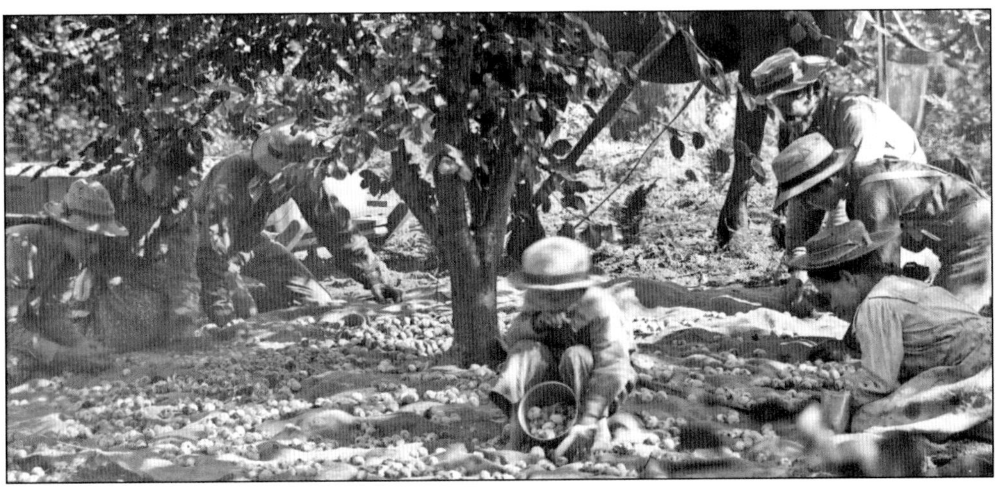

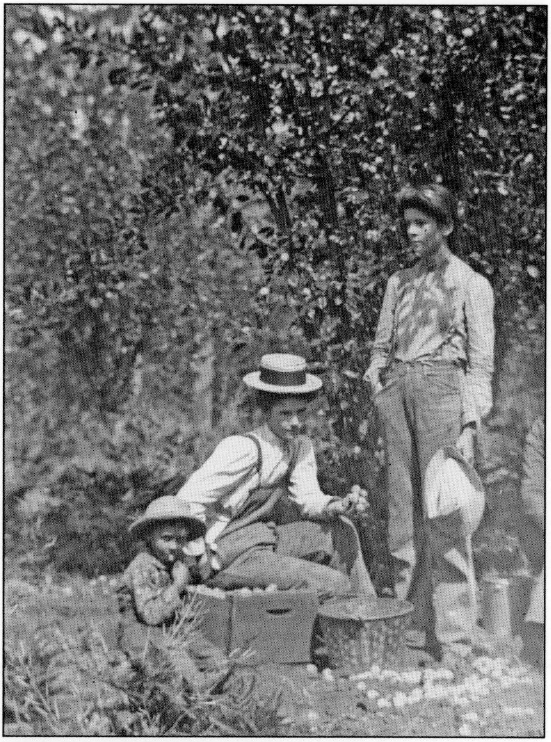

Harvesting the fruit became the new industry in Annapolis. While the Gualala River area was being logged, as well as some areas of Annapolis, other land areas were used for orchards. These orchards were quite successful. George Batt said it best in 1915: "We have tens of thousands of acres along the coast just adapted for this fruit and the man or woman is wise that will buy and plant . . . our Gravensteins will run 96 percent free of worms while nearly all other varieties are more than half wormy."

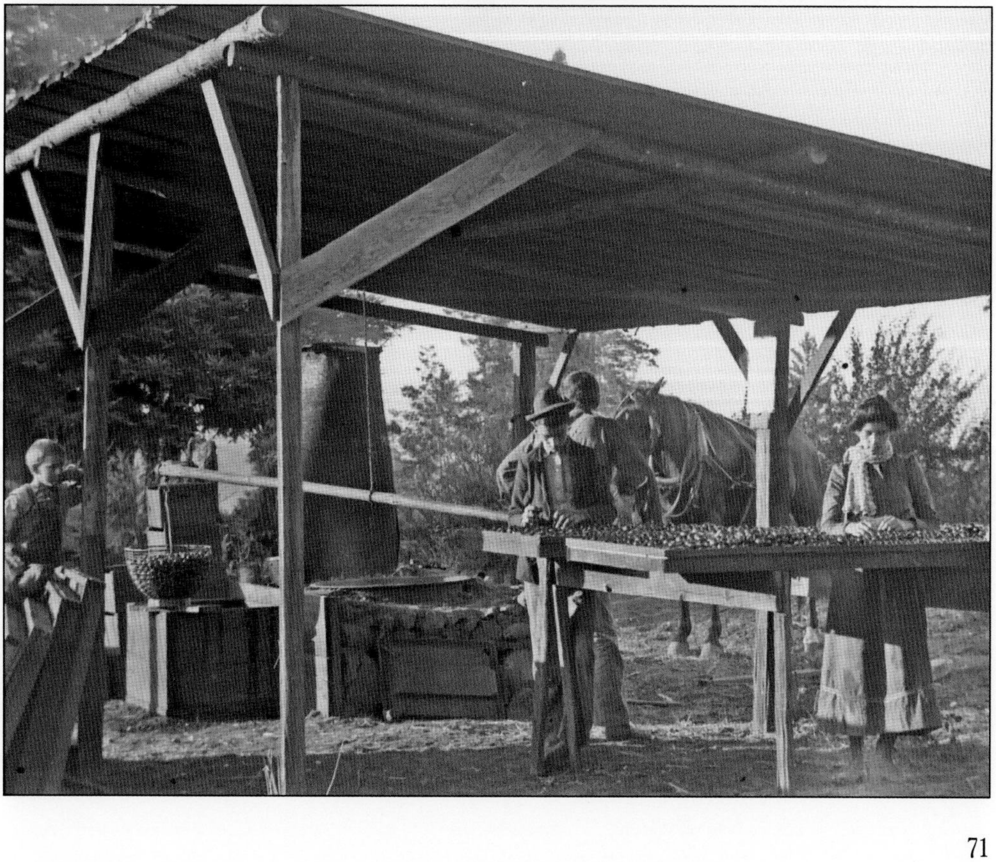

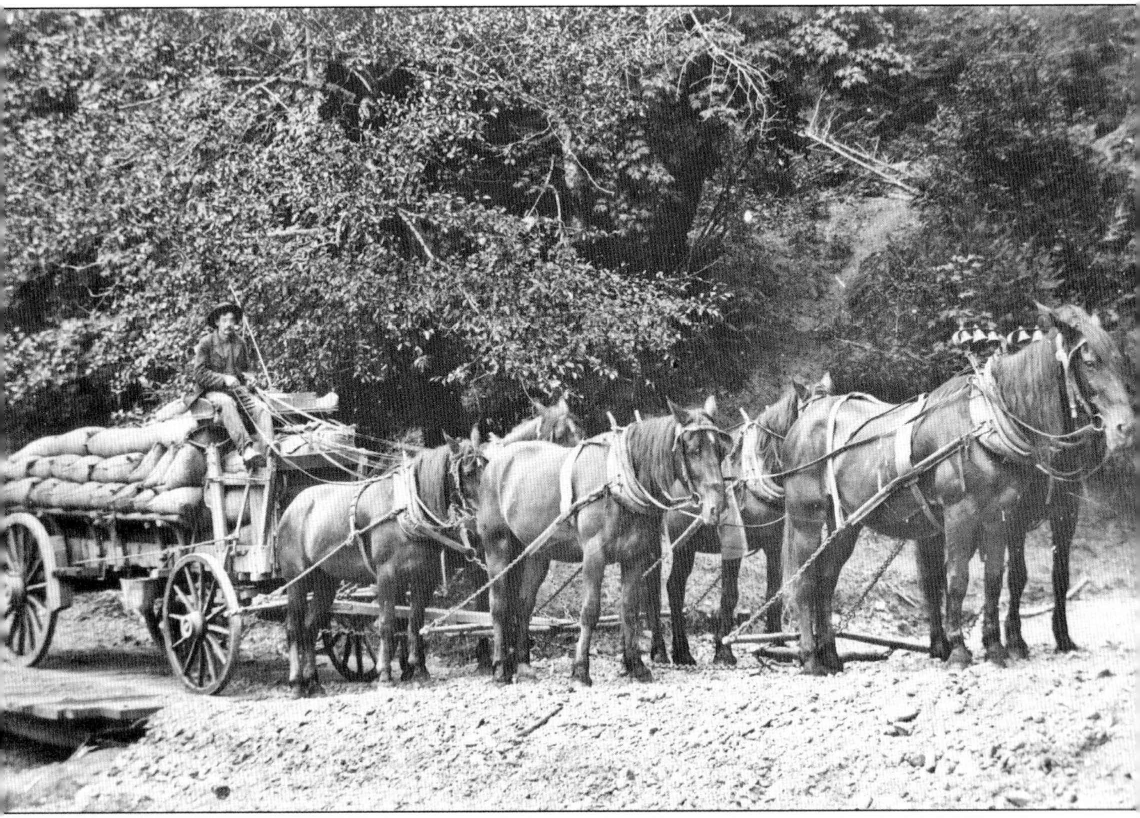

Hiram McMillen was the eldest son of Henry McMillen and sister to Molly McMillen Fiscus. He was well known for apple production. He also was the mail carrier. George Batt reported on May 19, 1915: "During the recent rain storm, for three days our mail carrier, Hyrum McMillen could not cross the river."

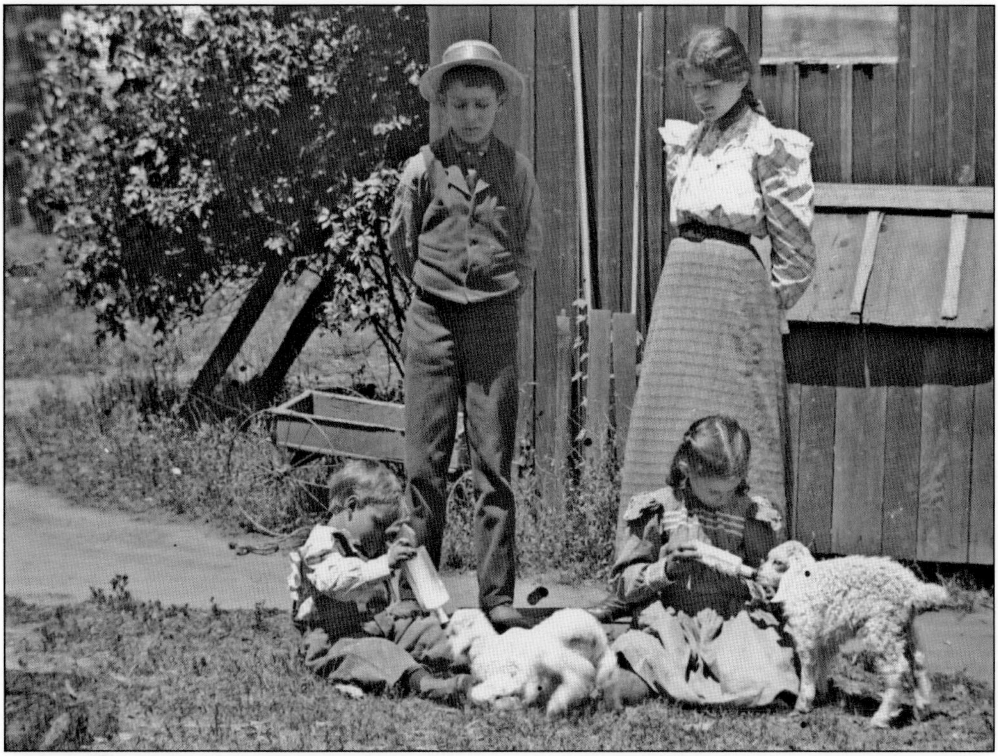

The Fiscus children, Charley, Fred, Grace, and Lois, are seen feeding their lambs. The Fiscus Ranch is still involved in lamb raising today.

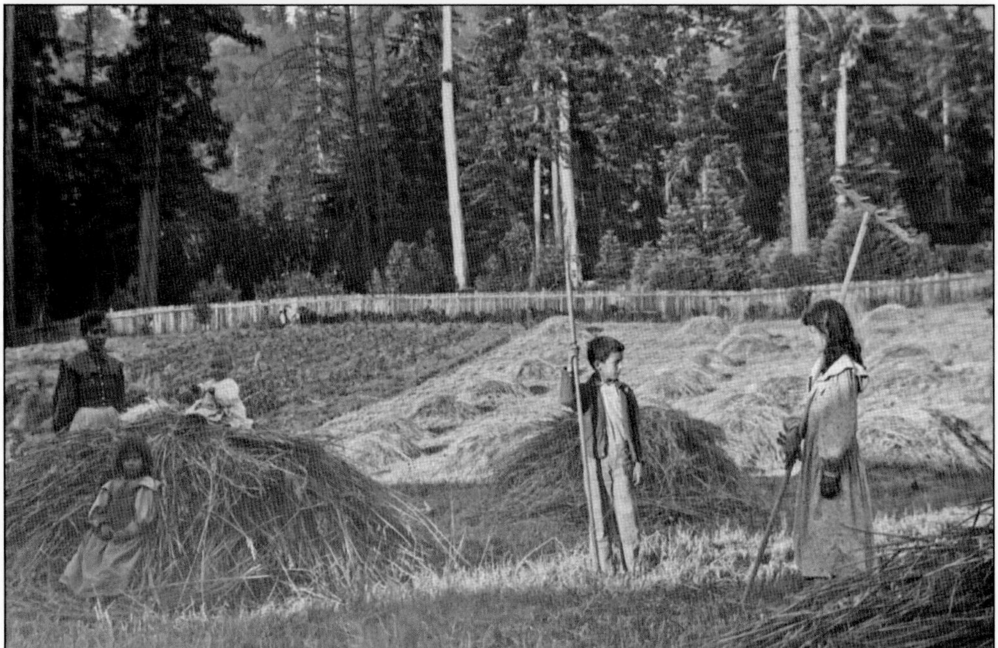

Many Annapolis families had large families to help with farm chores. The Batt family had 14 children, the McMillens had 10, and the Patchett family had 10.

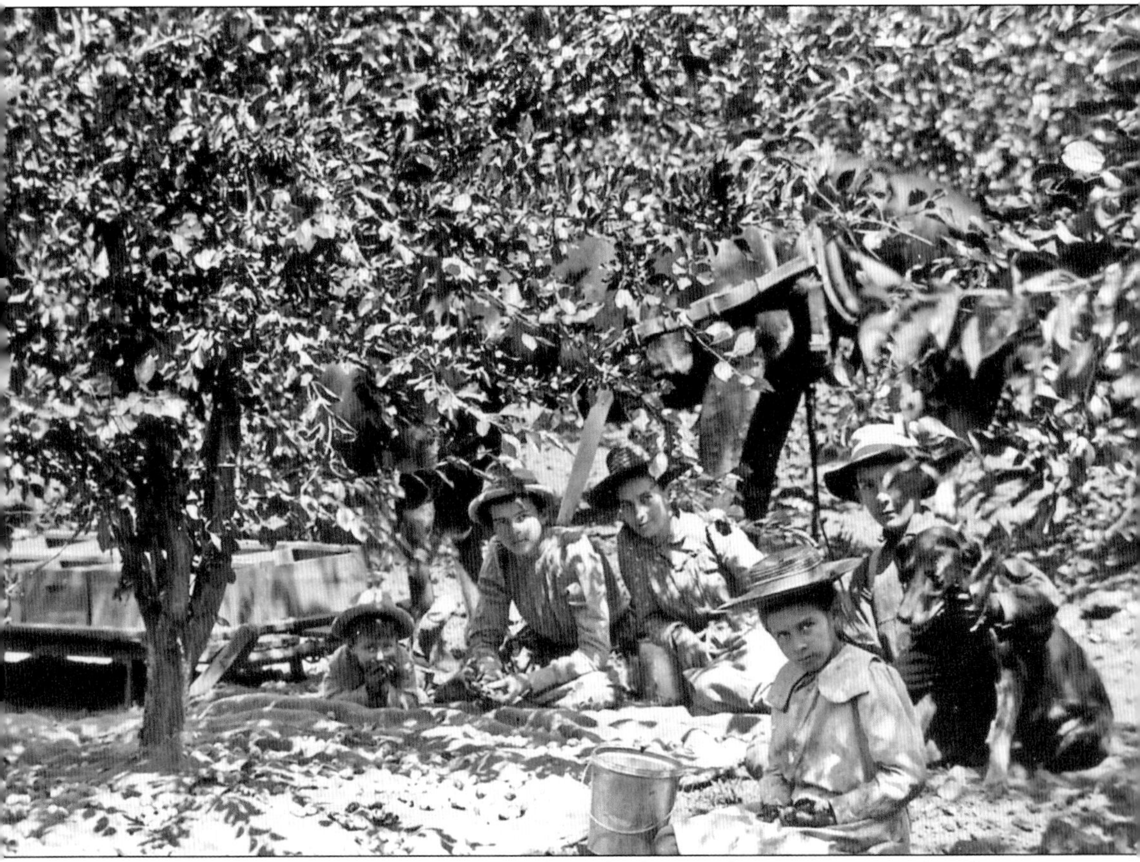

On December 26, 1911, George Batt wrote about the fruit production in Annapolis, "Our prunes are hard to beat and our plums are rich and beautiful. . . . Now if this is not paradise, point us to the beacon light showing the way. . . . And the best crop of all is our healthy, happy children."

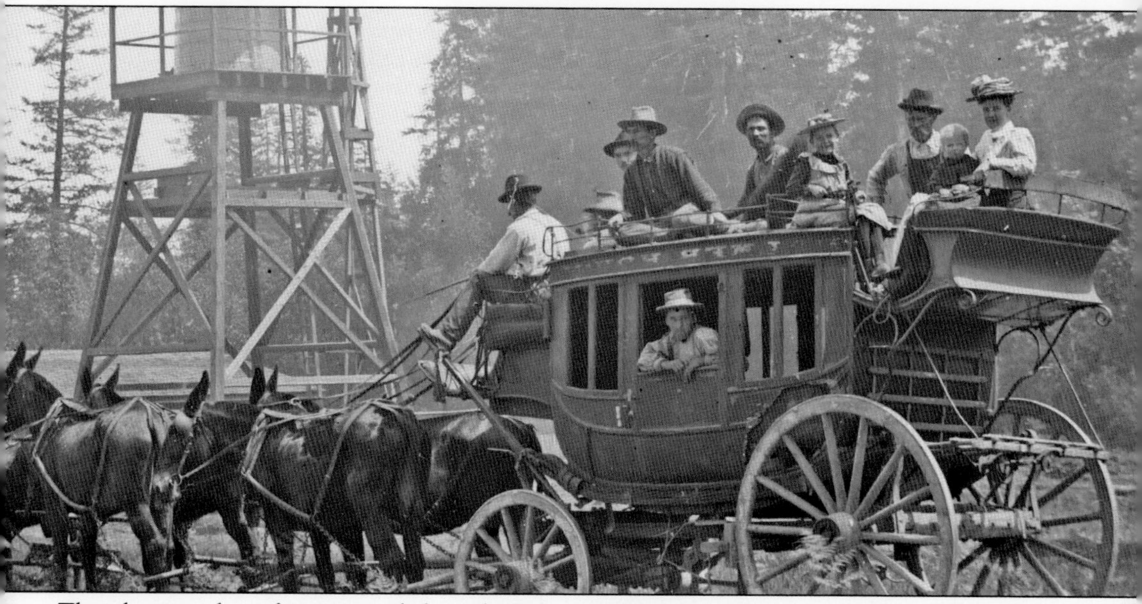

This photograph is of a stagecoach from the Palace Hotel in San Francisco brought to Wetmore's apple orchards in Annapolis. It is unknown exactly why the stagecoach travelled to the orchards, as there was not a stagecoach route in Annapolis.

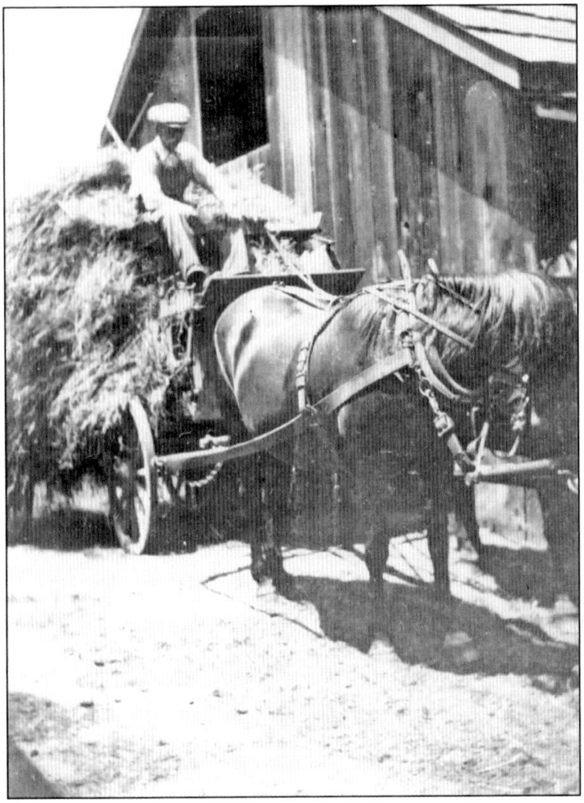

In later years, George Fiscus still worked on his ranch. Here he is shown beside his cow barn.

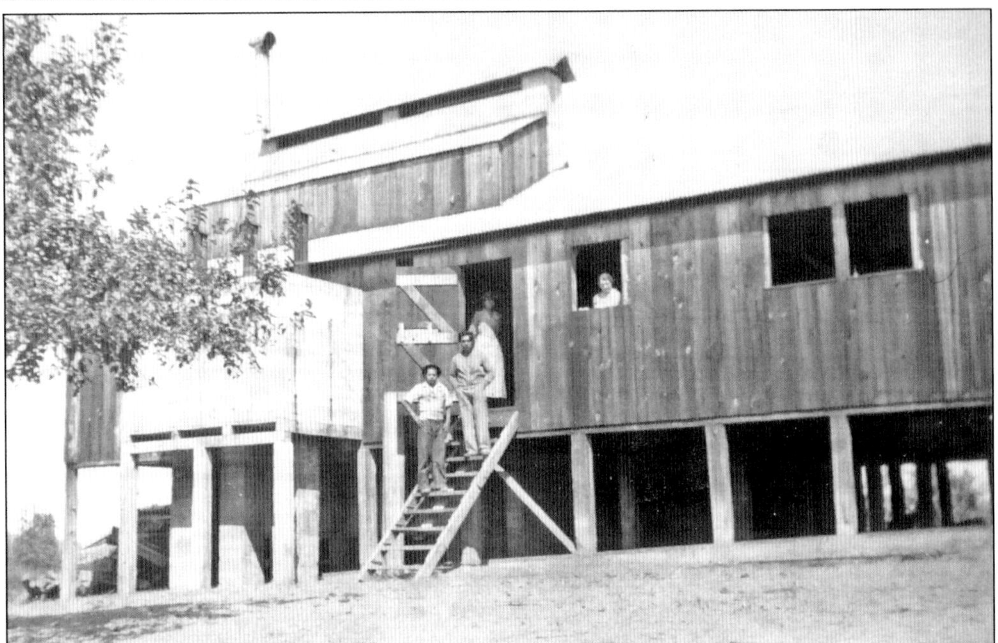

This apple dryer, in a photograph from the 1930s, shows that apple dryers were used for many years in the area. This dryer from the Ohlson Ranch was new and, according to the notes on the photograph, cost about $2,000.

Five

Schools and Family Life

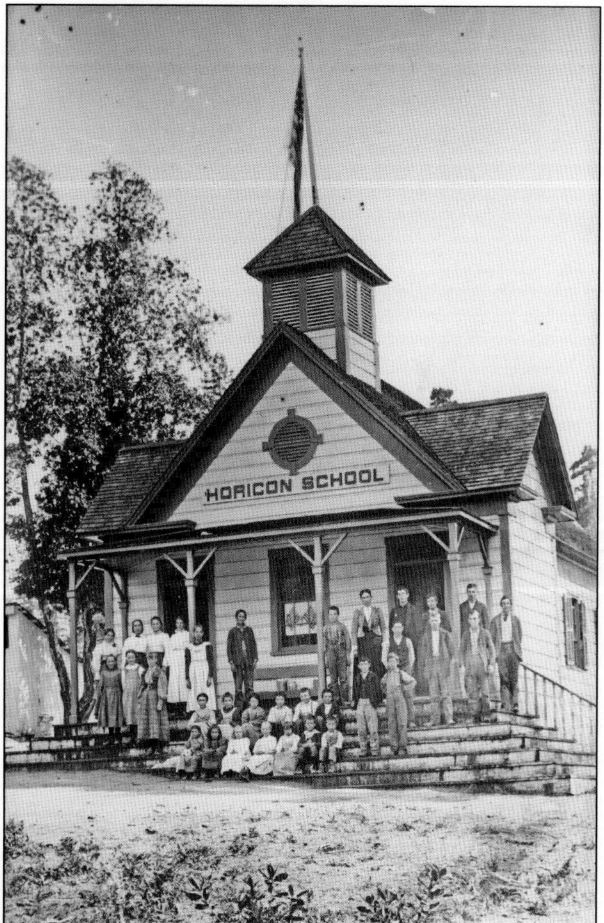

Horicon School, seen here about 1900, began around 1877 and is still operating. This historical schoolhouse is no longer used as the school and is now the home of the Annapolis Historical Society. Local families sent their children here and many later became the teachers, such as Docia Patchett.

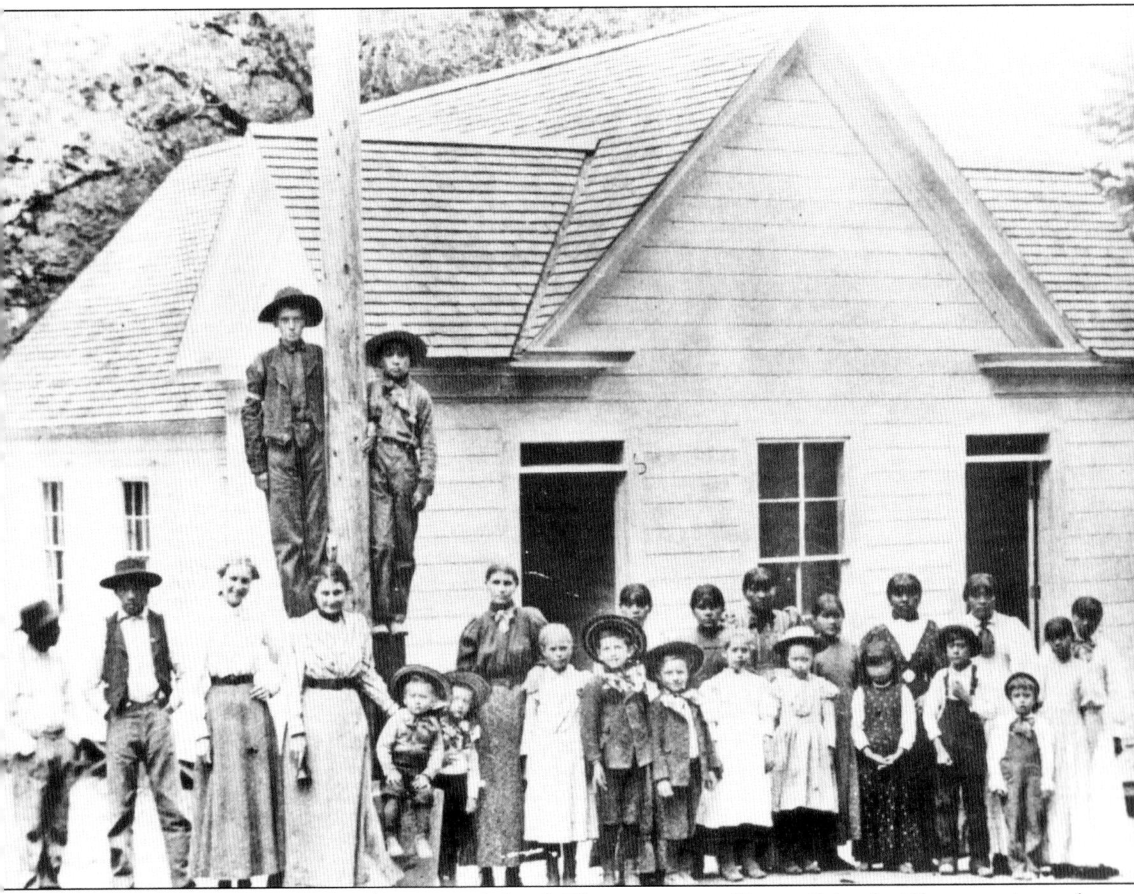

Another local school was the Dirigo School. There were two Dirigo Schools. The one pictured above is the second Dirigo School in 1897 or 1898. Pictured are children from the Antone, Johnson, Finsterbusch, Marshall, Jarvis, Haupt, Hicks, Reynolds, Ohlson, Pinole, and Williams families. The teacher was Josee Carson. (Courtesy of Charlene and Junior Ohlson.)

Since 1877, Horicon has maintained their school records, which illustrate the population patterns for the area.

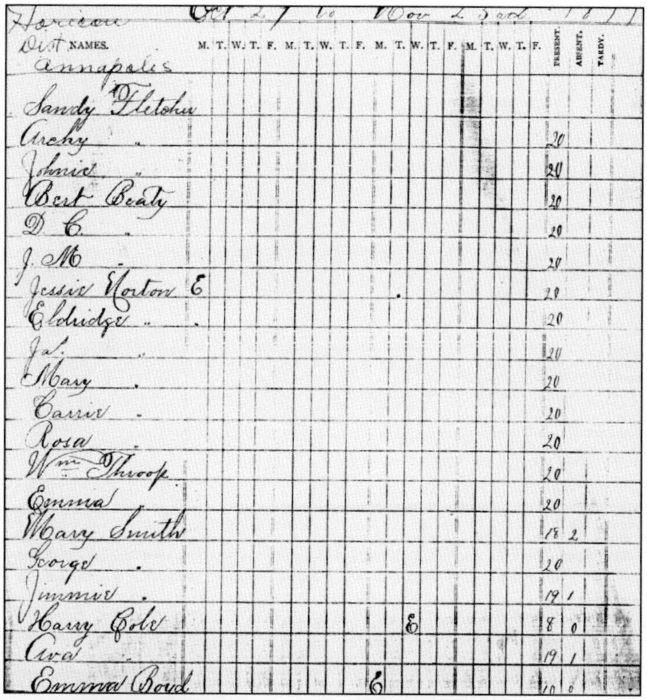

Horicon Oct 27 to Nov 23rd 1877
Dist NAMES. M. T. W. T. F. M. T. W. T. F. M. T. W. T. F. M. T. W. T. F. PRESENT. ABSENT. TARDY.
Annapolis
Sandy Fletcher
Archy " 20
Johnie " 20
Bert Beaty 20
D. C. " 20
J. M " 20
Jessie Norton E 20
Eldridge " 20
Ja. " 20
Mary " 20
Carrie " 20
Rosa " 20
Wm Throop 20
Emma " 20
Mary Smith 18 2
George " 20
Jimmie " 19 1
Harry Cole E 8 0
Ava " 19 1
Emma Boyd E 10 0

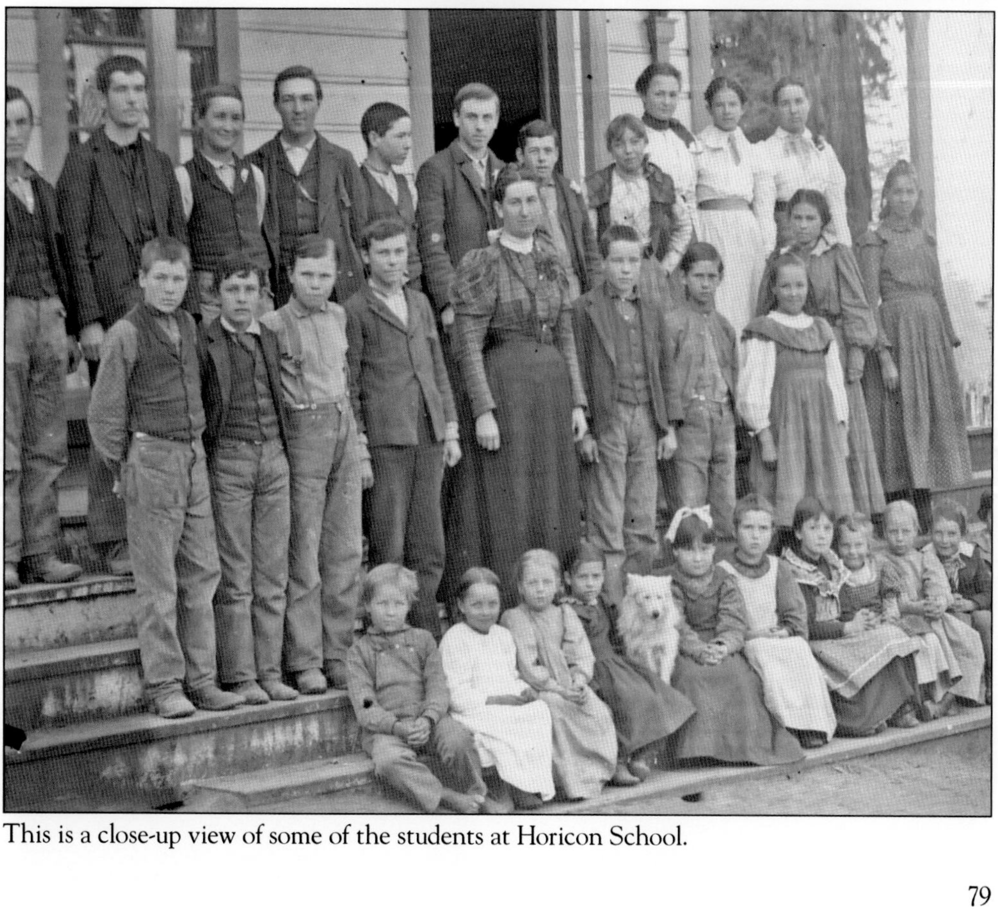

This is a close-up view of some of the students at Horicon School.

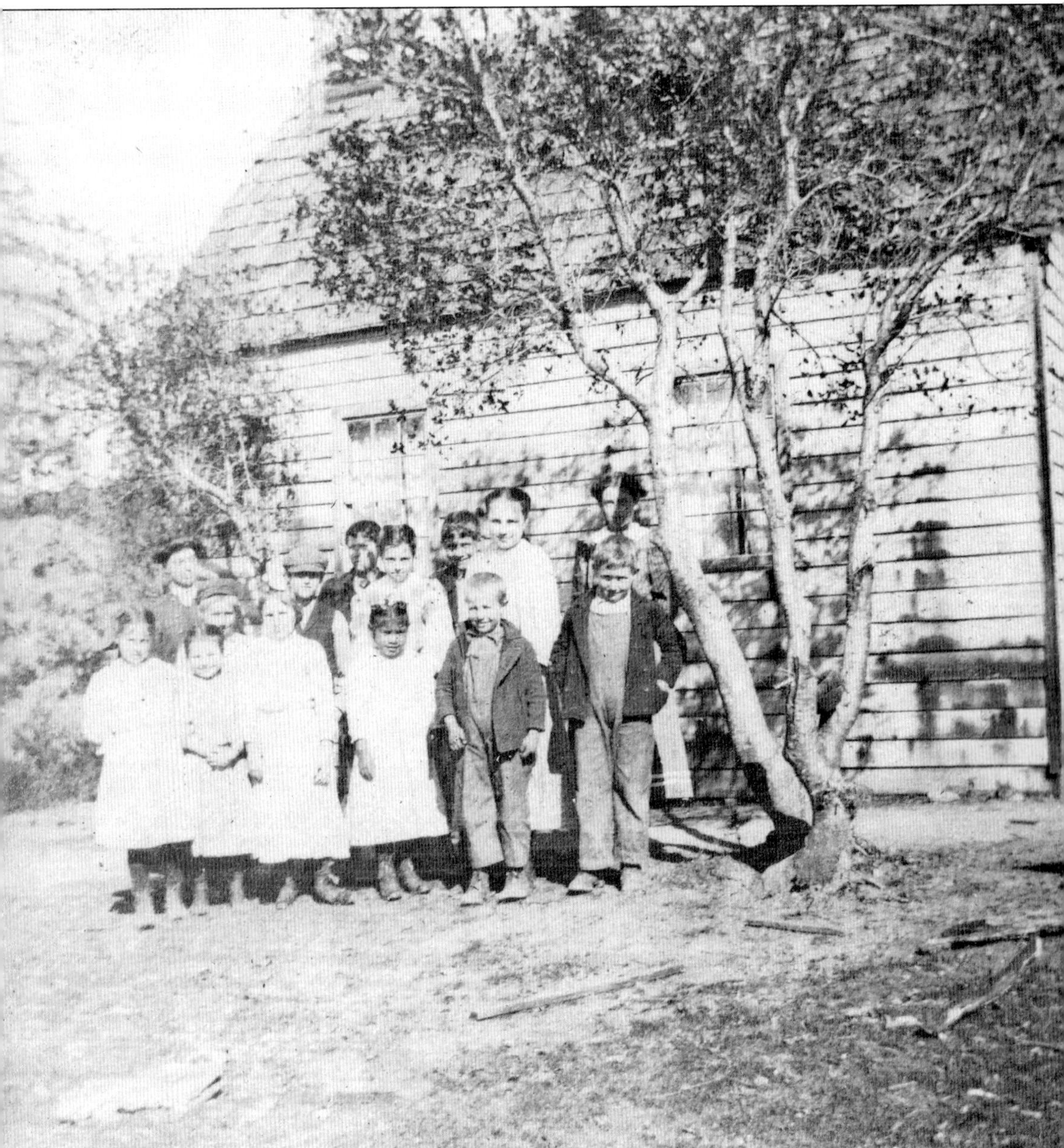

After the new Dirigo School was built, the old Dirigo School was renamed the McMillen School. Many of the children who attended the school were from the McMillen family. This school continued until at least 1916 and was then combined with Horicon School. George Batt reported in 1915: "At the McMillen School, while hard at play on Friday, Floyd McMillen broke his arm. His father and mother took him to Dr. Pitts at Point Arena." (Courtesy of William McMillen Kramer.)

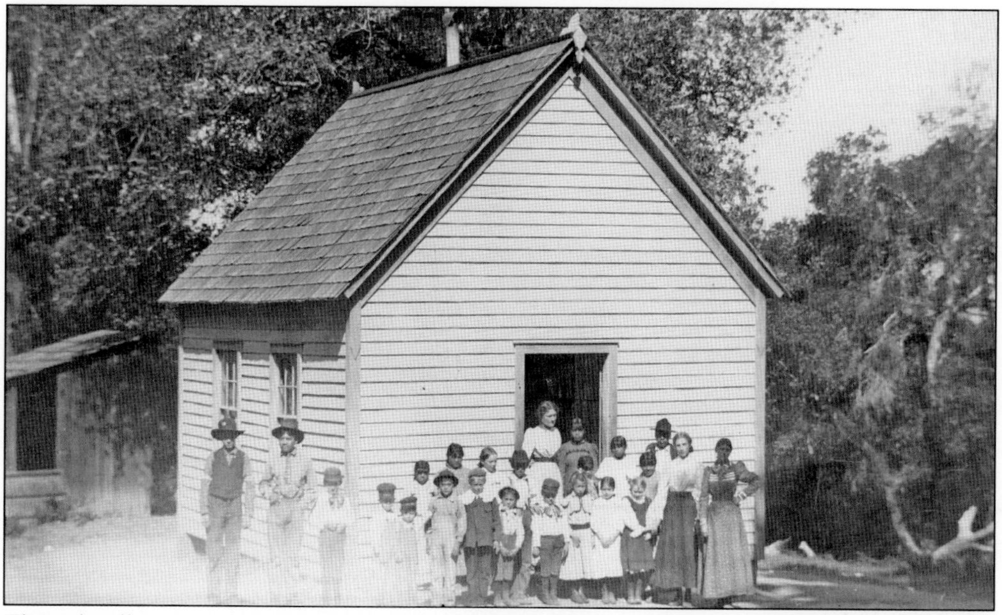

This schoolhouse was built by George Fiscus on the Ohlson ranch. The Ohlson boys, as well as the Haupt children, attended this school. It was called the Dirigo School, later known as the first Dirigo School.

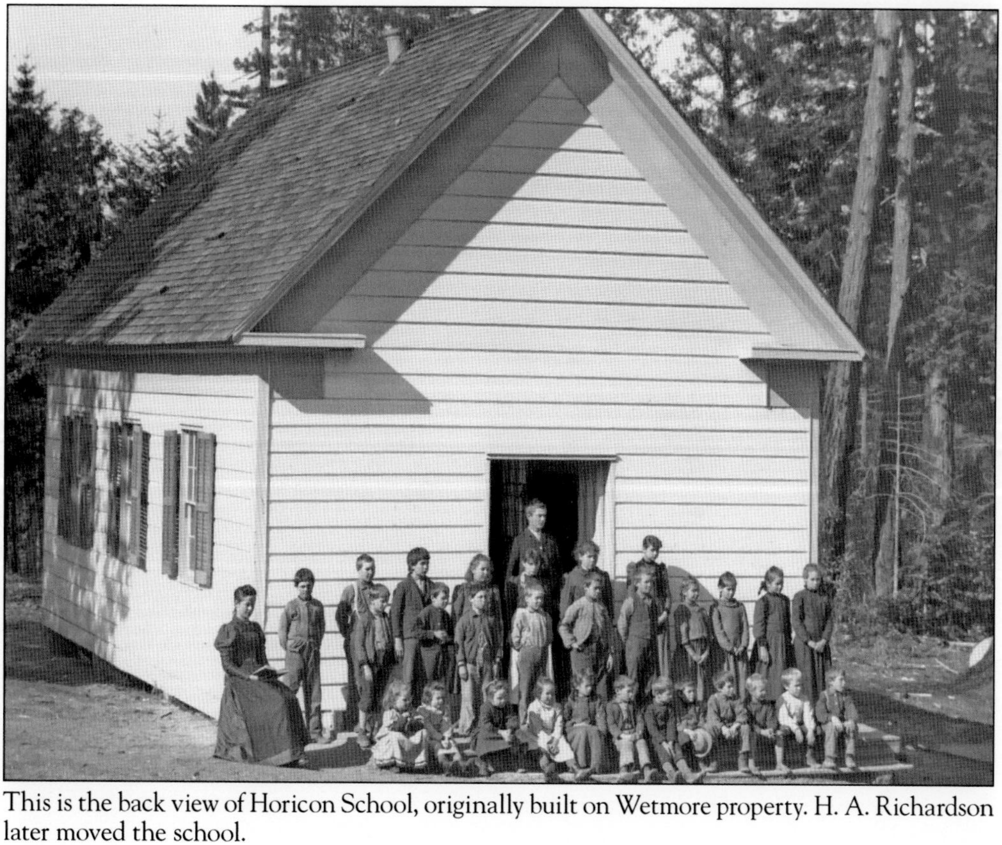

This is the back view of Horicon School, originally built on Wetmore property. H. A. Richardson later moved the school.

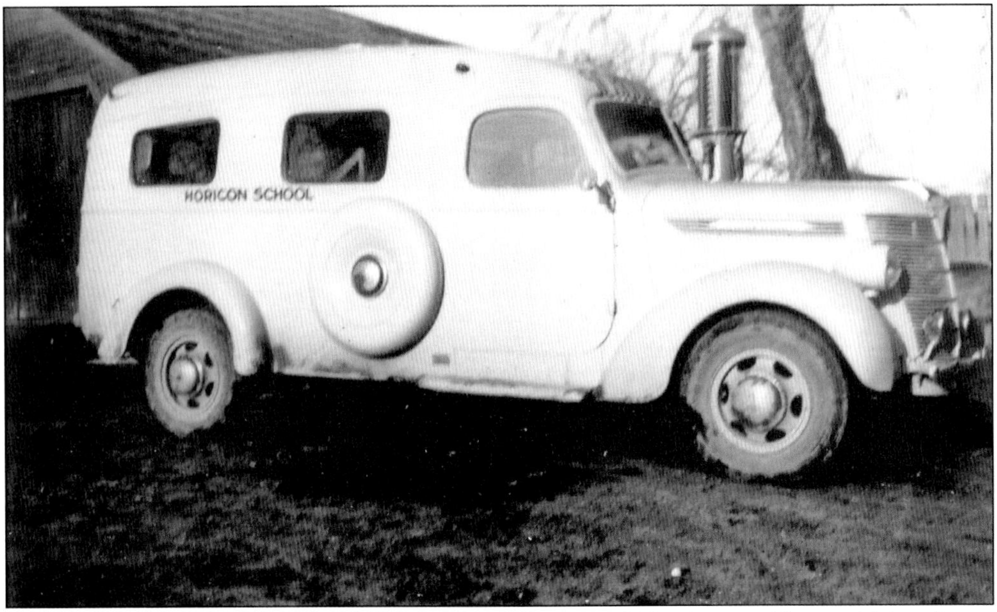

Horicon School got its first school bus in 1940. (Courtesy of Charlene and Junior Ohlson.)

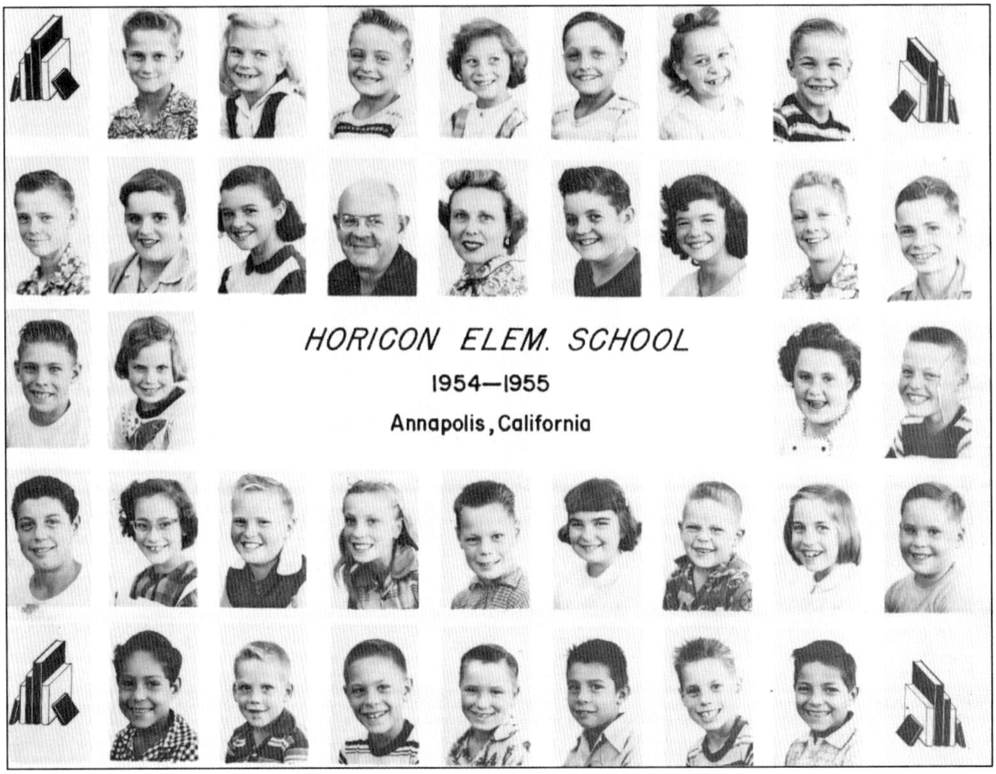

The Horicon Elementary School photograph from the 1954–1955 school year has William Conroy as teacher. The school was still quite small with only 33 students. Among those pictured are Mary, Paul, and Johnny Stibi and Karen Campbell. In later years, Conroy was instrumental in preserving the historic schoolhouse. (Courtesy of the Annapolis Historical Society.)

Inside the Horicon classroom, Conroy is looking over the desk of Pete Radtkey. Pete Radtkey later grew up and drove logging trucks in Annapolis. His children also attended Horicon School. (Courtesy of the Annapolis Historical Society.)

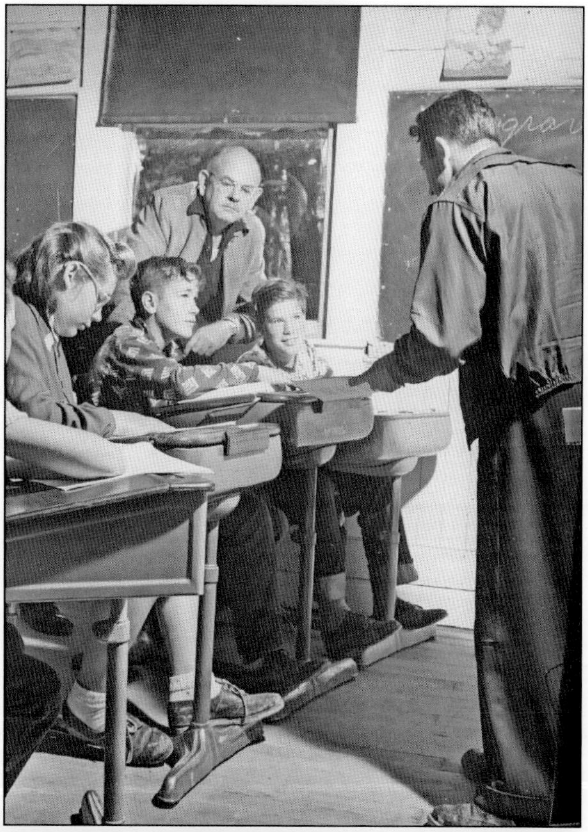

Conroy taught at Horicon School for many years. In this school photograph from the 1949–1950 school year, there are 36 students. (Courtesy of the Annapolis Historical Society.)

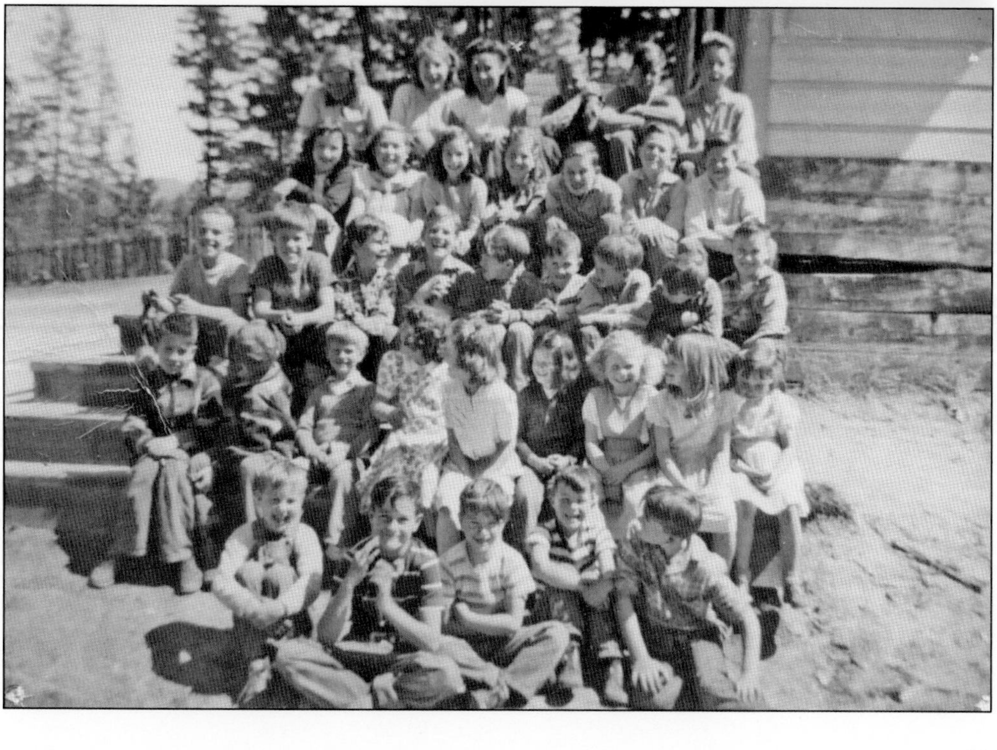

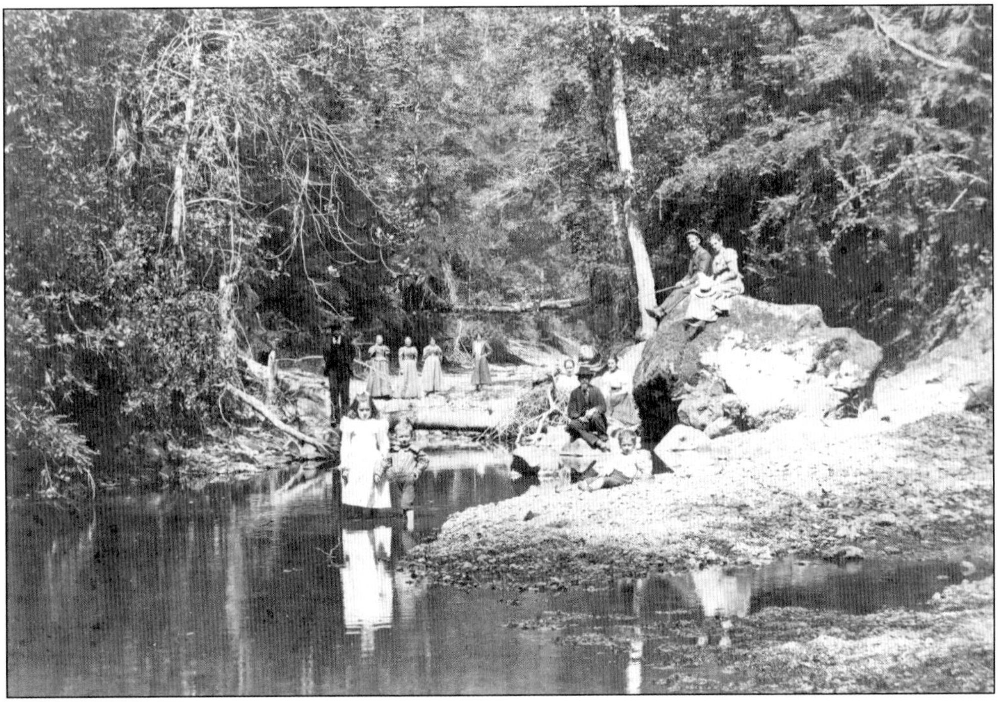

This photograph was taken August 28, 1898, at Buckeye Creek near Soda Springs in Annapolis. In this time period, it was common to picnic near this big rock. Soda Springs was considered a special site, in that there were mineral springs.

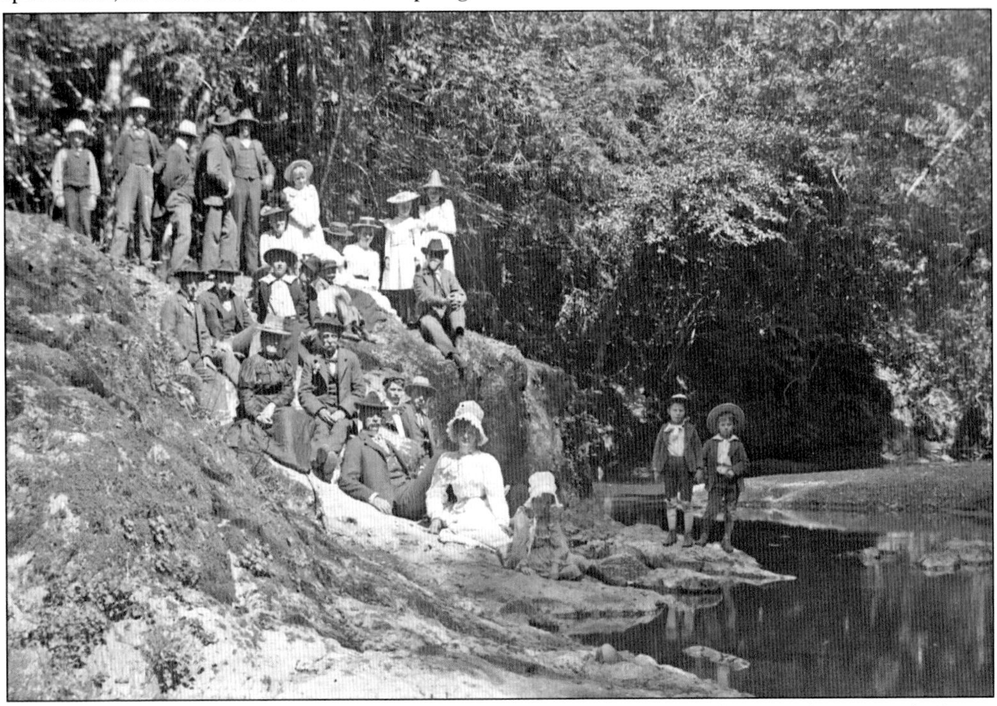

This large gathering of Annapolis residents poses against the big rock in Buckeye Creek. Since everyone is dressed up, it may be a special day celebration such as Fourth of July.

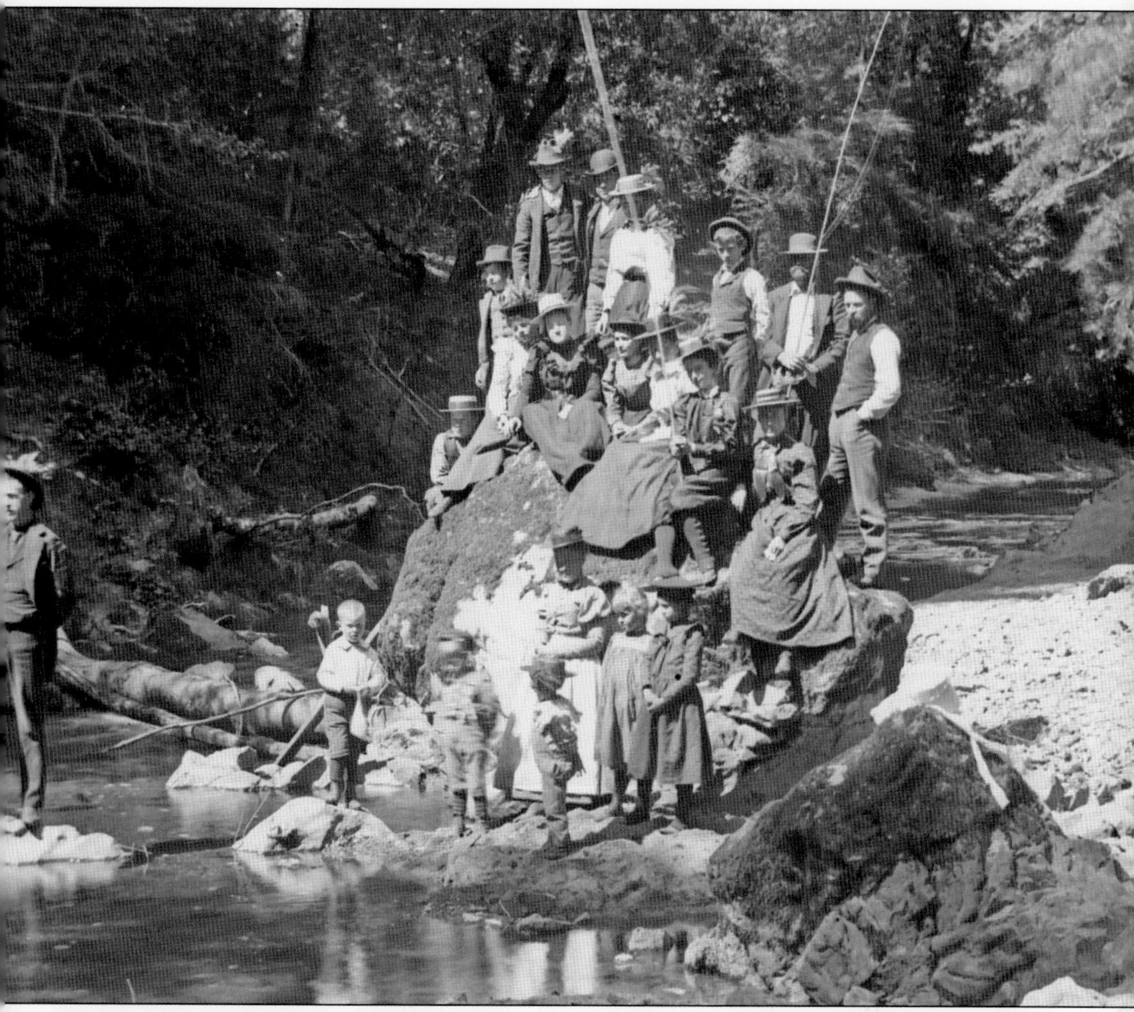

The area where Soda Springs (a natural mineral spring) flows into Buckeye Creek was considered a special spot. Pictured are members of the Batt, McMillen, Cole, Fiscus, and Stibi families.

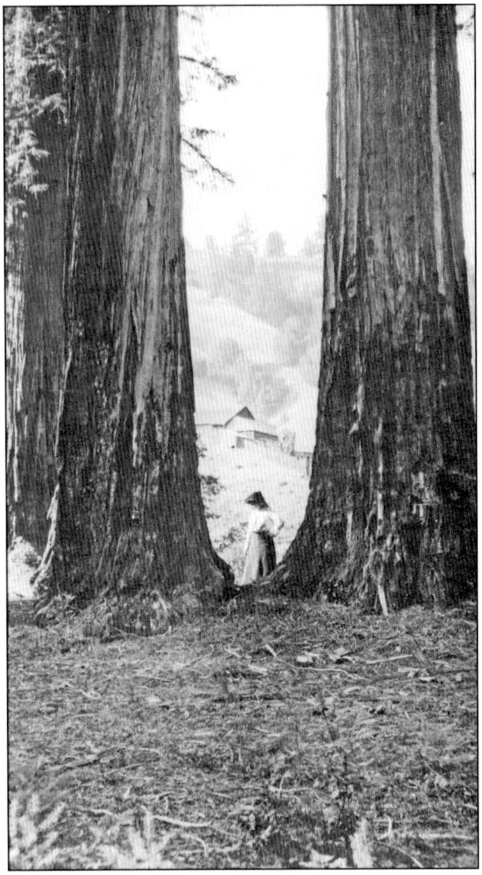

In 1913, George Batt wrote: "John Paul Stibi and Lillian Ellen Batt were married . . . Nineteen years ago, the people of Annapolis held a picnic at the mineral spring down on the beautiful Buckeye stream. Mrs. Stibi was there with her little boy and as the writer was holding his little Lillian, the good woman [said], 'what a sweet little baby; I must have her for my little Johnnie.' The years have come and gone and I never doubted the fulfillment of those words." In the photograph at left, Lillian Batt Stibi is pictured looking toward the Stibi ranch.

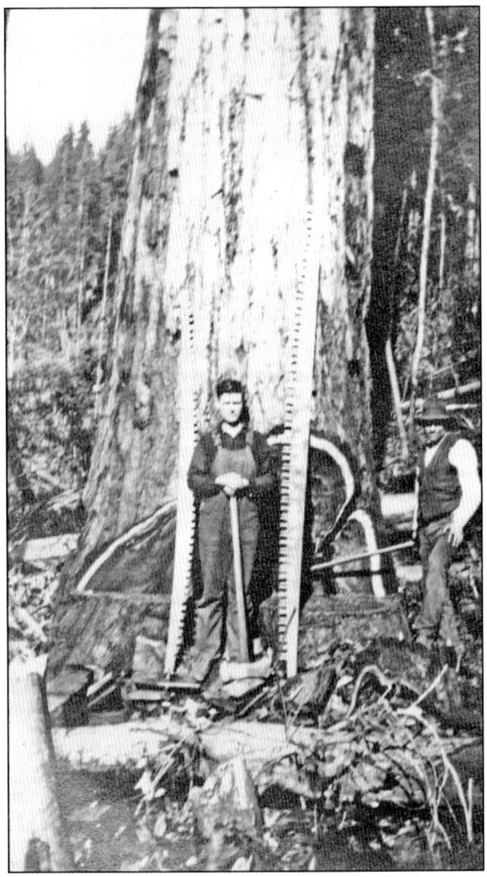

Taken in 1919, this photograph shows the size of the saws that were often used to harvest the timber. Even in 1919, there were still many large trees tucked into the woods around Annapolis and the river. (Courtesy of Arline Hamilton.)

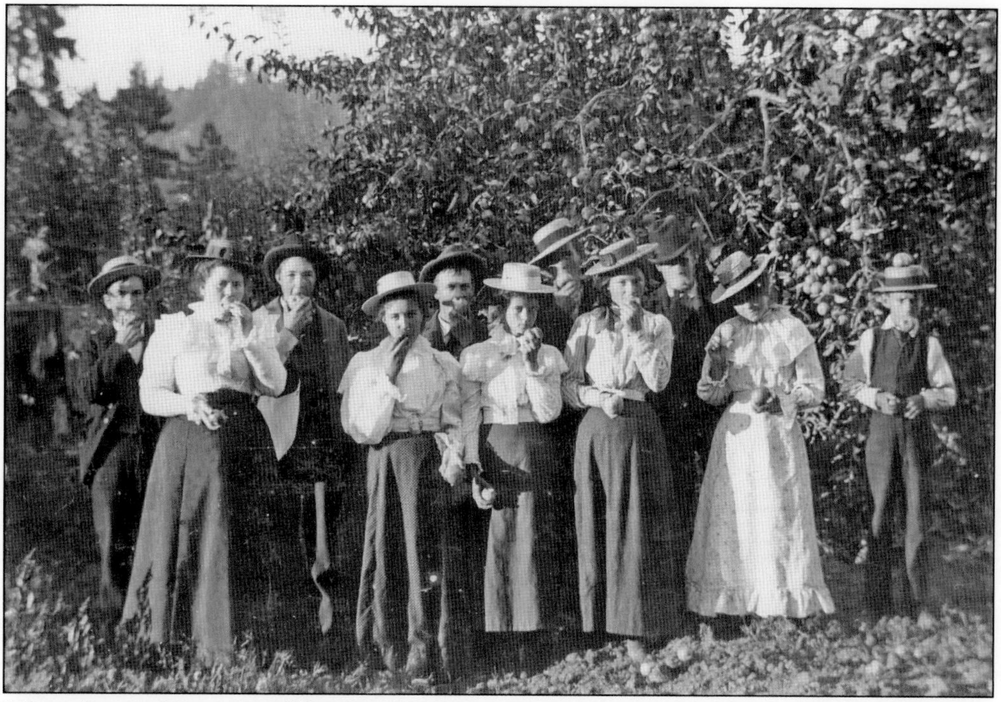

Life in Annapolis was not all hard work. Numerous celebrations took place, including gatherings like this one during a fruit harvest.

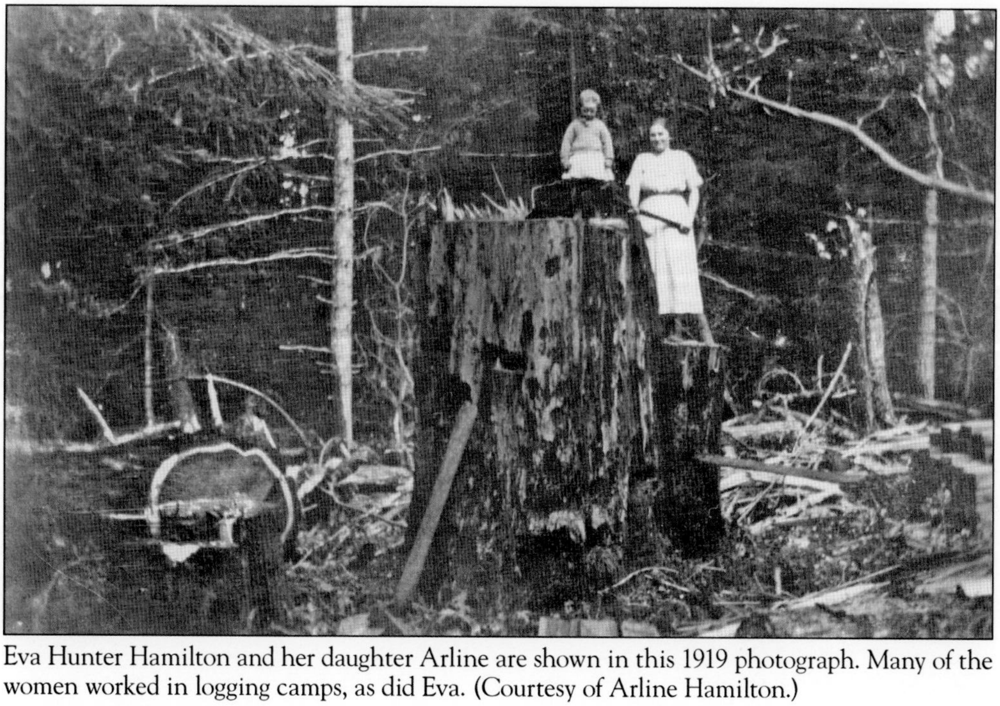

Eva Hunter Hamilton and her daughter Arline are shown in this 1919 photograph. Many of the women worked in logging camps, as did Eva. (Courtesy of Arline Hamilton.)

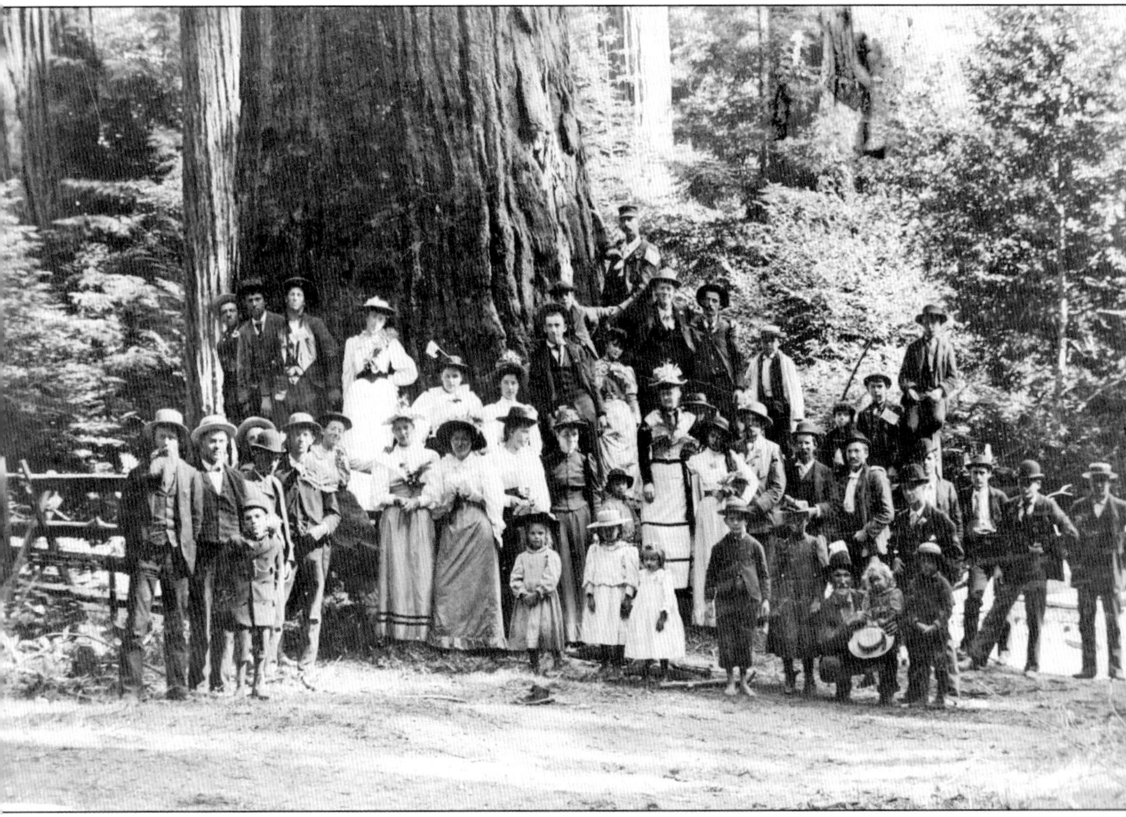

The Fourth of July was always celebrated in a big way. Many times, picnics were held by the biggest trees.

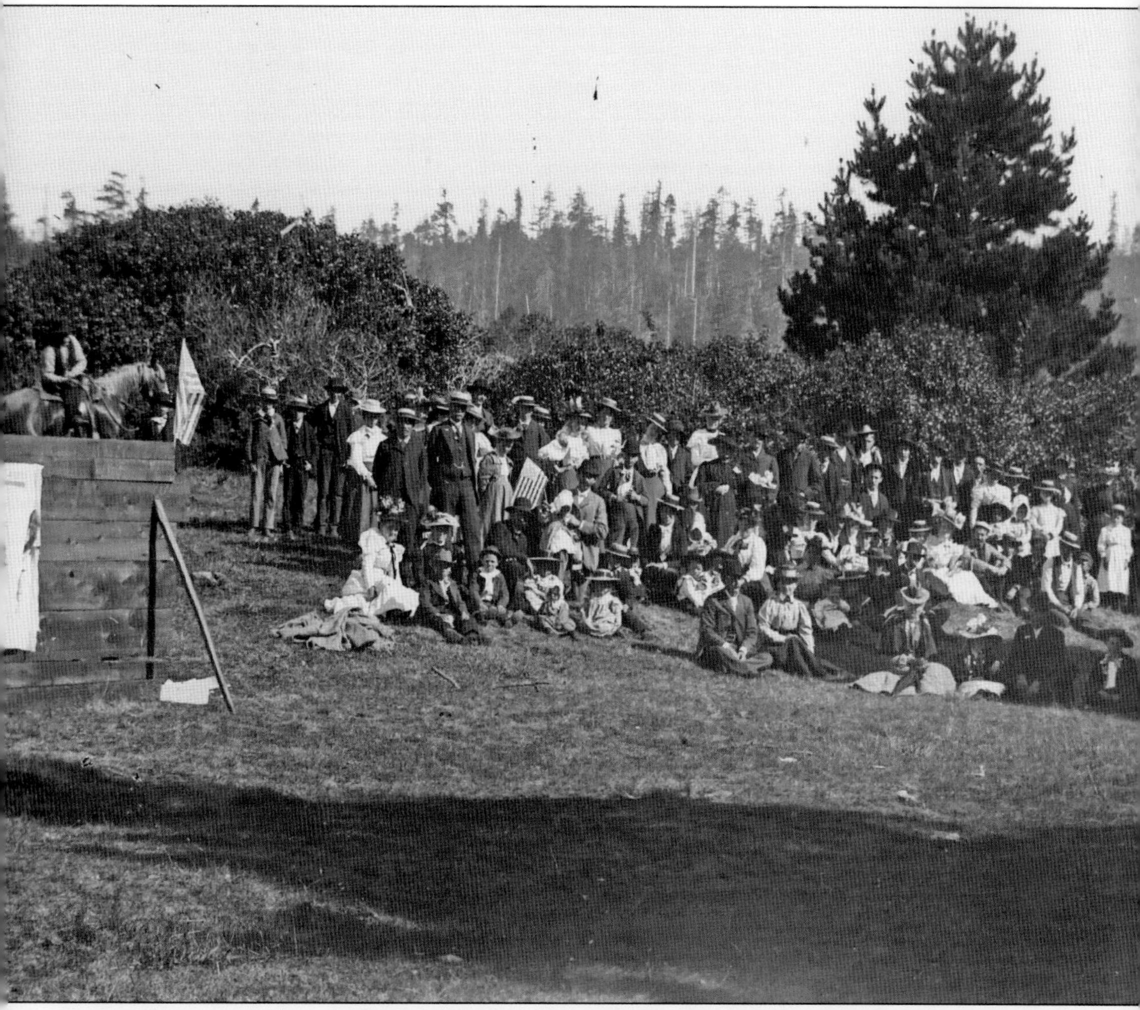

George Batt reported on the Fourth of July, 1915: "The glorious Fourth passed by the people of Annapolis enjoying themselves at different places. About 55 spent the day on the Buckeye and freely drank of the water at the famous mineral spring. There was singing of songs and recitations and a number of fine cornet solos by Ulysses Patchett."

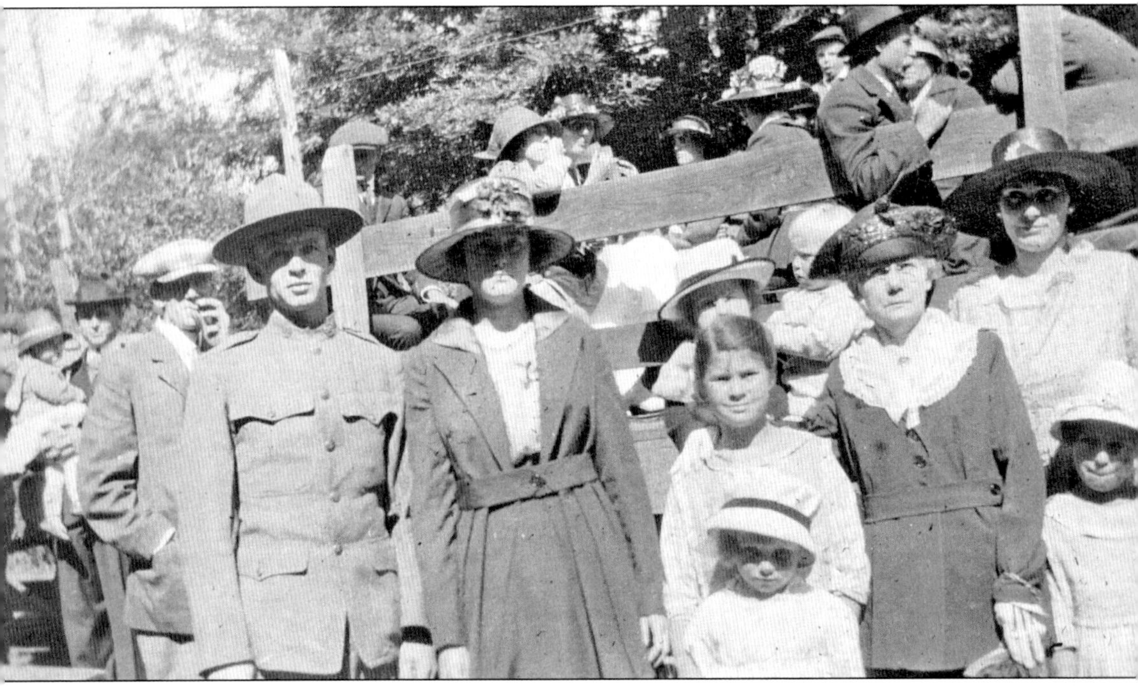

Taken July 4, 1919, members of the Hunter and Hamilton families are loading up for the annual picnic on the Gualala River. (Courtesy of Arline Hamilton.)

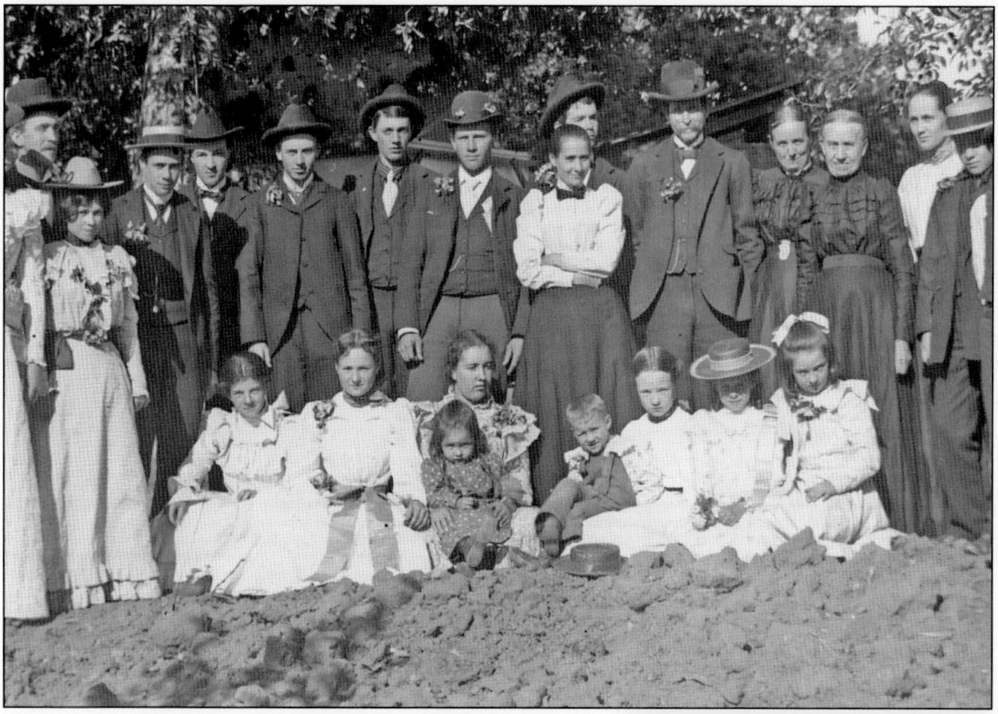

This is a wedding photograph from the 1900s. Pictured are members of the Patchett and Hickman families.

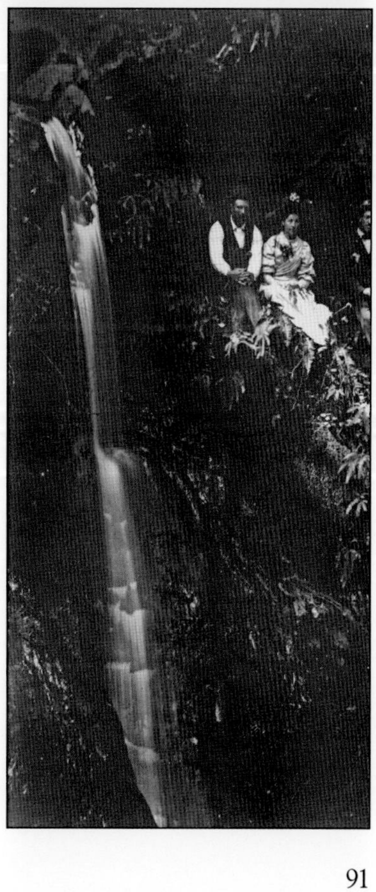

This photograph is at the waterfalls at Fuller Creek. The bride and groom are posing against the falls.

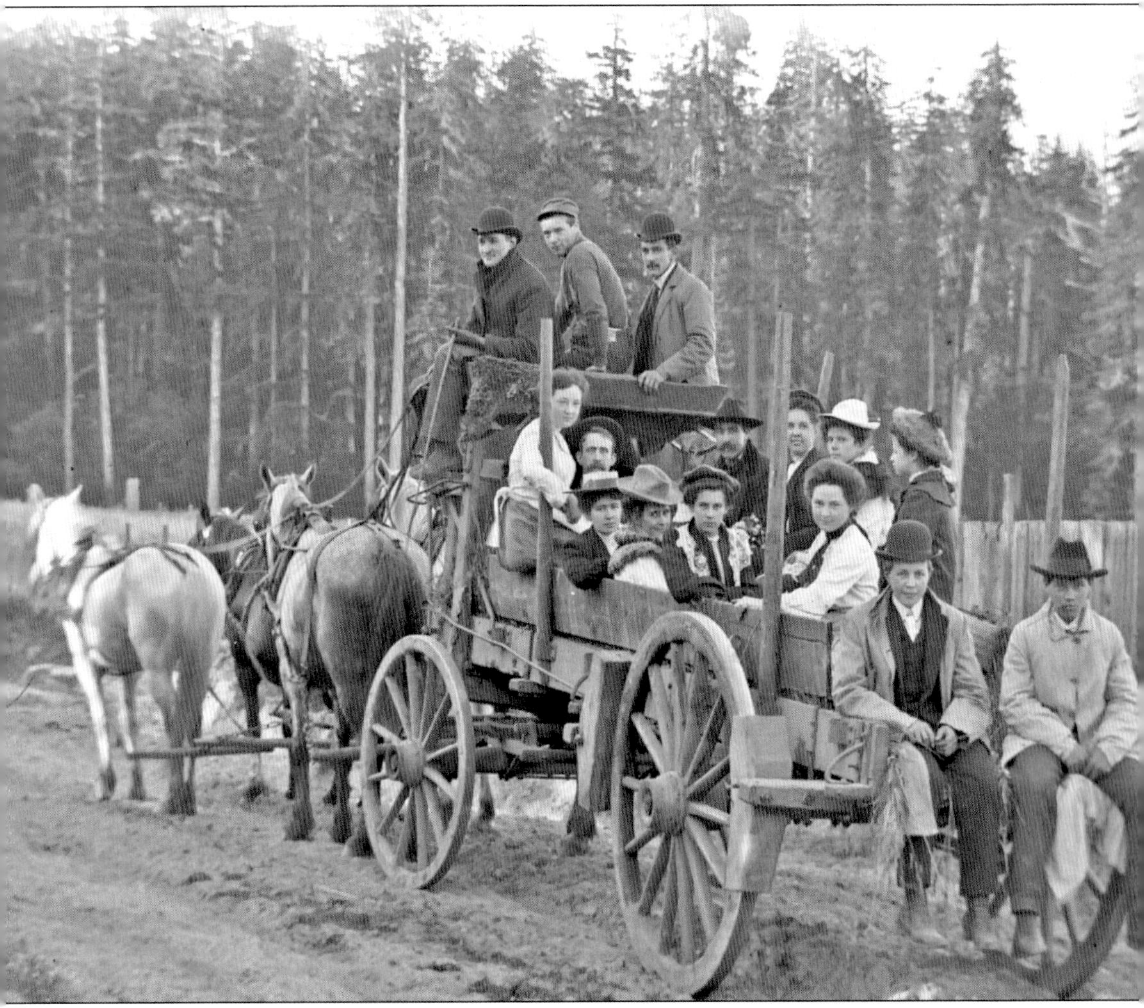

Black Point had a hotel and saloon. This wagonload of people was on the way to a dance at Black Point.

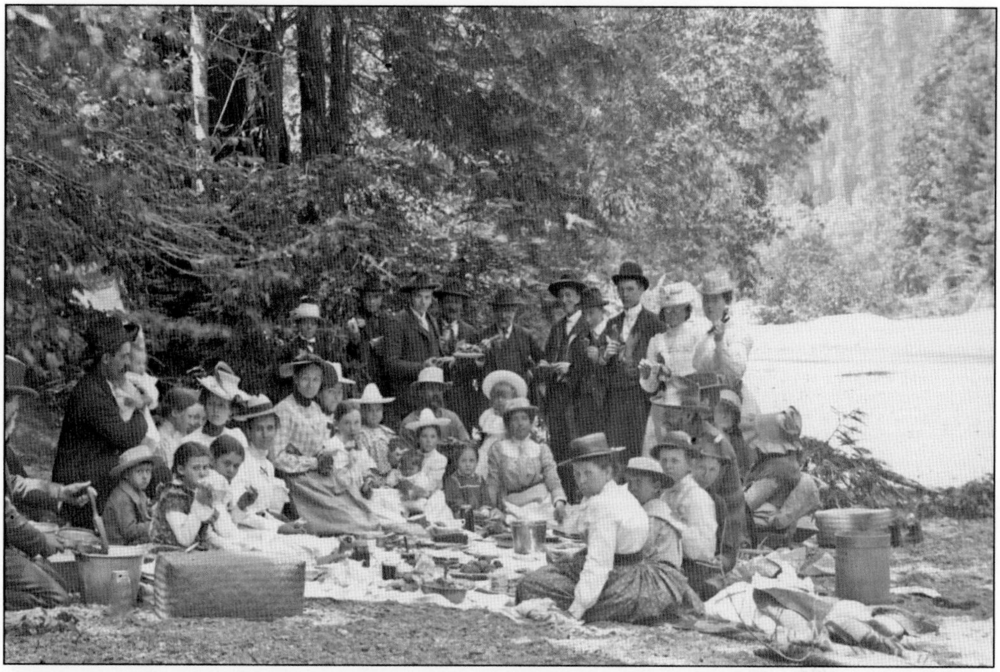

This picnic, alongside the Gualala River, shows the tall timbers in the background. The Gualala River was known as a vacation spot for many people, even those outside the area.

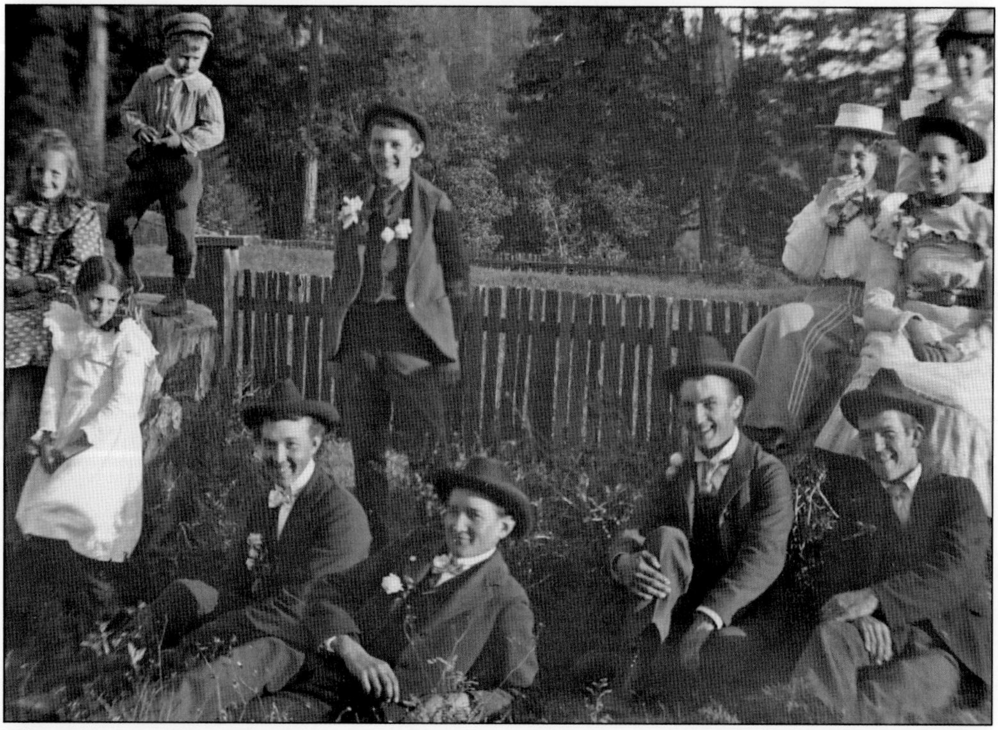

This photograph, probably from a wedding celebration, was taken in the early 1900s. Weddings were widely reported in the local newsletters and newspapers, as they were cause for great celebration.

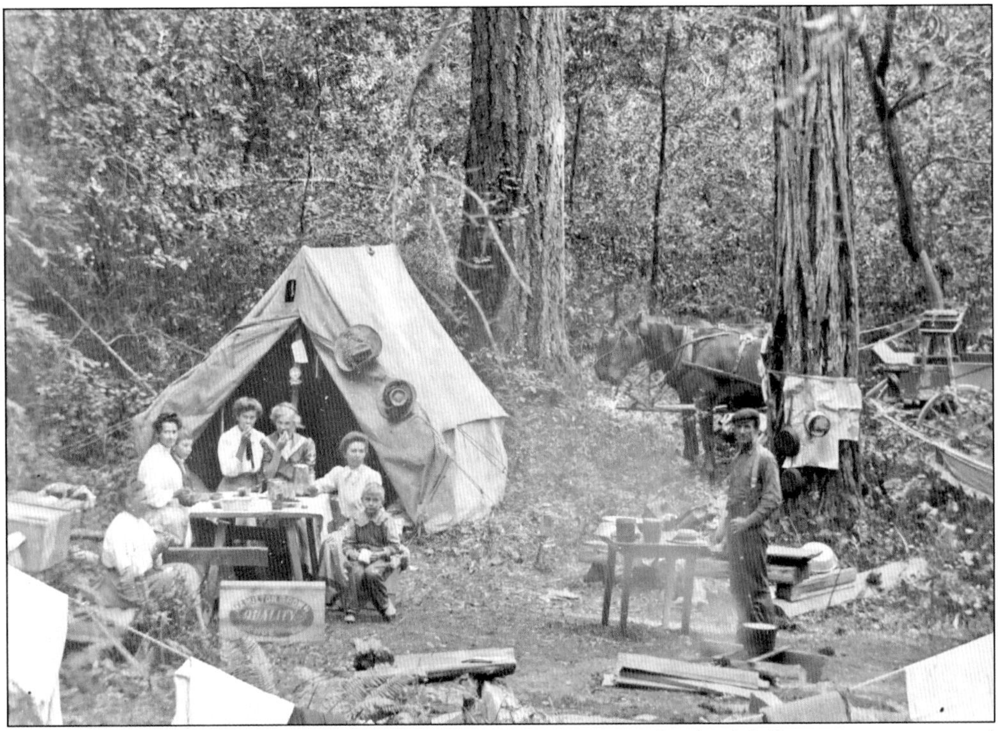

These photographs show camps that families often set up. Families had different camp areas and named the camps. Although they were camping, the women still wore skirts. Some of the camps were more established than others.

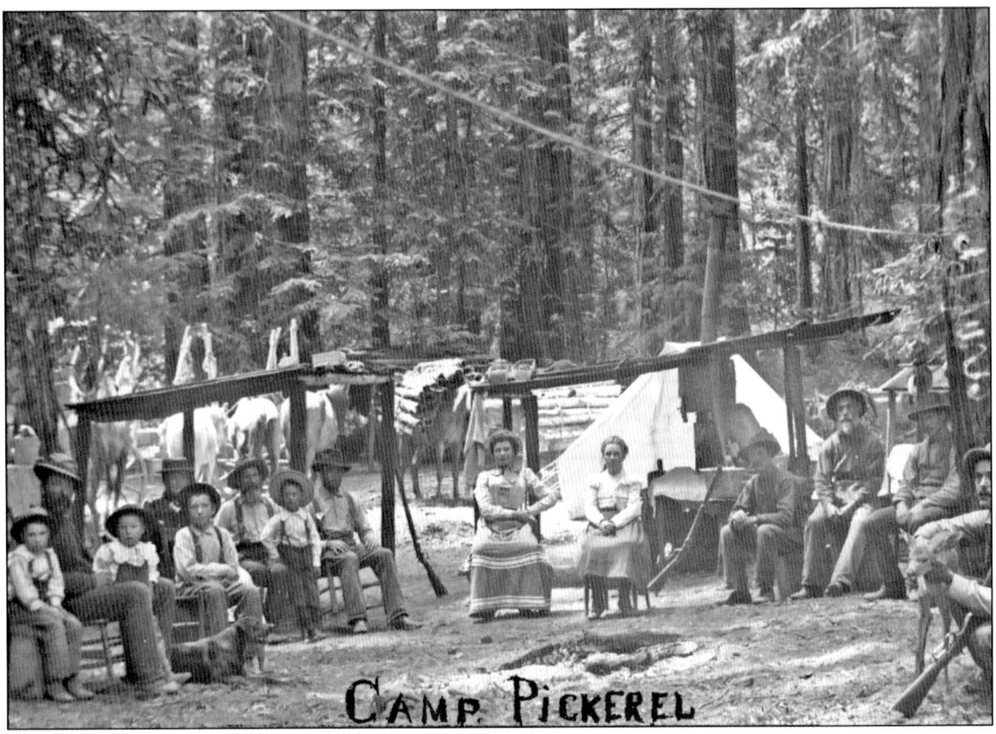

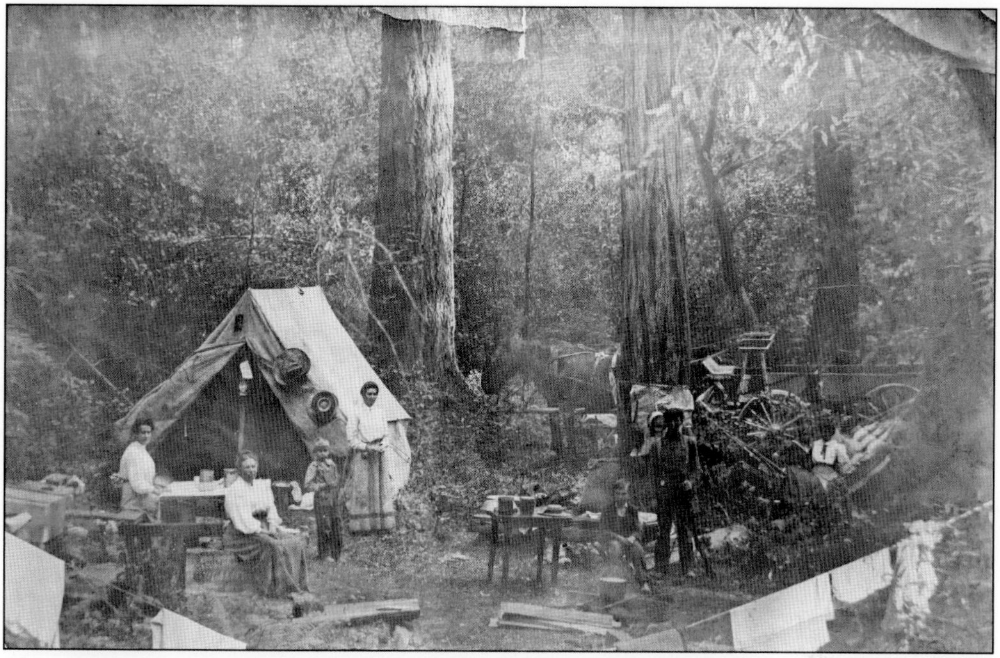

There was great focus on the family and the children. This snow scene is probably from the Lookout area, which is high on a ridge in Annapolis, thus having a higher elevation and more of a chance for snow during colder conditions.

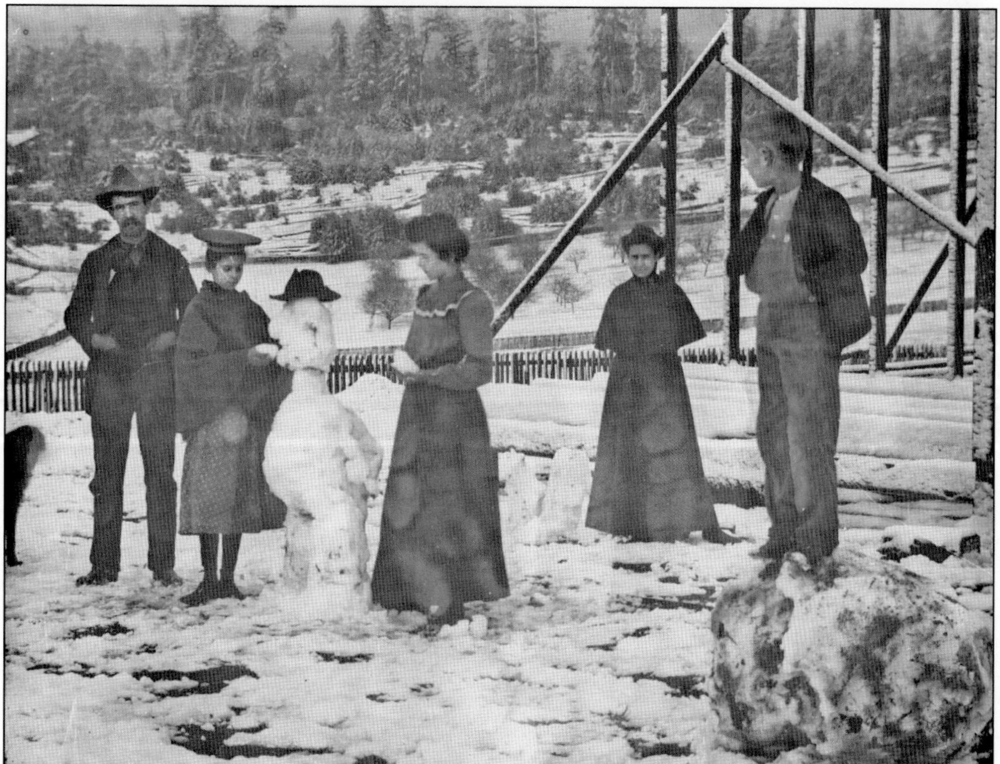

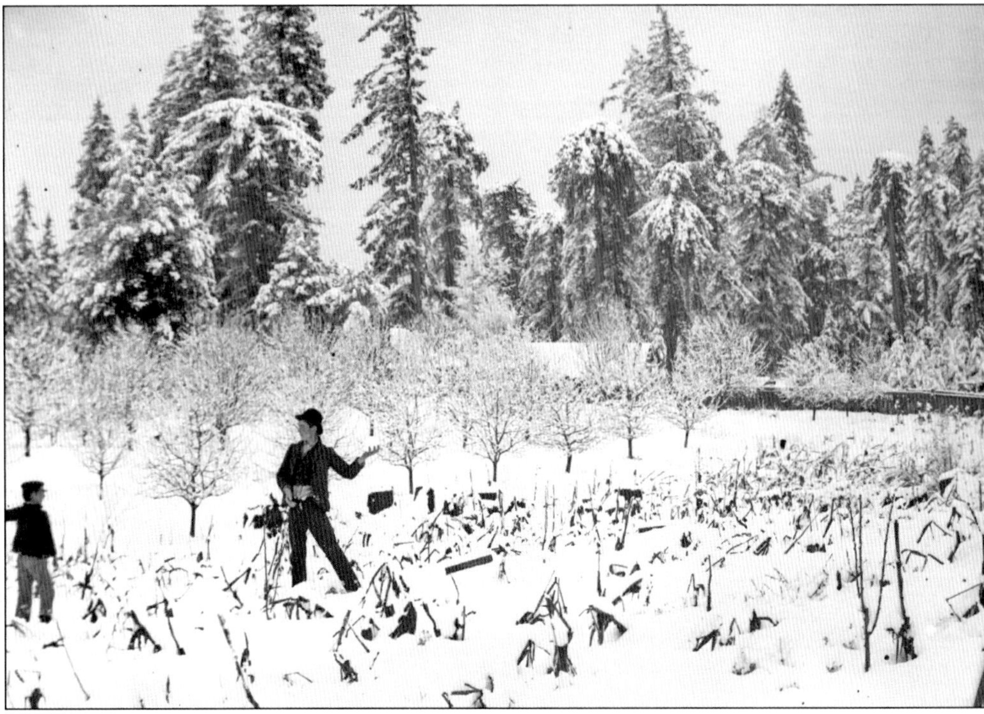

When it snowed, it was a big deal in Annapolis.

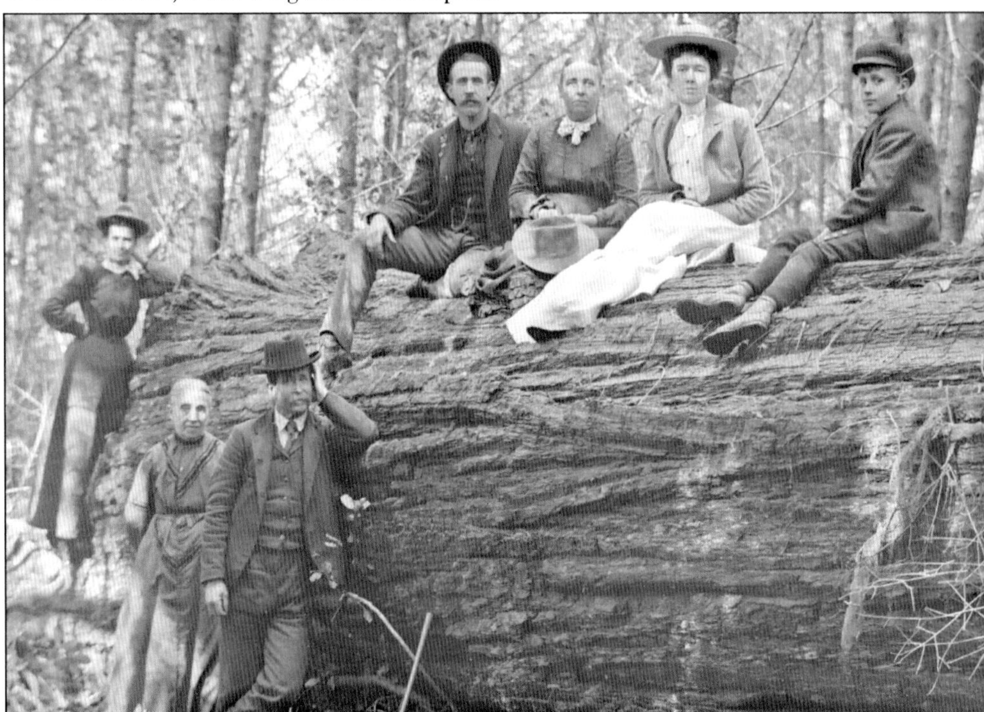

This photograph was taken at the Hickman ranch. Because the size of the trees was so surprising to people from other areas, many photographs were taken with the trees in the background.

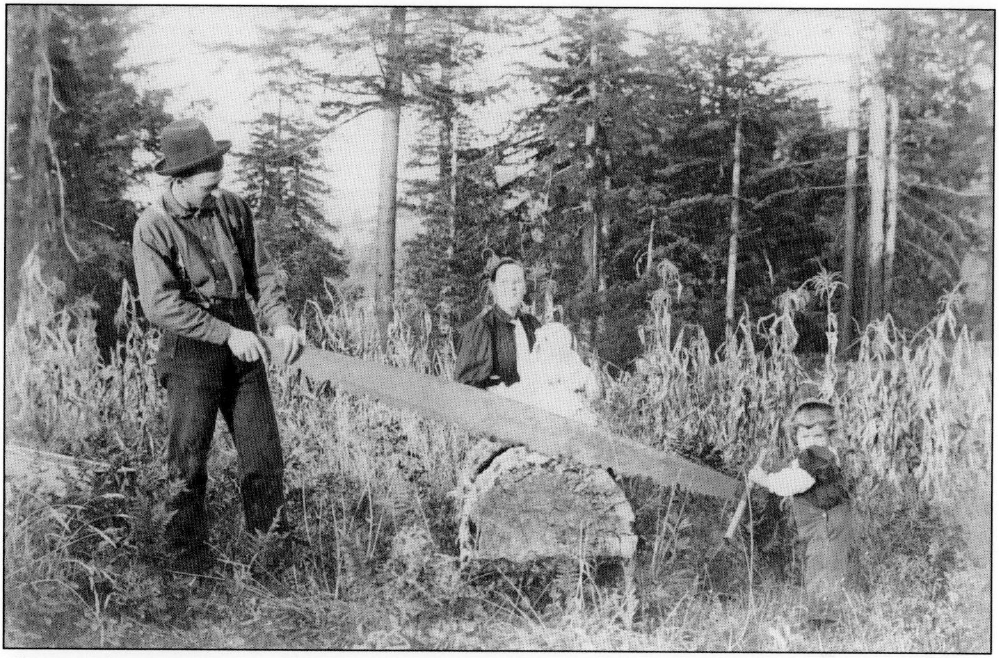

This is a photograph of the Charley Wetmore family. The Wetmores were so successful with their apple business that they eventually had over 100 acres of apple trees, all bearing fruit, and had to rent other orchards to keep up with the demand.

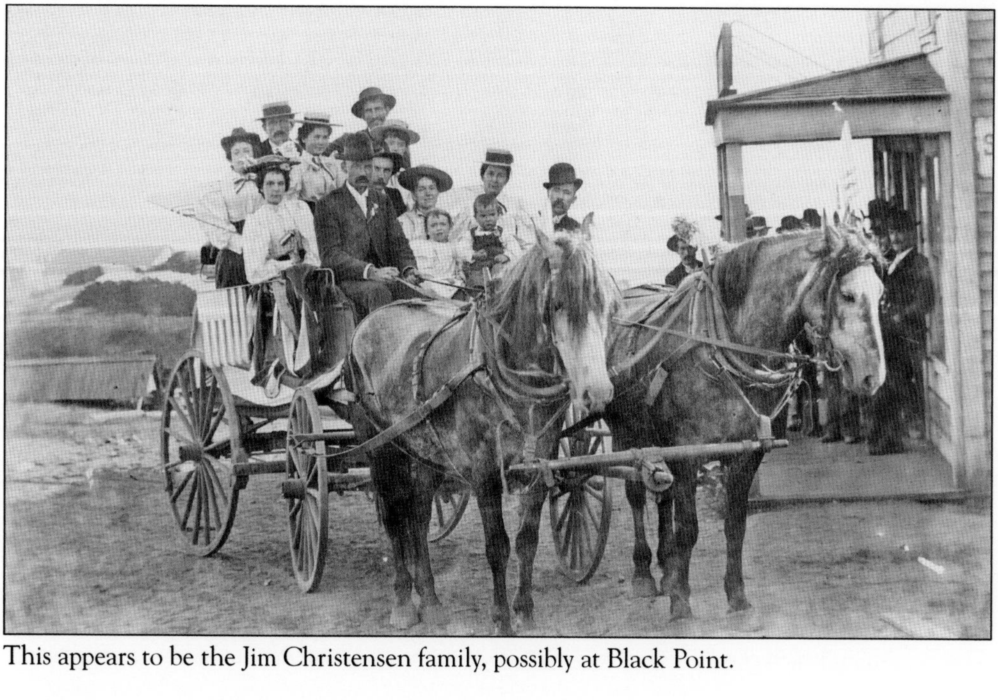

This appears to be the Jim Christensen family, possibly at Black Point.

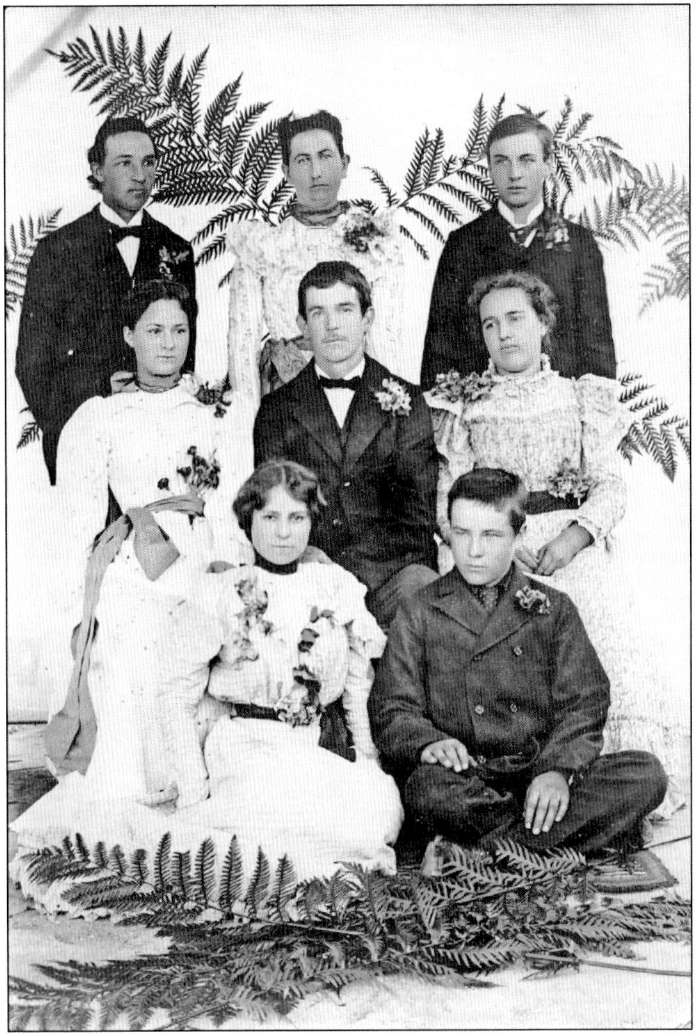

Pictured are, from left to right, (first row) Faith Batt and Bob Cole; (second row) Elise Cole, Horace Hickman, and Olive Patchett; (third row) Bert Patchett, Maud Merrit, and Aldolph Johnson.

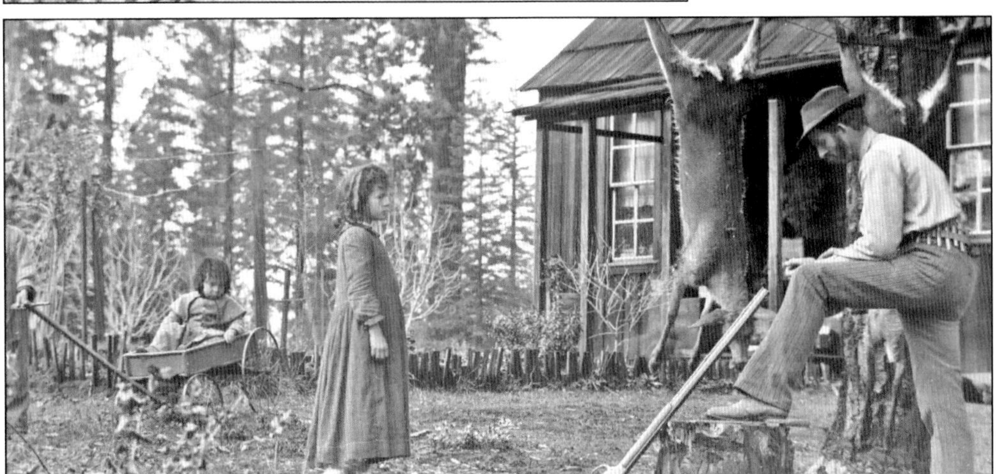

The Fiscus family is shown in everyday living. Deer hunting is still very common in this area.

George is showing his young son Fred how to hunt. A deer is even visible in the brush. This photograph was taken approximately 1895.

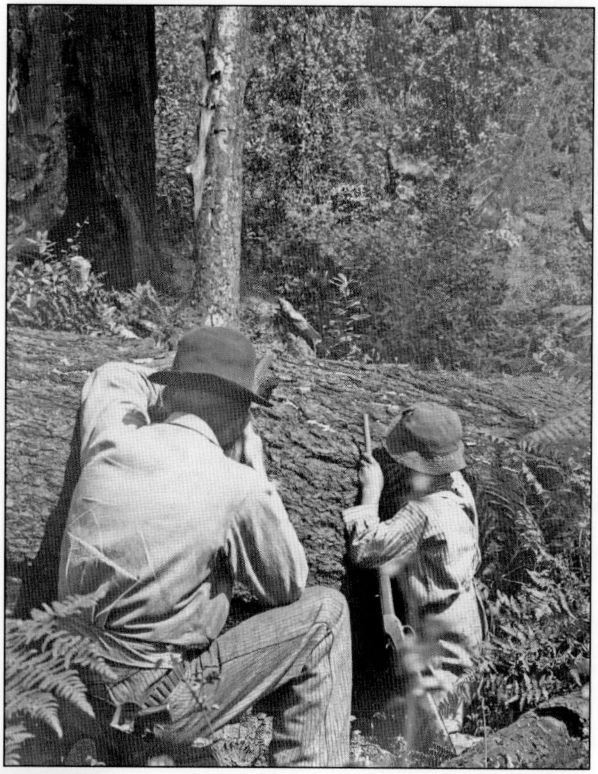

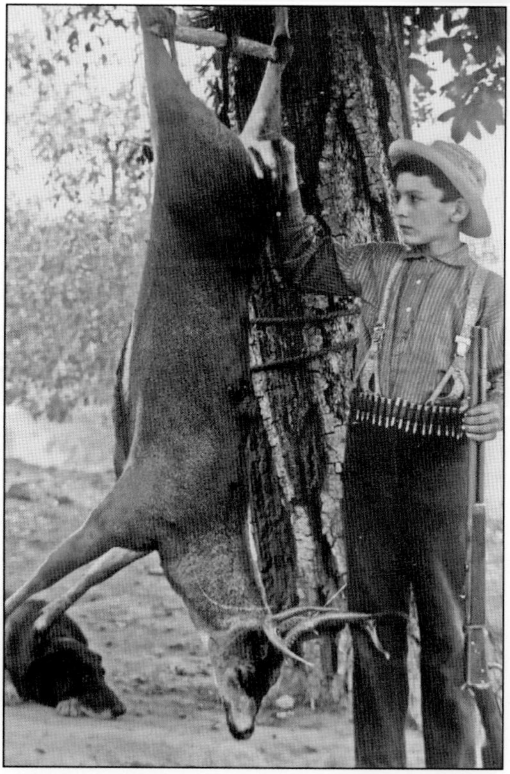

This photograph was labeled "Fred with his first deer." It was probably taken around 1900.

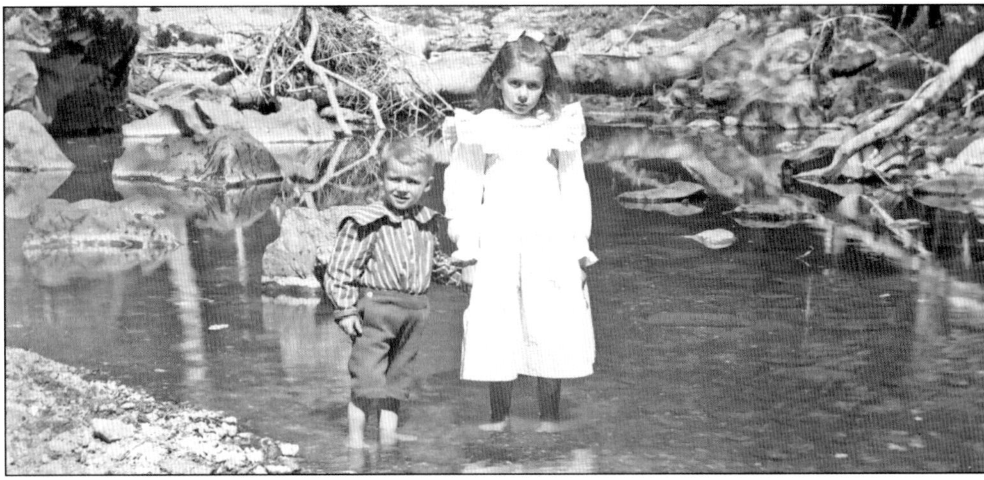

Buckeye Creek is a tributary to the Gualala River, and it flows through Annapolis. Seen here about 1900 are Charley and Lois Fiscus.

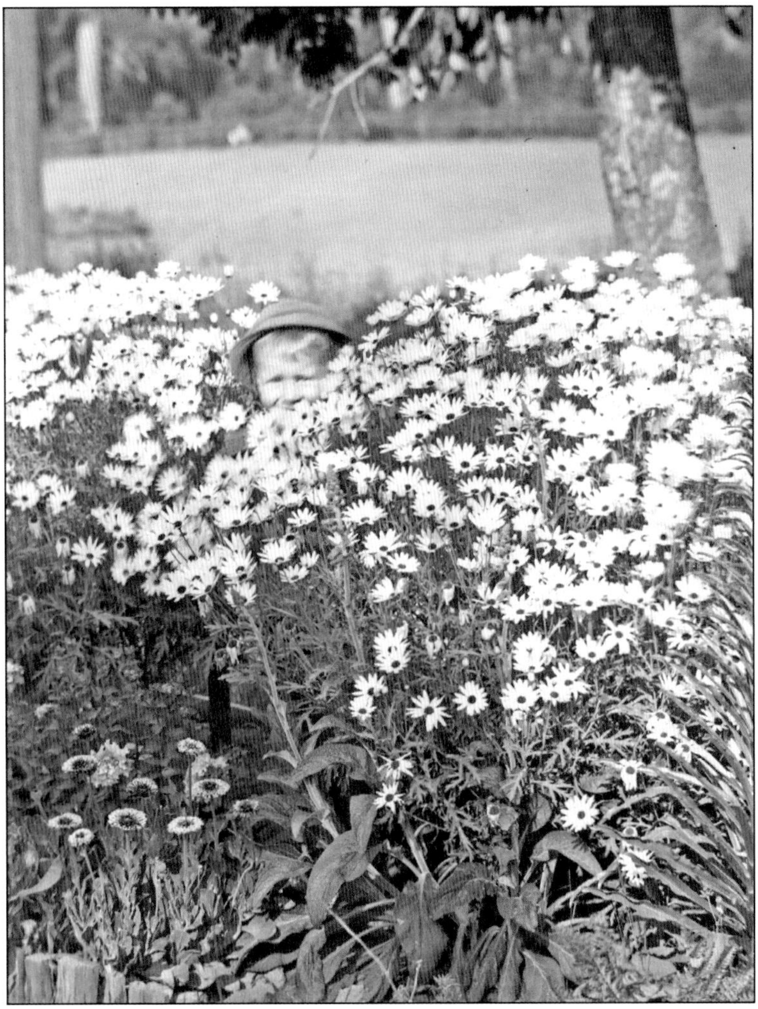

A young Charley Fiscus is seen hiding in the flowers.

When the negative for this photograph was discovered, it was labeled "Charley's new boots." Charley definitely looks happy in his new boots, even if they are on the wrong feet!

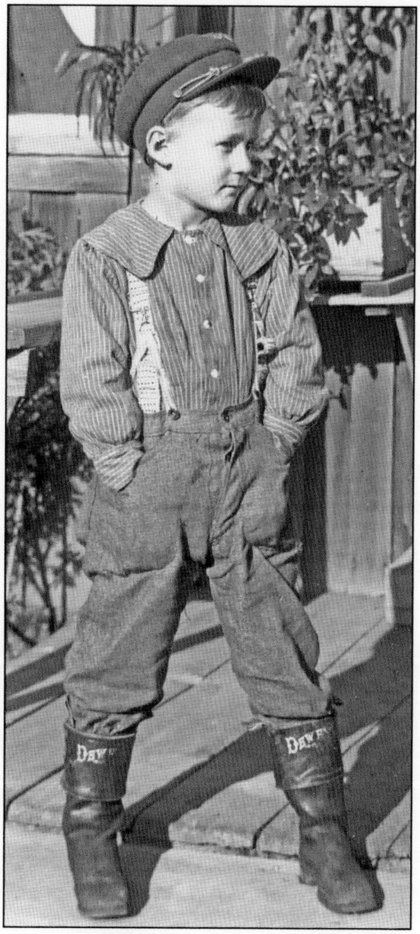

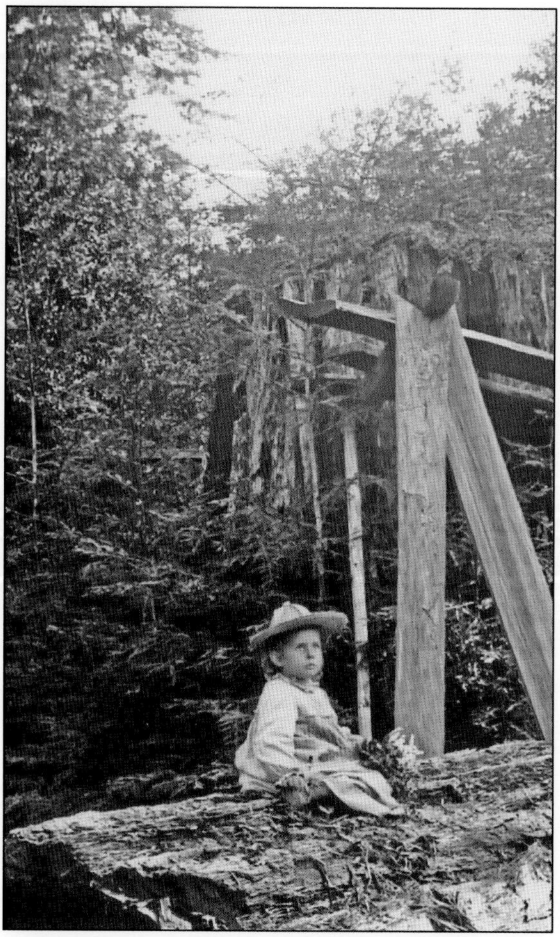

Children at the turn of the century in rural Annapolis helped their parents on all projects. Even the youngest members of the families were involved and helped in their own way.

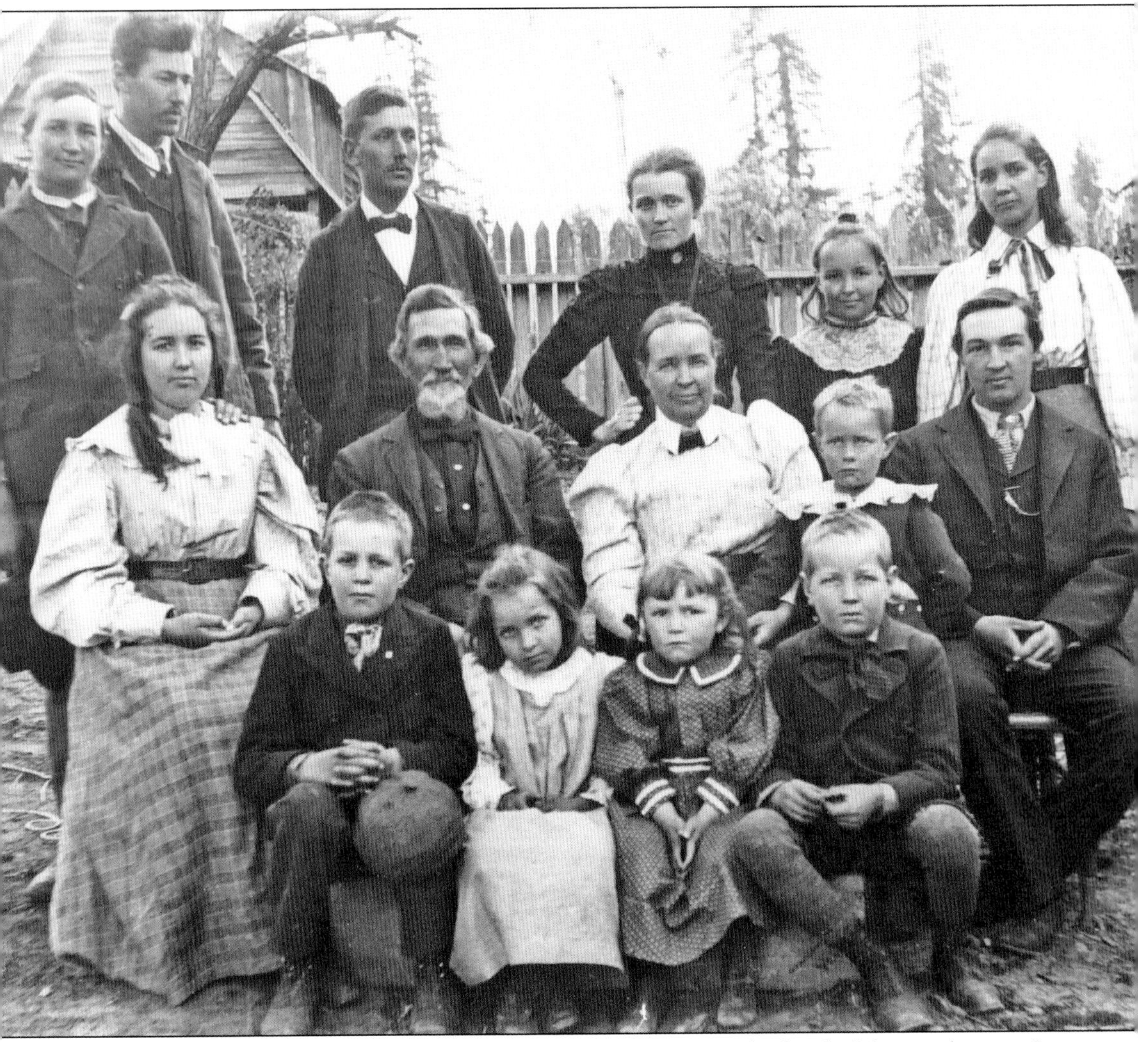

John A. Patchett and his wife, Mary, were an important Annapolis family. John was born in Iowa and they came to California before 1890. One daughter, Docia, became a teacher at Horicon. (Courtesy of the Annapolis Historical Society.)

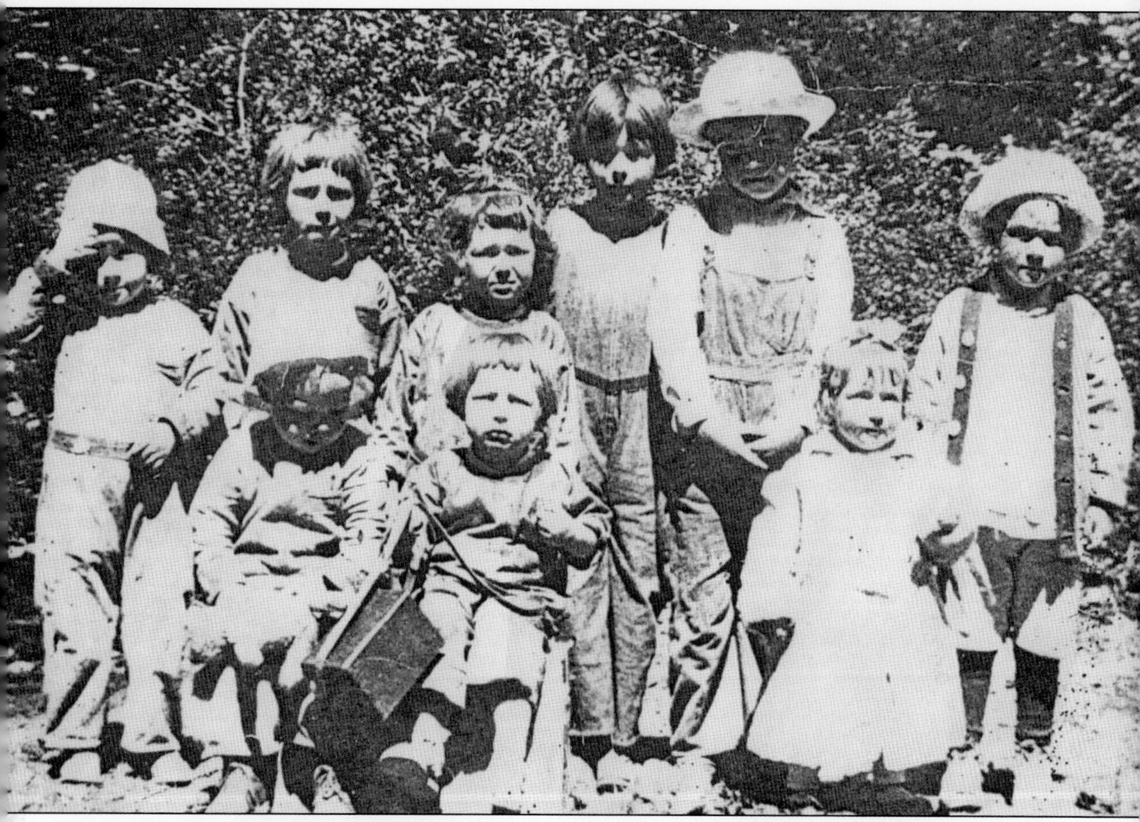

George Batt immigrated to the United States from the United Kingdom in 1876. He and his wife, Ellen, had 14 children. This photograph shows the third generation of Batt cousins. From left to right are (first row) Albert Stibi, Dorothy Batt, and Lorena Evans; (second row) Alice Stibi, Ruth Batt, Marguerite Batt, Leona Batt, Elmer Evans, and George Evans. (Courtesy of the Annapolis Historical Society.)

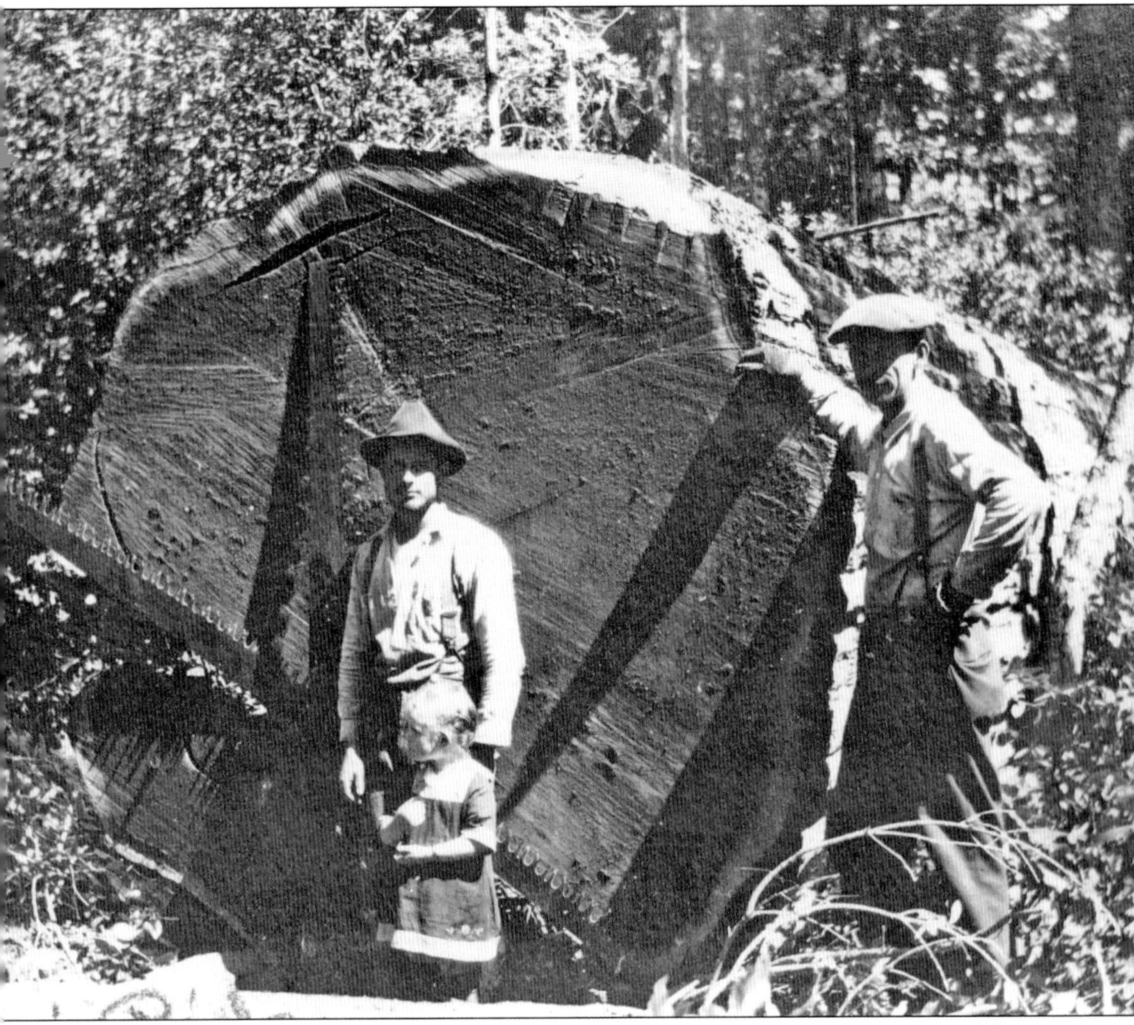

Lovel Hamilton (left), Arline Hamilton (center), and Silas McMillen examine one of the many large redwoods harvested on the McMillen land in 1919. (Courtesy of Arline Hamilton.)

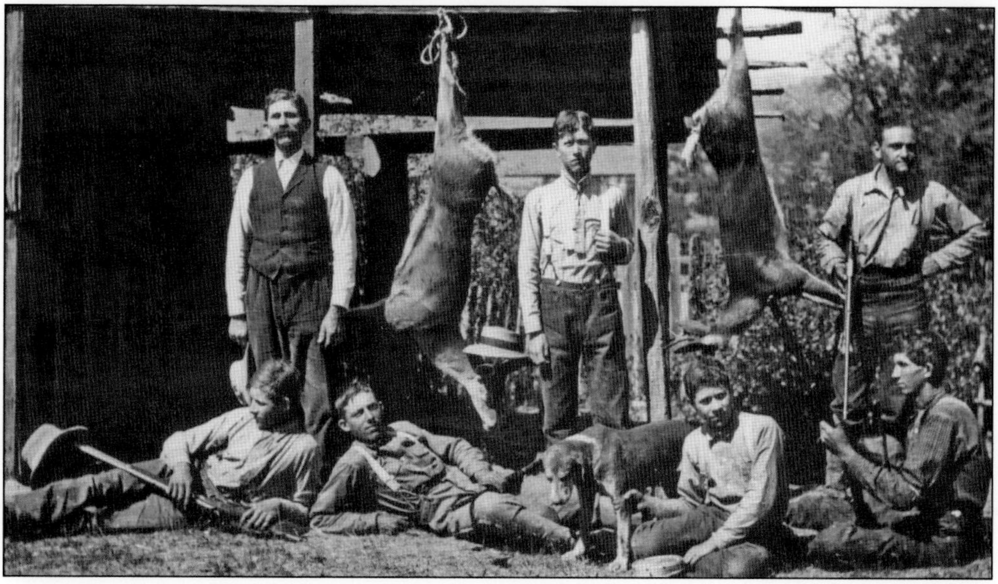

John E. Ohlson was born in 1859 and married Margret in 1891. The photograph above is of the Ohlson family at their ranch after hunting. Pictured are, from left to right, John, Ernie, Will L., Chester, Henry Matheson, Elmer, and Ed. The Ohlson family is also shown below in another view at their home. (Both, courtesy of Charlene and Junior Ohlson.)

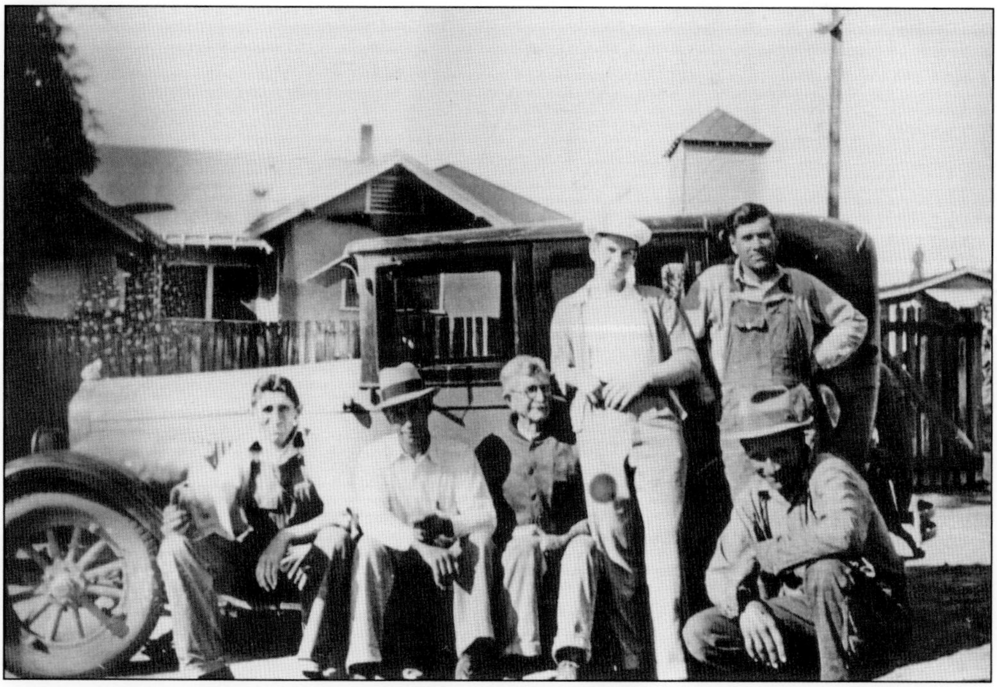

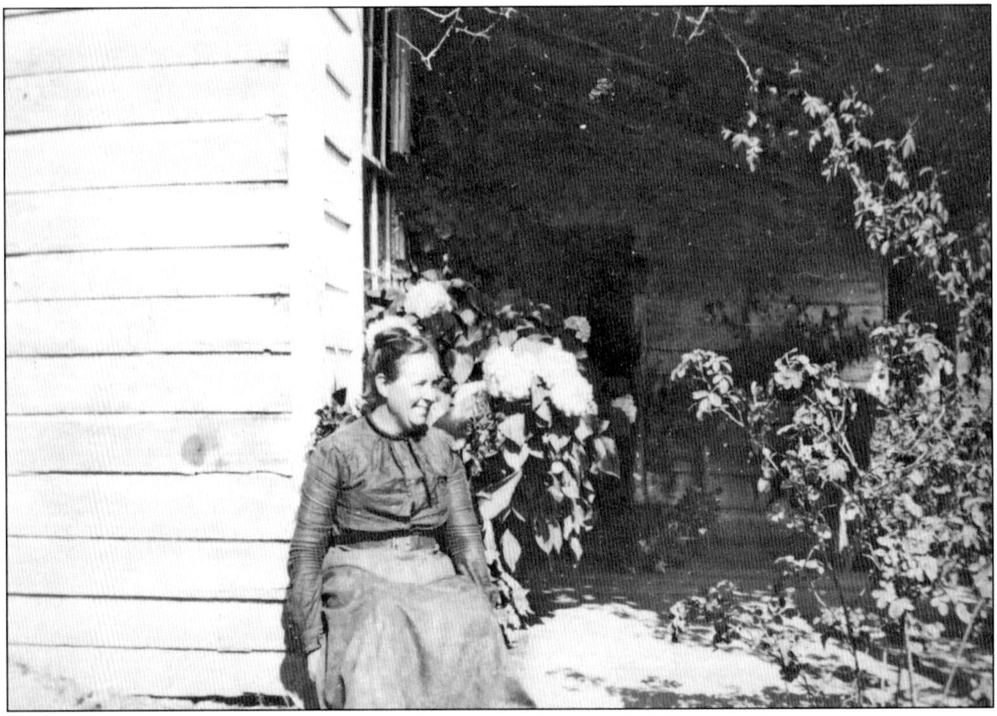

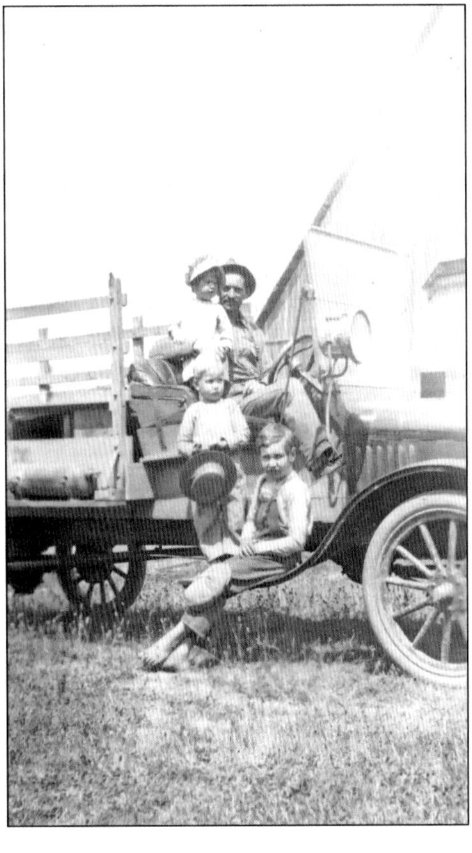

Olive May Patchett (born in 1882) married Claus Petersen. Her daughter, Mary Petersen, married Ernest Ohlson. This is a photograph of Olive May, or Grandma Patchett, at the Ohlson home. (Courtesy of Charlene and Junior Ohlson.)

After Claus Petersen died on the ranch in 1911, Olive married Peter, Claus's brother. They had three more children: Peter W., Anne, and Olive Irene. Pictured here are Peter Petersen (in driver's seat), Anne, Peter W. (standing), and Jack at the Nob Hill Ranch. (Courtesy of Sandra Petersen.)

This photograph, taken about 1910, shows Mary Petersen (left) and Margrete Petersen at the Nob Hill Ranch in Annapolis. (Courtesy of Charlene and Junior Ohlson.)

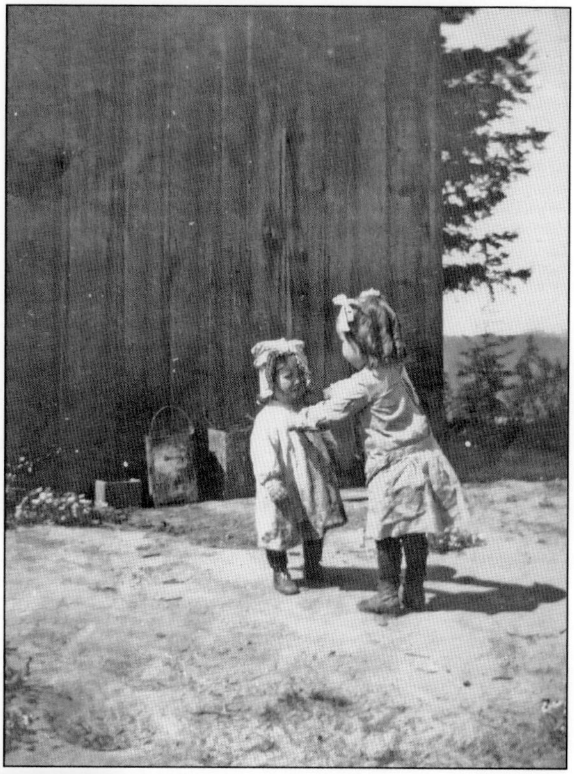

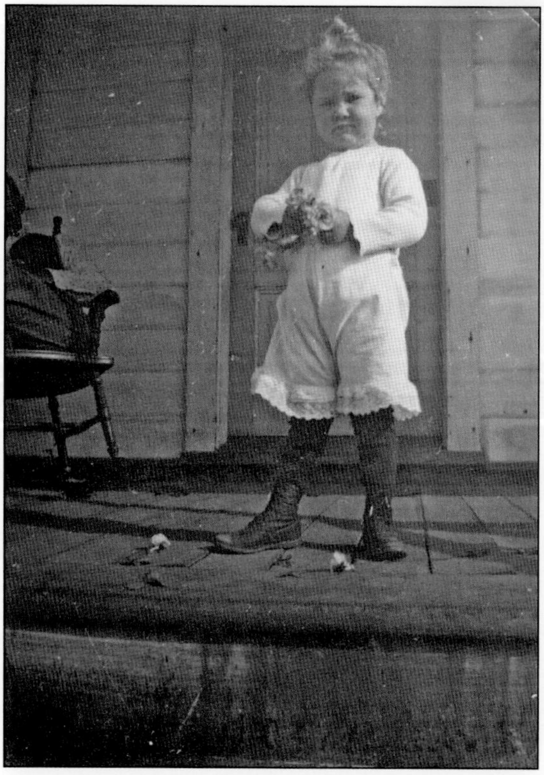

This is a photograph of Mary Annette Petersen, daughter of Olive May Patchett and Claus Petersen. She later married Ernest Ohlson, the third son of John and Margrete Ohlson. (Courtesy of Charlene and Junior Ohlson.)

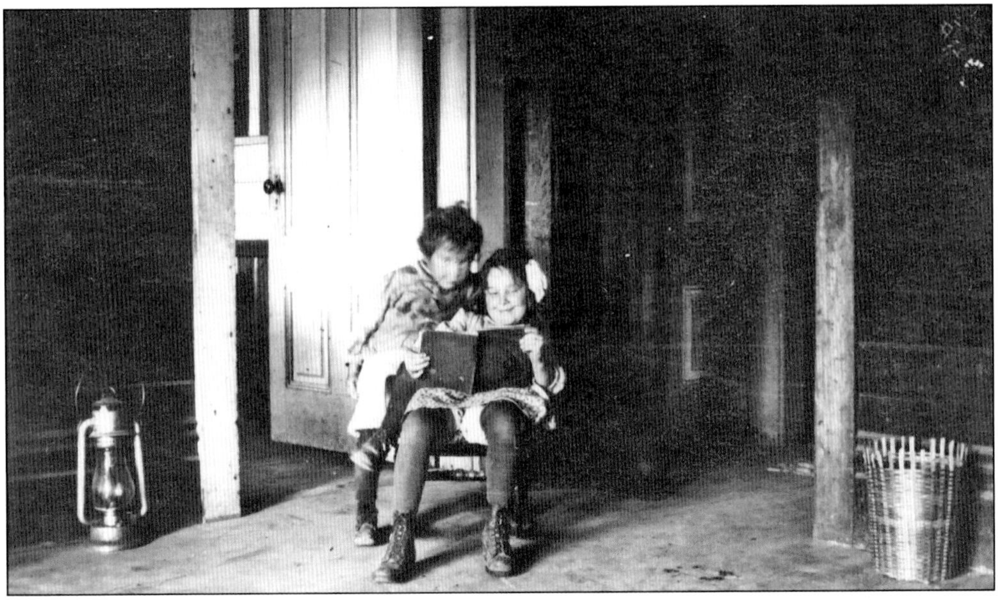

Jack and Mary Petersen are reading a book at the Nob Hill Ranch in Annapolis. The Petersens purchased the Nob Hill Ranch from the sea captain Sunberg. (Courtesy of Charlene and Junior Ohlson.)

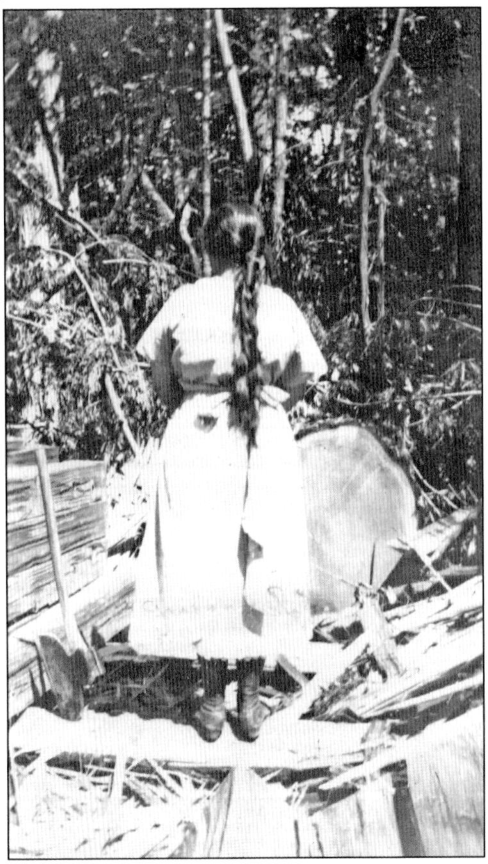

Eva Hunter Hamilton, May 1919, works in the woods alongside her husband, Lovel Hamilton. (Courtesy of Arline Hamilton.)

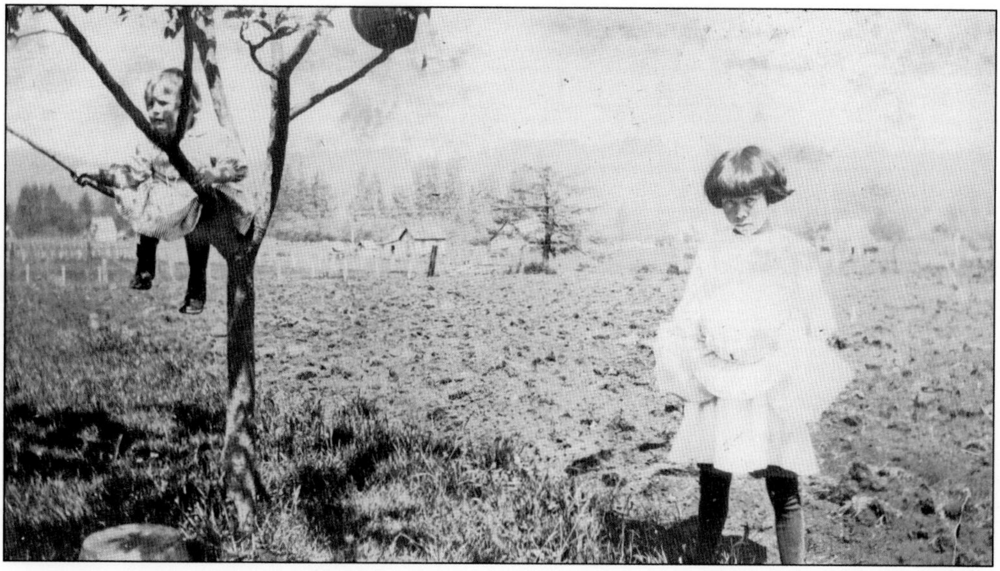

Since most early Annapolis families were large, older children often entertained the younger children. Playgrounds were stumps and trees. Arline Hamilton (above) is not happy about being placed in the tree by her cousin. However, the children in the photograph below seem to enjoy playing school on a redwood stump. (Both, courtesy of Arline Hamilton.)

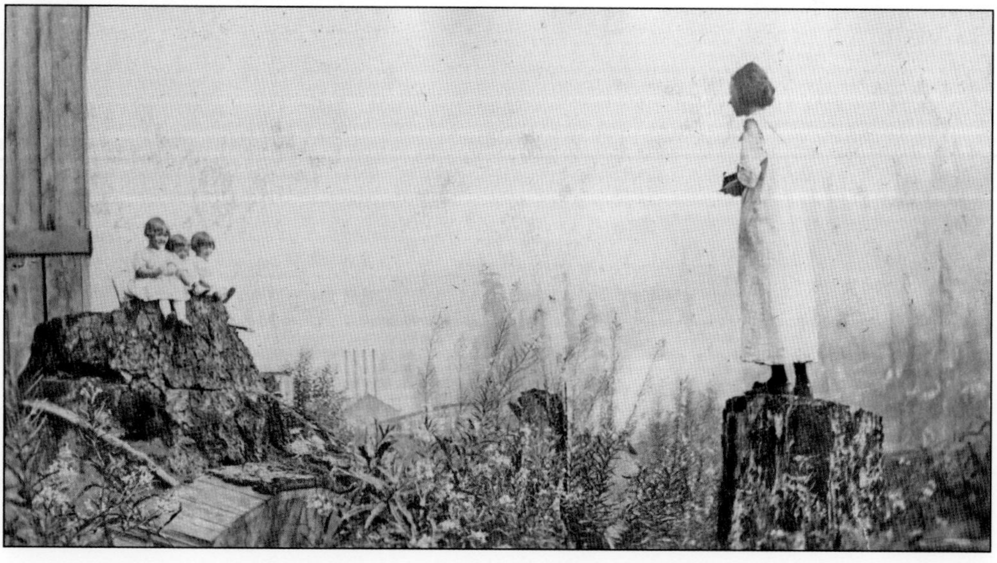

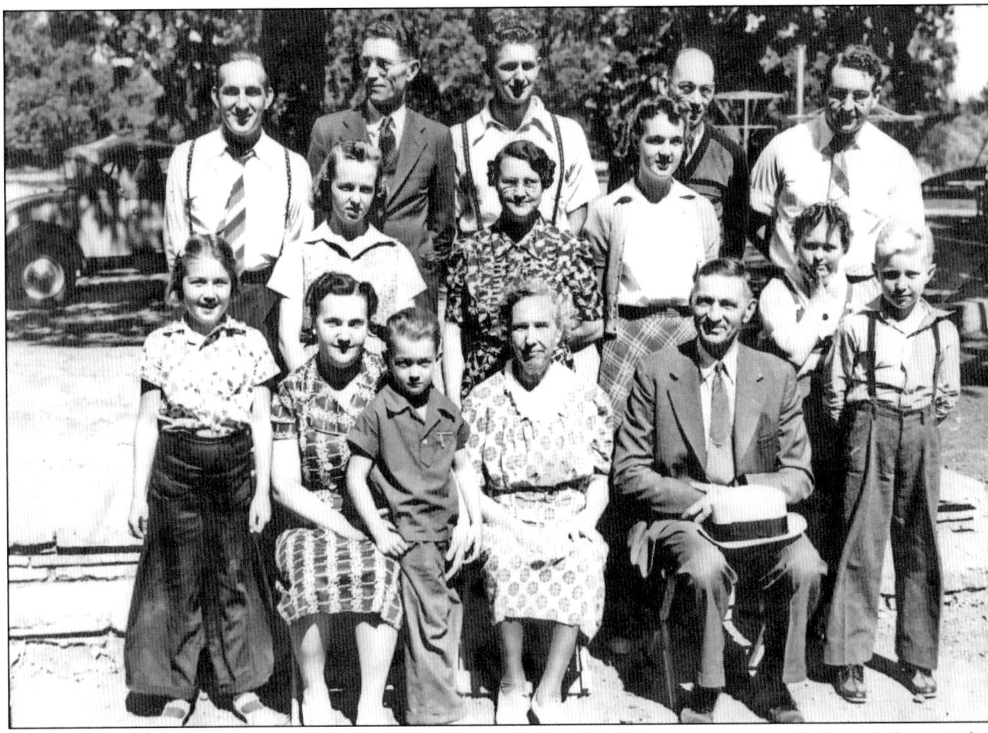

The Patchett family held a reunion in Santa Rosa in 1939. They are pictured, from left to right, as follows: (first row) Gwennie Begley, Marg Begley, Gilbert Begley, Olive May Petersen, Peter Petersen Sr., and Junior Ohlson; (second row) Edna Petersen, Mary Ohlson, Anne Petersen, and Olive Irene Petersen; (third row) Peter Petersen Jr., Ernie Ohlson, Bill Chenoweth, Marcus Begley, and Jack Petersen. (Courtesy of Sandra Petersen.)

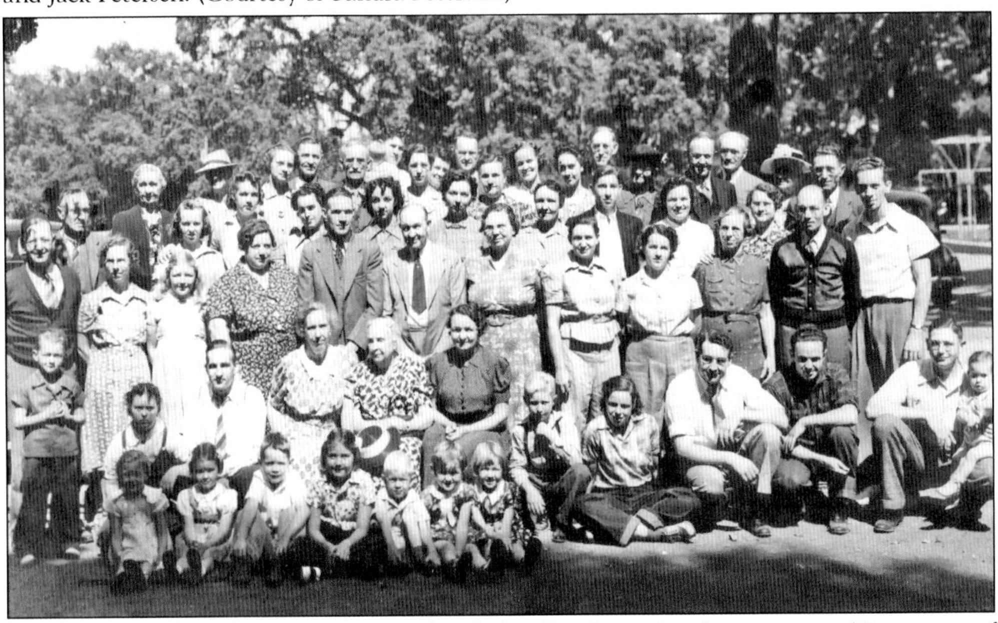

This is a more inclusive photograph of the Patchett family reunion. (Courtesy of Sandra Petersen.)

Posing by some of the largest trees was commonplace in early photographs.

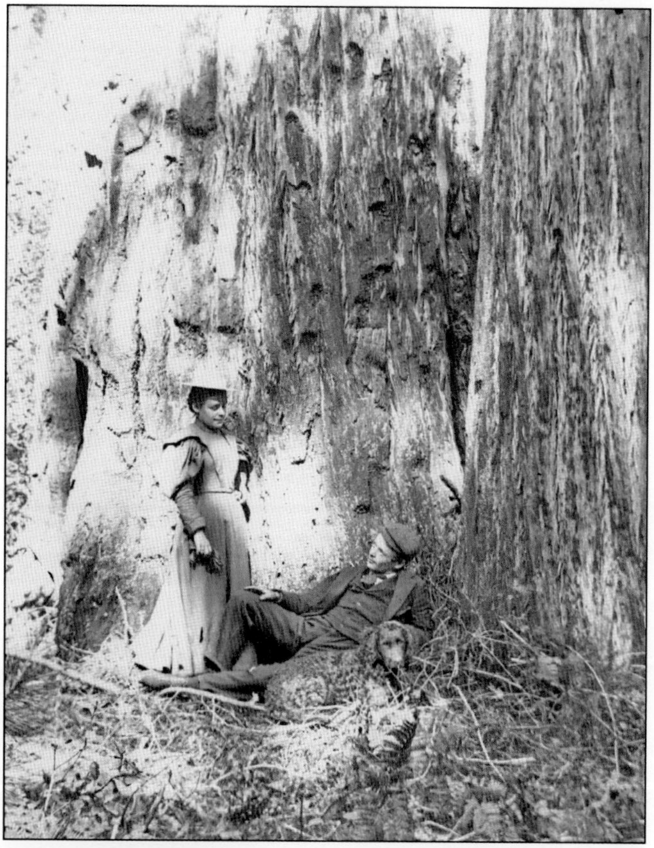

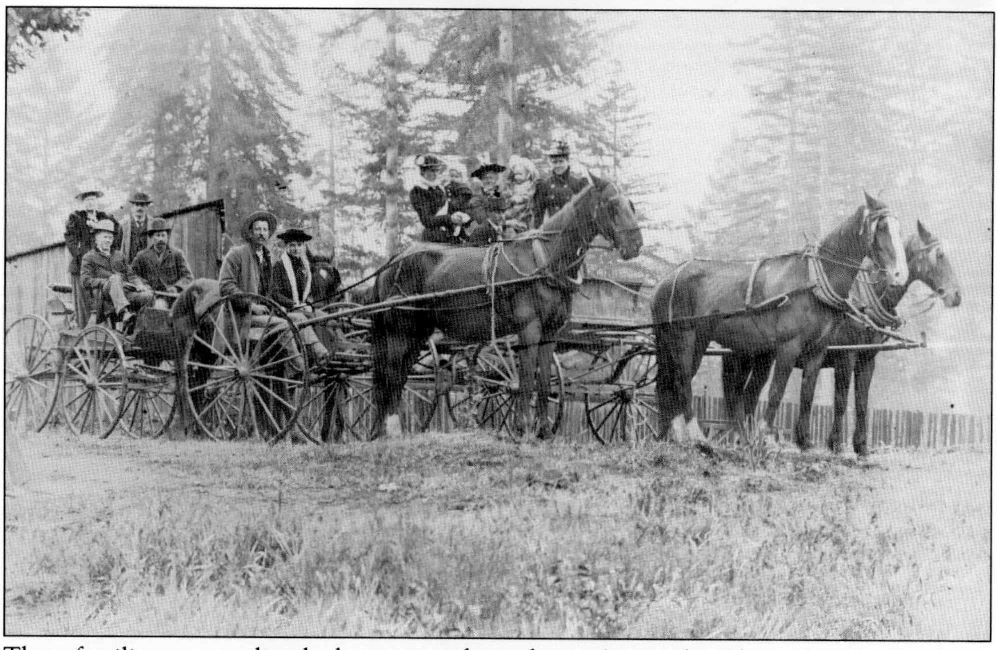

These families are traveling by buggy on a foggy day in Annapolis. These photographs depict everyday life in Annapolis, showing the difference 100 years can make.

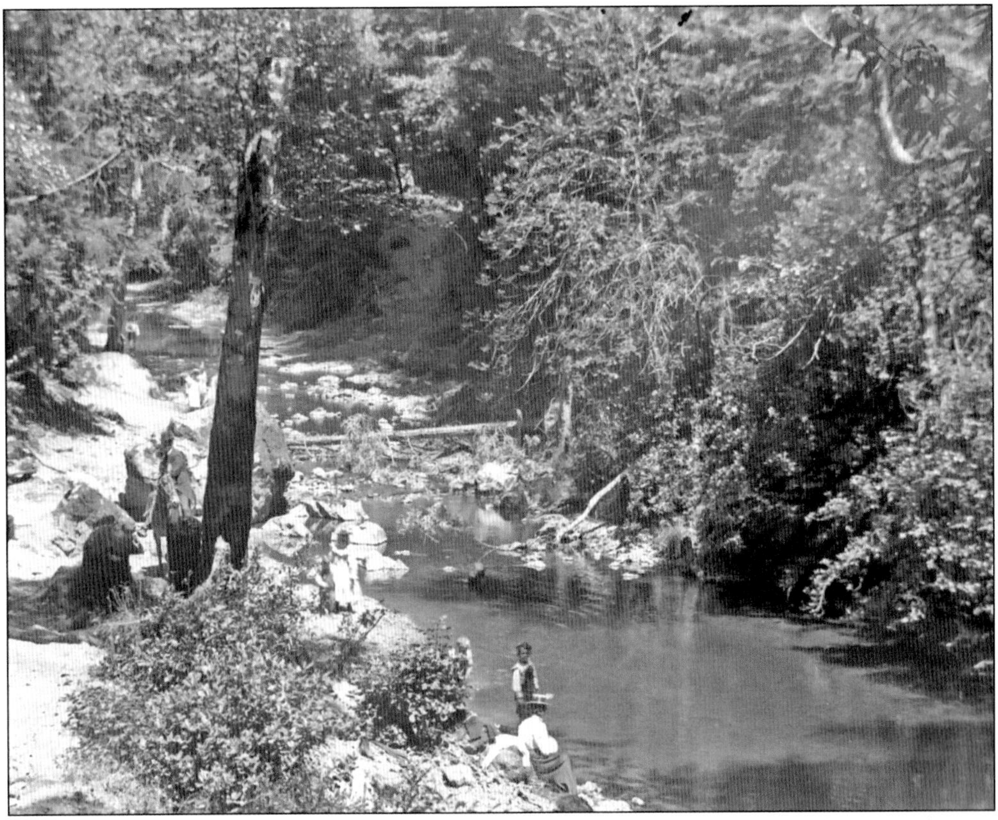

This is most likely Buckeye Creek in Annapolis. Today the water flow in Buckeye is much less.

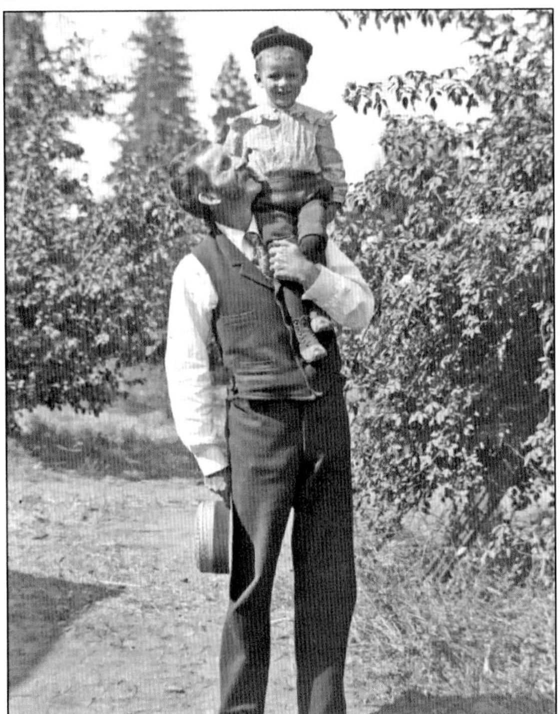

George and Charley Fiscus are in the orchard.

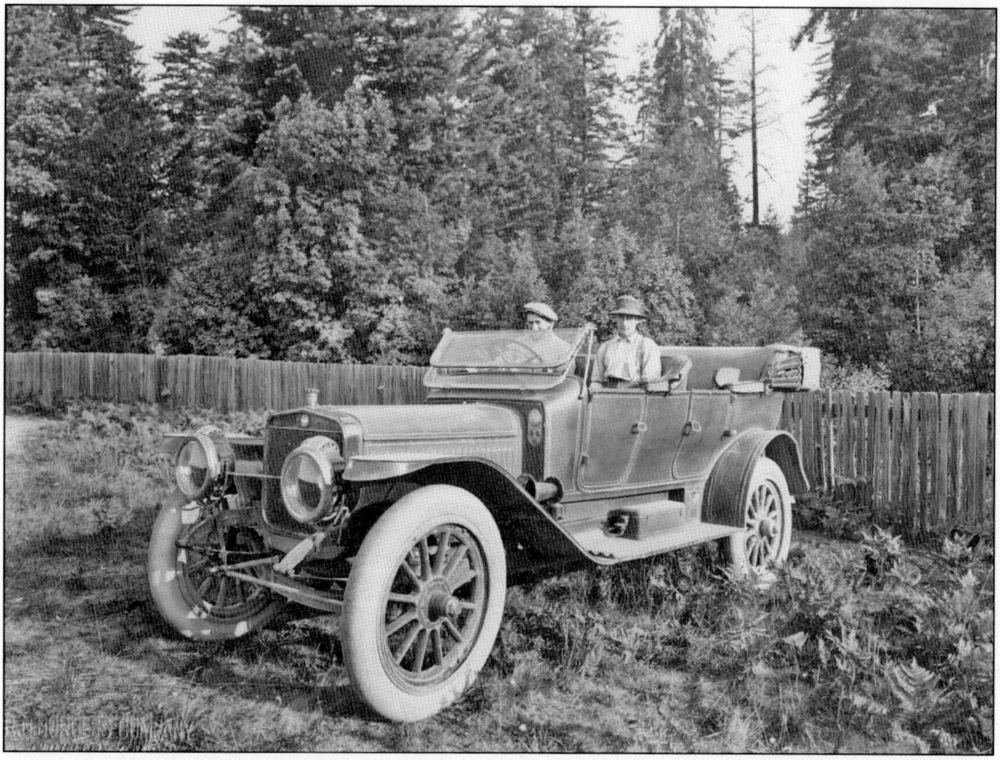

Automobiles eventually made it to the Annapolis area. Seen above in the driver's seat is Charley Fiscus in George Fiscus's first car. It was unique in that the steering wheel was on the right side. The car was used in Point Arena's Fourth of July parades. Seen below is Harold Hunter's car on Highway 1. (Below, courtesy of Joyce Hamilton Pratt.)

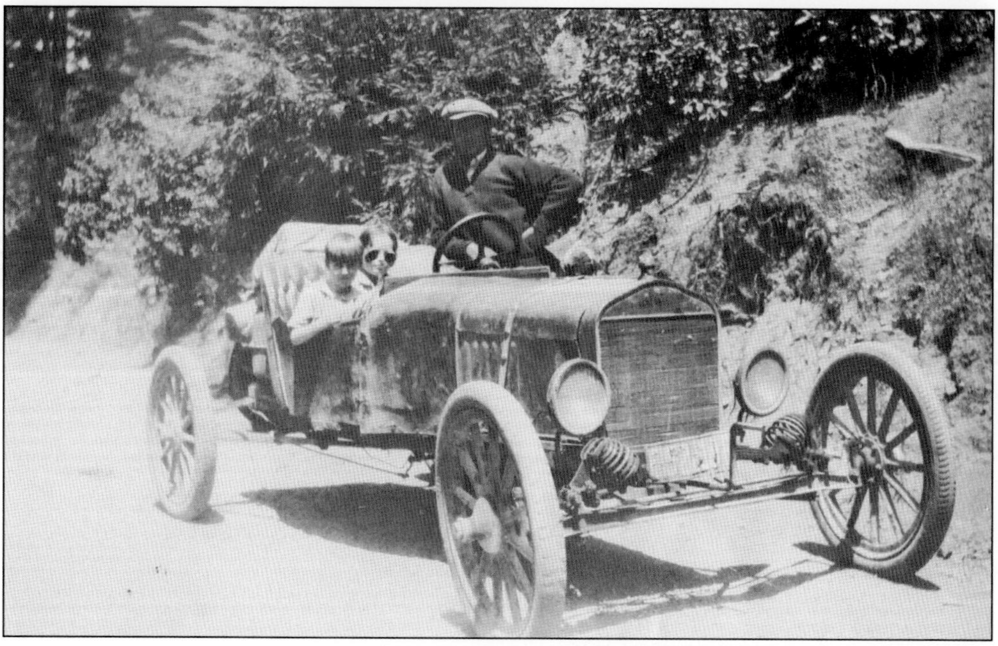

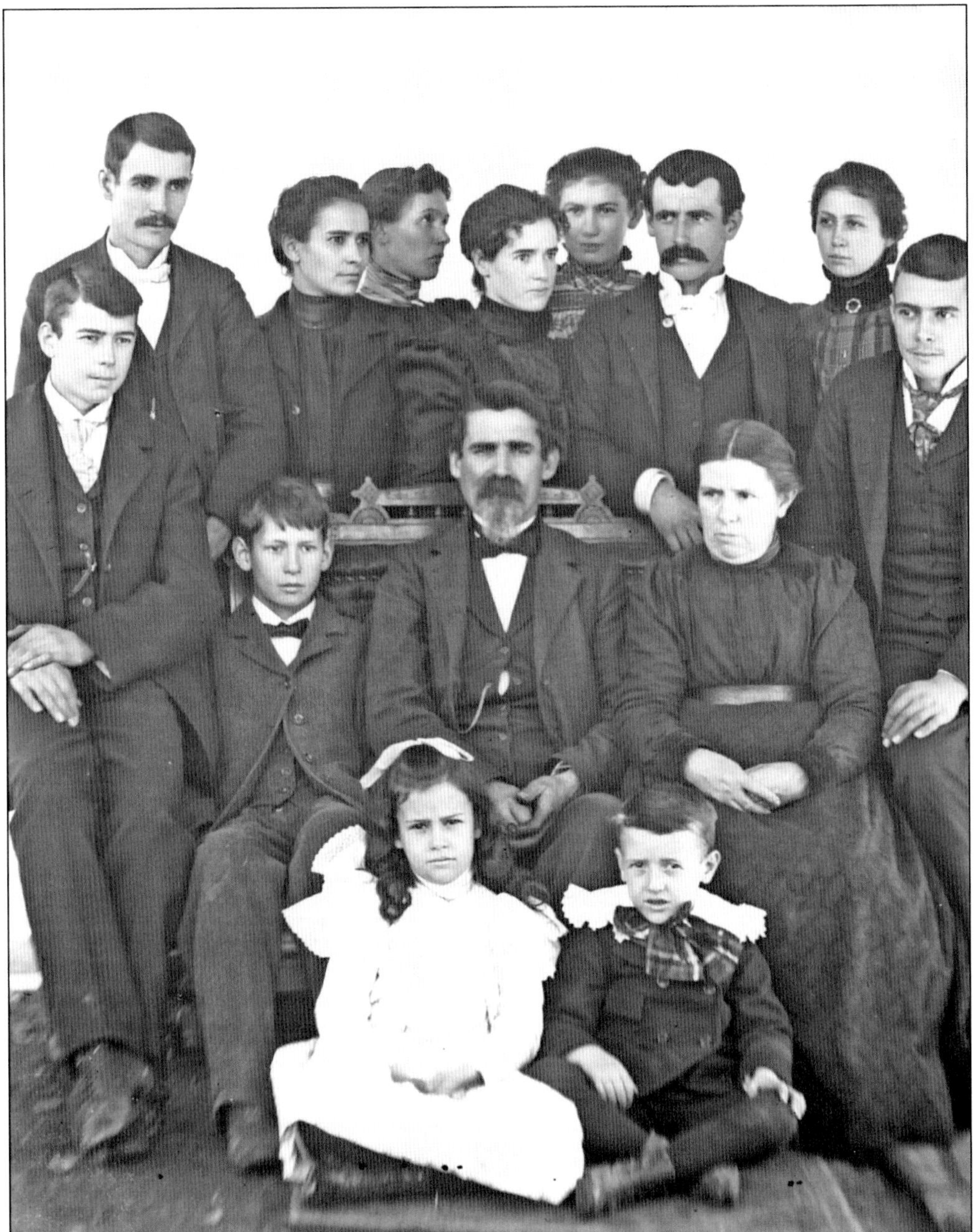

Henry and Mary (Parks) McMillen settled in Annapolis in the 1880s and several of their 12 children were born there. Some of their children grew up to work in the woods. Abe drove a team of horses hauling posts, pickets, and tan bark to Stewart's Point. Pictured here are, from left to right, (first row) Clara and Alfred; (second row) Abraham, Silas, Henry, Mary, and Edward; (third row) Hiram, Gertrude, Vinnie, Belle, Cora, John, and Mary Elizabeth.

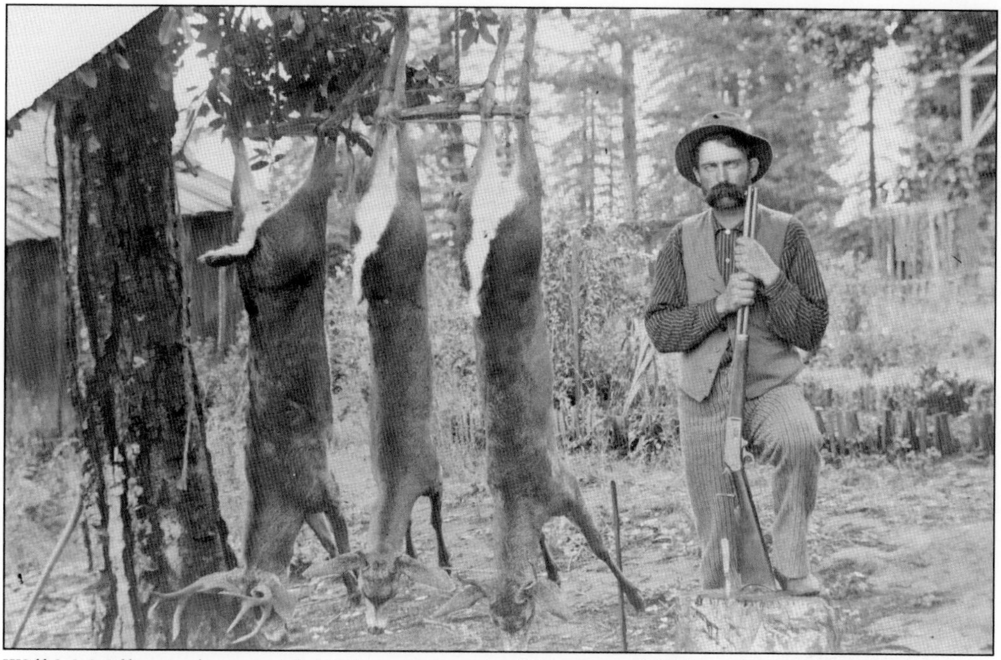

Will McMillen is shown with his hunting catch. (Courtesy of William McMillen Kramer.)

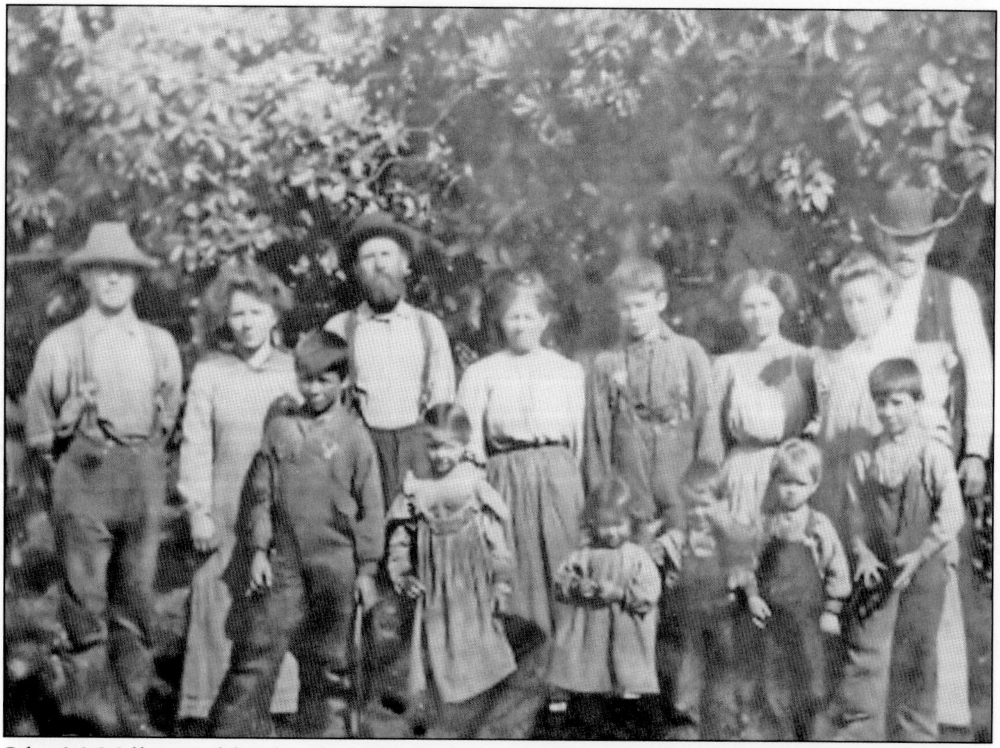

Silas McMillen and his brother Abraham married two sisters from the Parkins family of Bloomfield. Their children were double cousins because of this relationship. (Courtesy of William McMillen Kramer.)

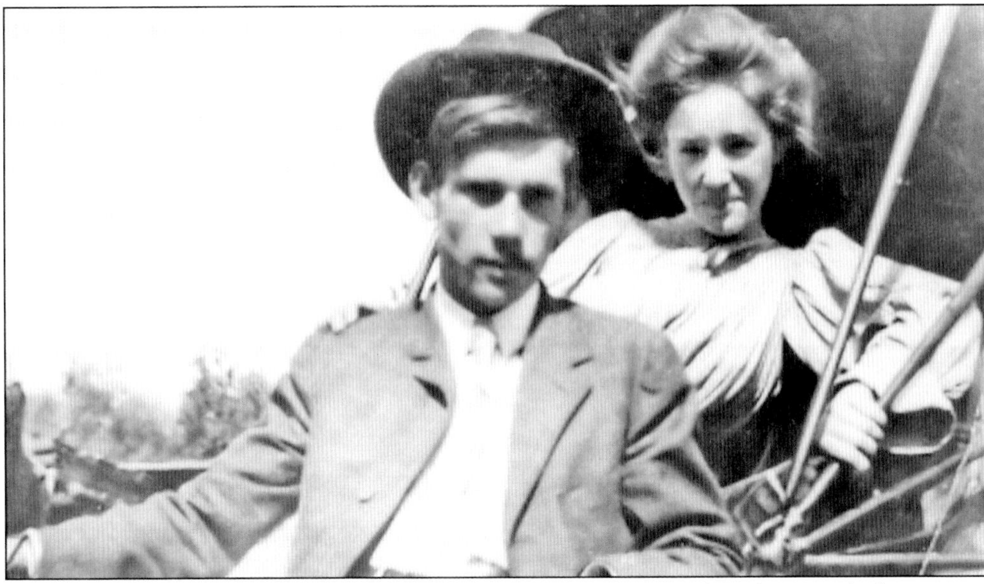

This photograph shows Silas McMillen and Irina Parkins on their wedding day. Silas and Irina had four children: Viola, Blanche, George, and Ruth. Tragically, Silas was killed in a logging accident in 1923 at age 36. (Courtesy of William McMillen Kramer.)

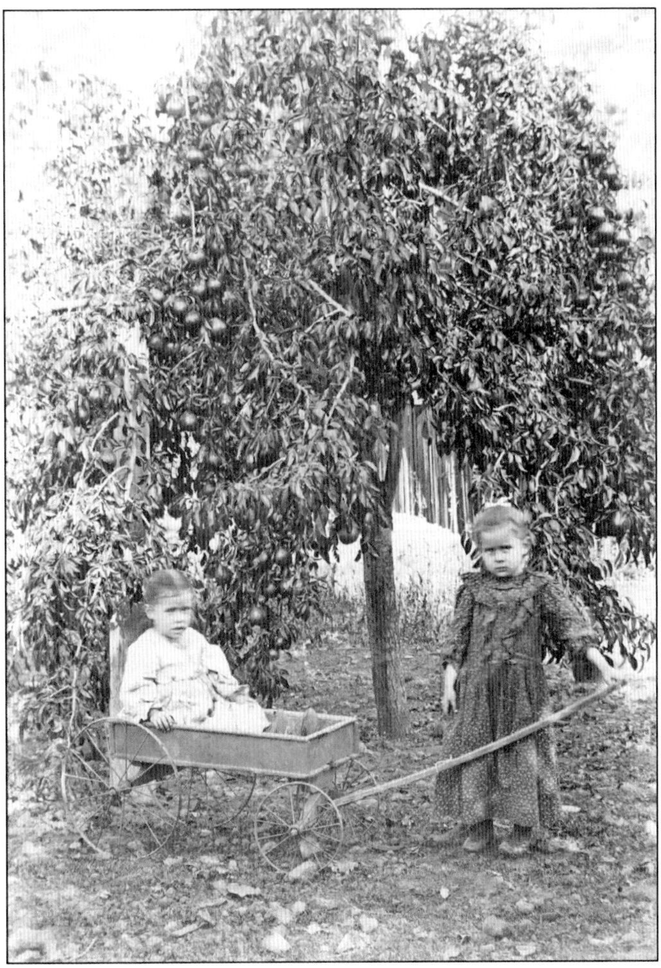

Many Annapolis families were related. Clara McMillen is pulling her cousin Lois Fiscus in a wagon.

Gertrude McMillen married George Ross. George Ross had many logging operations in the area.

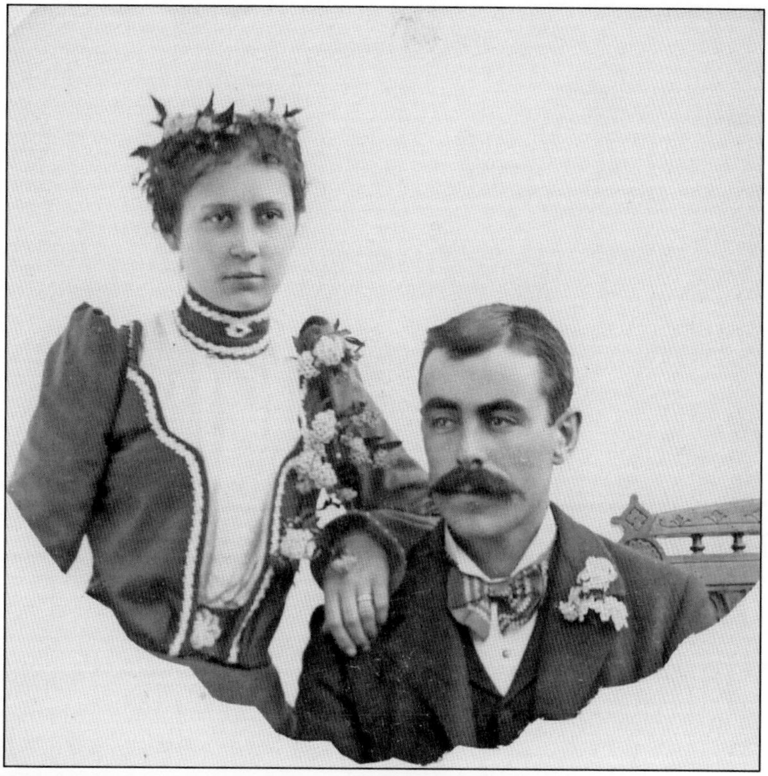

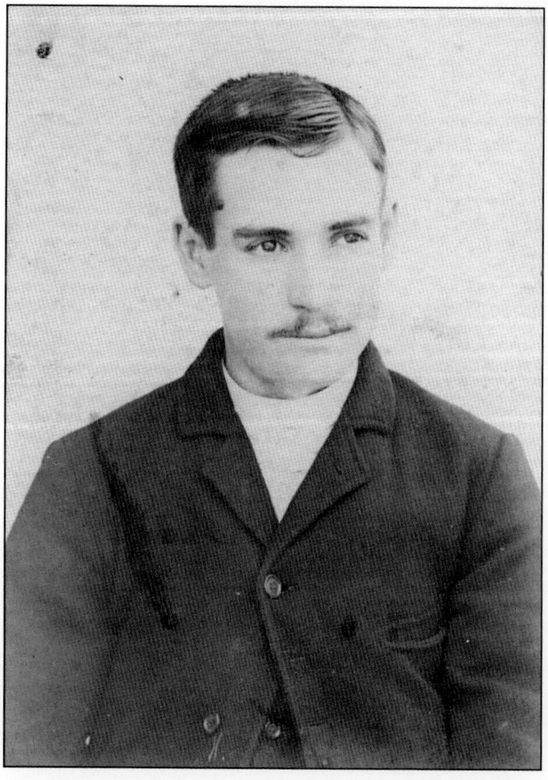

Hiram McMillen married Sadie Miller and was the father of Ralph, Lloyd, and Selma McMillen. Ralph later ran the Point Arena General Store.

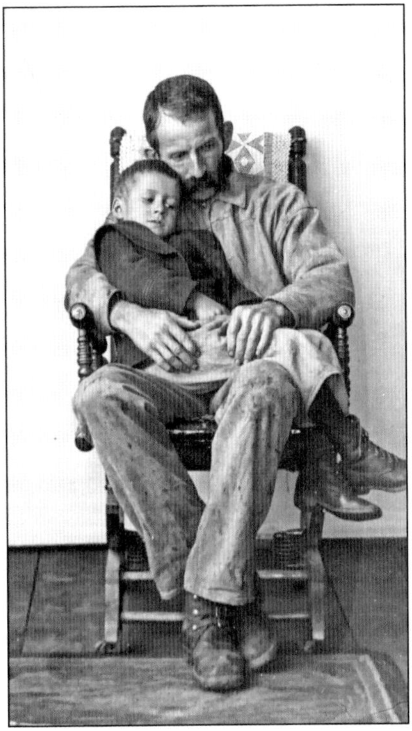

George Fiscus holds his young son Charley.

Mary McMillen Fiscus and her children are in the orchard sometime around 1900.

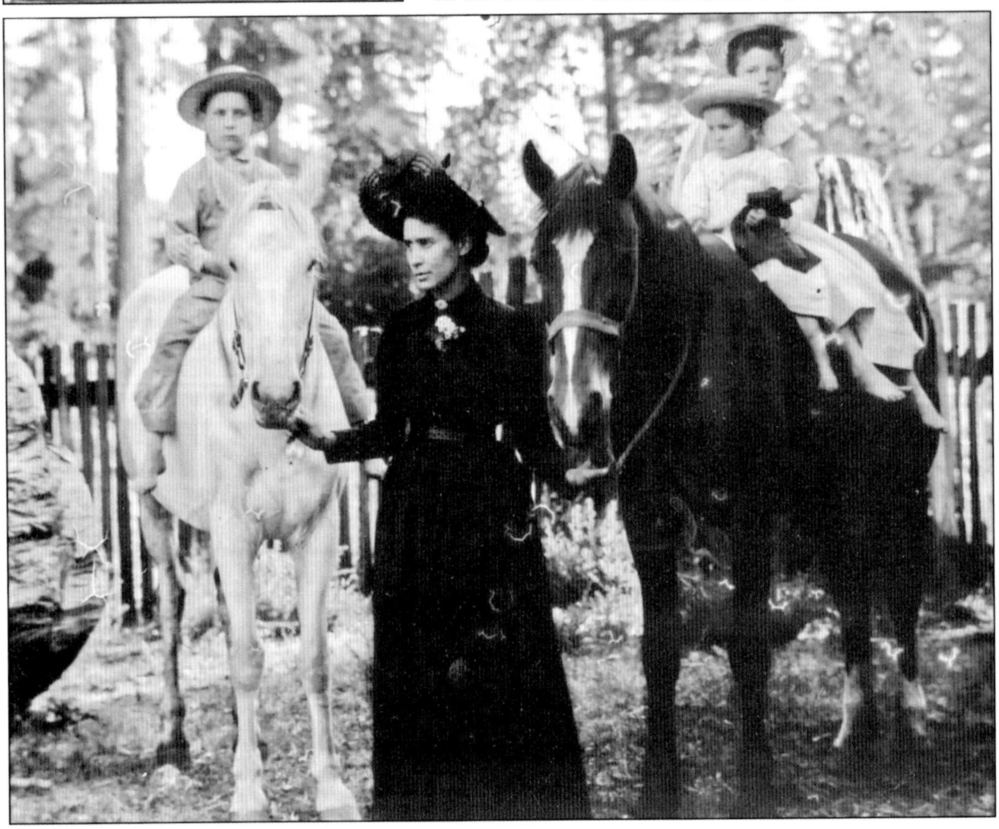

Grace Fiscus later became a teacher at the Del Mar School. This photograph is of her daughter.

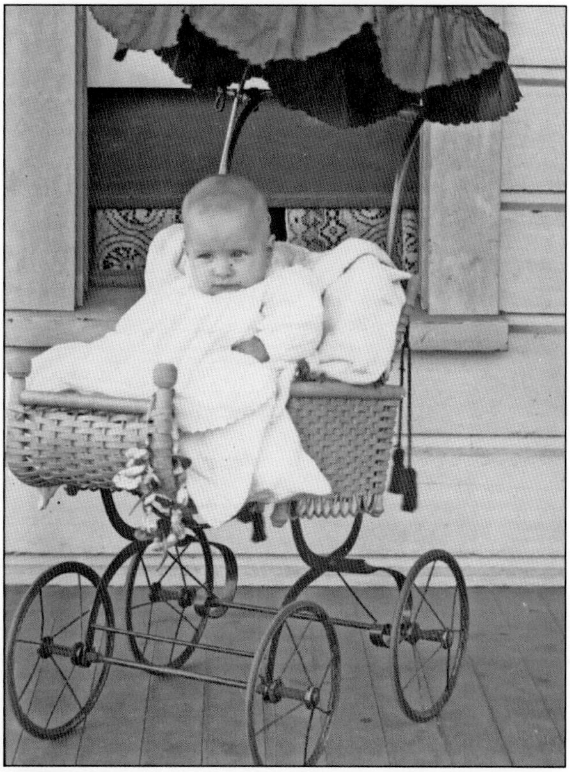

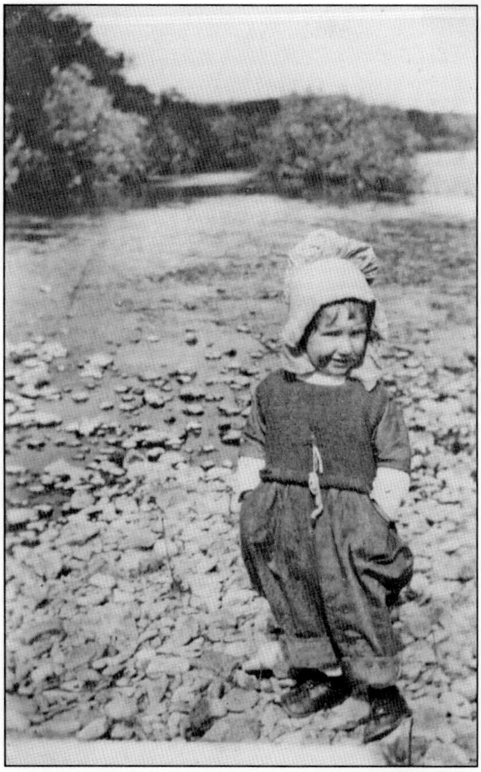

Many years ago, the Gualala River provided recreation to children. This is still true today. Seen here is Clara Hunter in the Gualala River. (Courtesy of Arline Hamilton.)

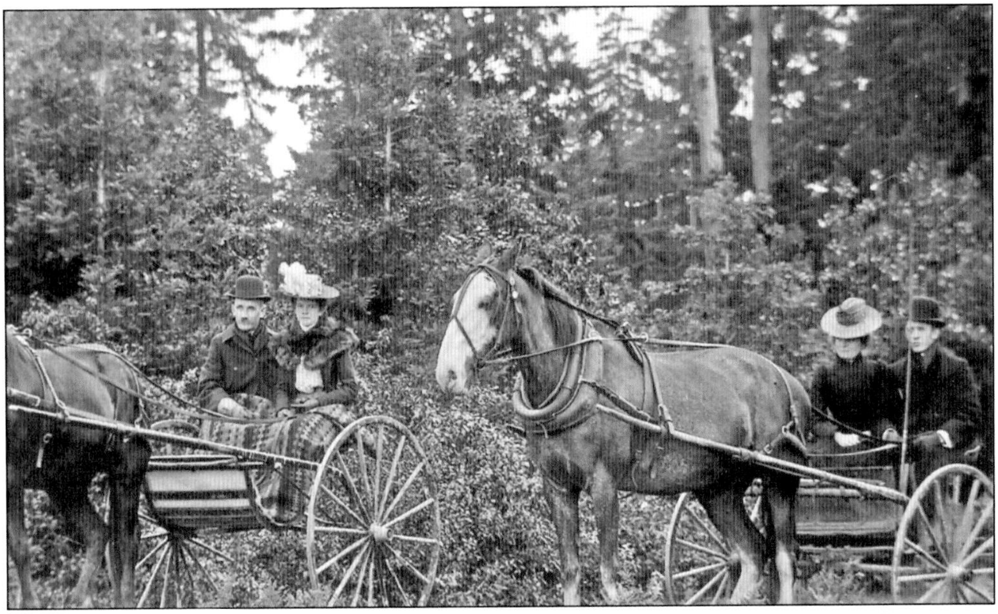

The roads in Annapolis provided a way to see the beautiful sites of the area. George Batt wrote: "Through the great country from Clark's Crossing on the Gualala River to Cazadero, via John Ohlson's, Charlie Haupt's, Joseph Irwin's, Chester Brown's, Child's, and Billy King's. The road leads up and down, not many yards of it is level and the most of it is very narrow. If a fellow ever gets drunk, it is the last road to take. In places the road leads along mountain ridges only just wide enough to hold you up, from the dizzy heights you look almost straight down, thousands of feet on either side . . . but the grandeur is so fascinating that I almost forgot that I was the teamster and being so near the clouds I just wanted to stop and study why this section."

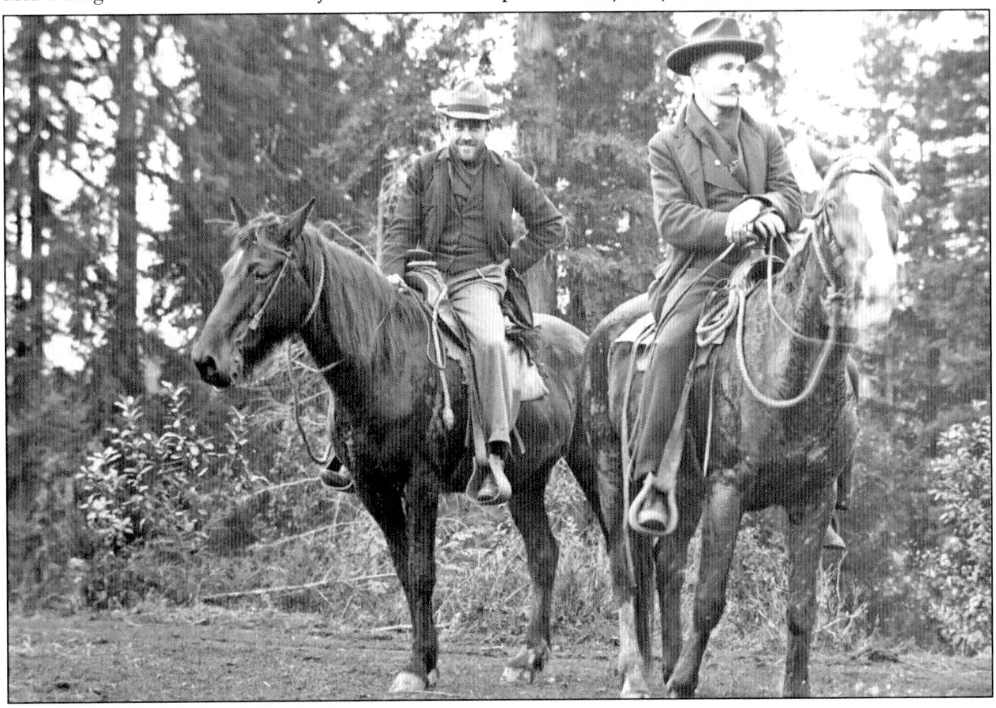

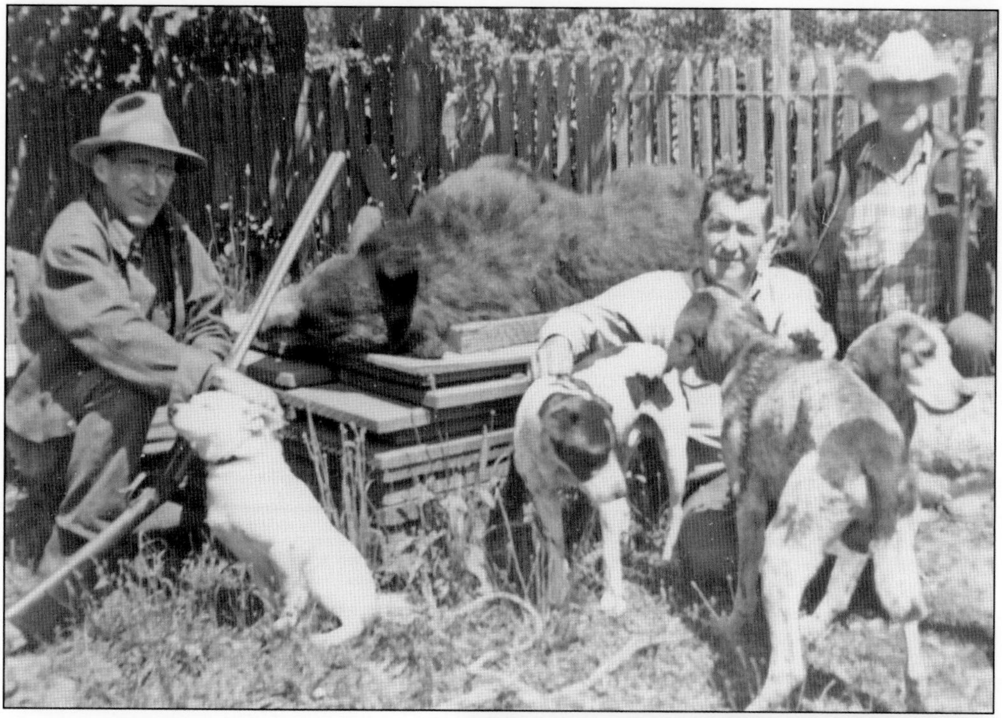

In some ways, times do not change. Although this photograph is from 1952, it could be from 100 years earlier. In this scene, two state troopers pose with a bear and Charley Fiscus (center).

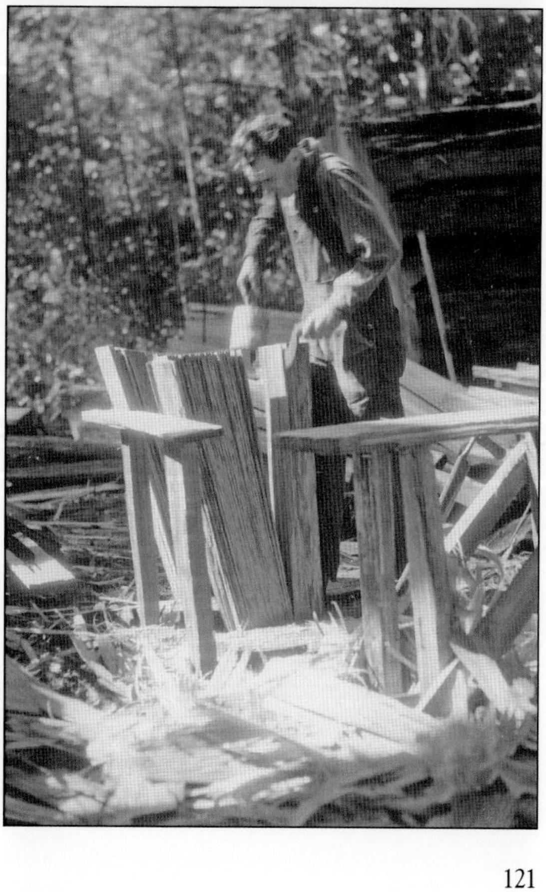

In later years, wood products were still being manufactured. Charley Fiscus makes shakes on the Ohlson ranch 1945.

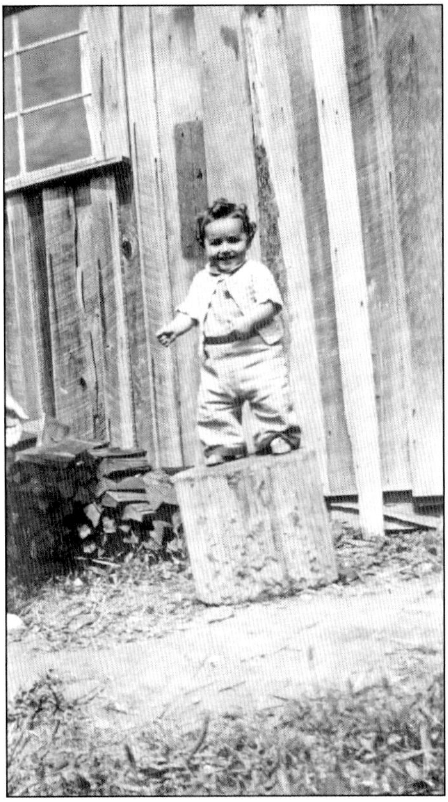

Many thanks are offered to this young Annapolis resident, Dorothy Fiscus Craig. She is seen here in her native Annapolis.

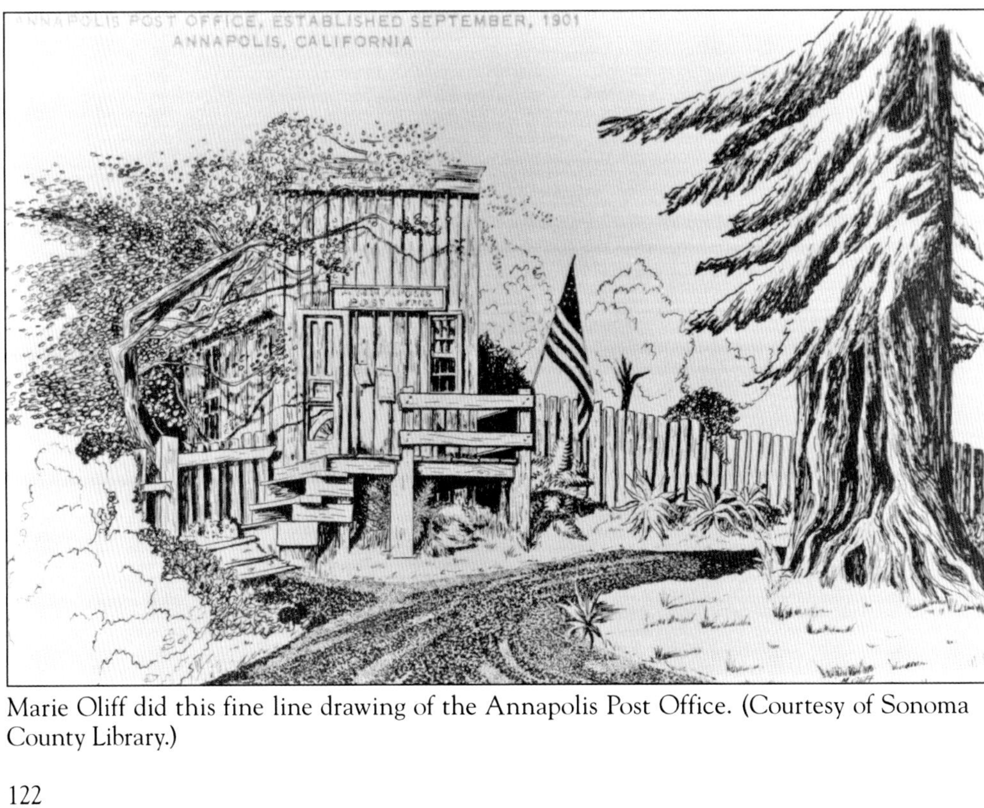

Marie Oliff did this fine line drawing of the Annapolis Post Office. (Courtesy of Sonoma County Library.)

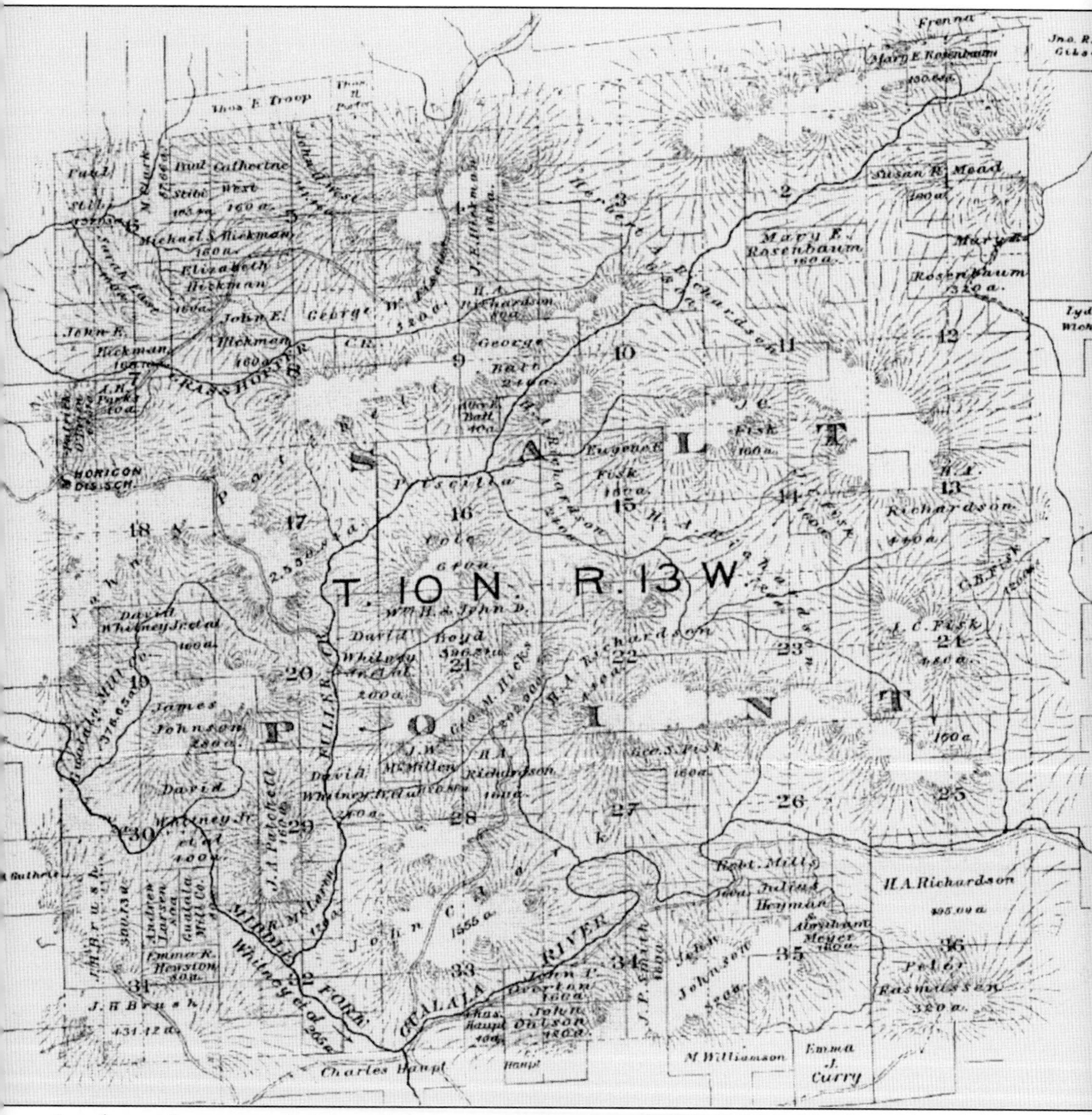

Land records are recorded according to special plot maps determined by the relationship of the land to certain landmarks such as meridians, range lines, base lines, and townships. The Annapolis area is in Townships 9 and 10 North, Range 13, and 14 West. This map from the 1898 edition of *The Illustrated Atlas of Sonoma County* shows the Gualala Mill Company land, Grasshopper and Fuller Creeks, the middle fork of the Gualala River, and plot land of early landowners such as the Hickmans, Batts, McMillens, and Richardsons. Horicon School District is also noted. (Courtesy of David Rumsey Maps.)

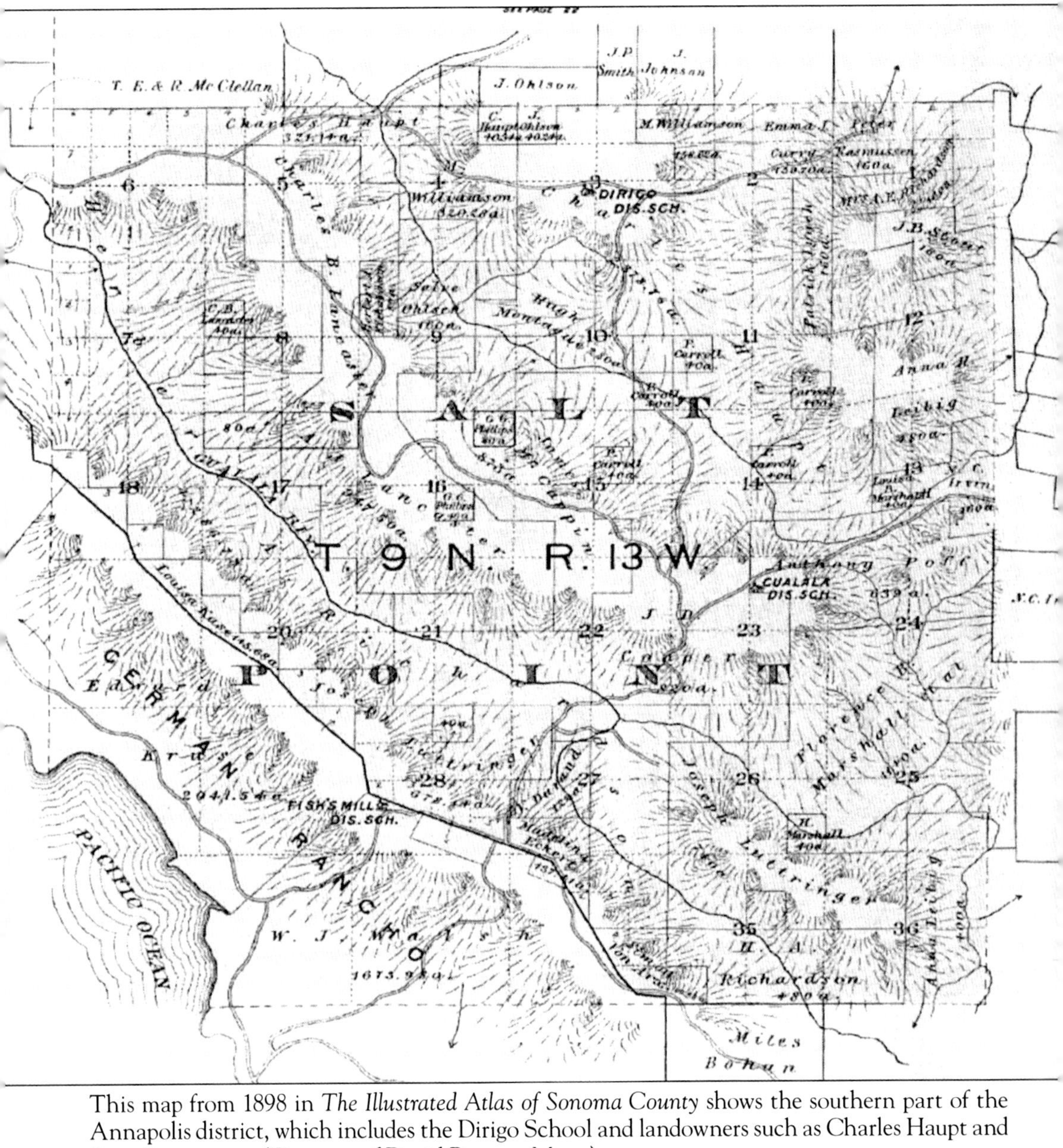

This map from 1898 in *The Illustrated Atlas of Sonoma County* shows the southern part of the Annapolis district, which includes the Dirigo School and landowners such as Charles Haupt and Peter Rasmussen. (Courtesy of David Rumsey Maps.)

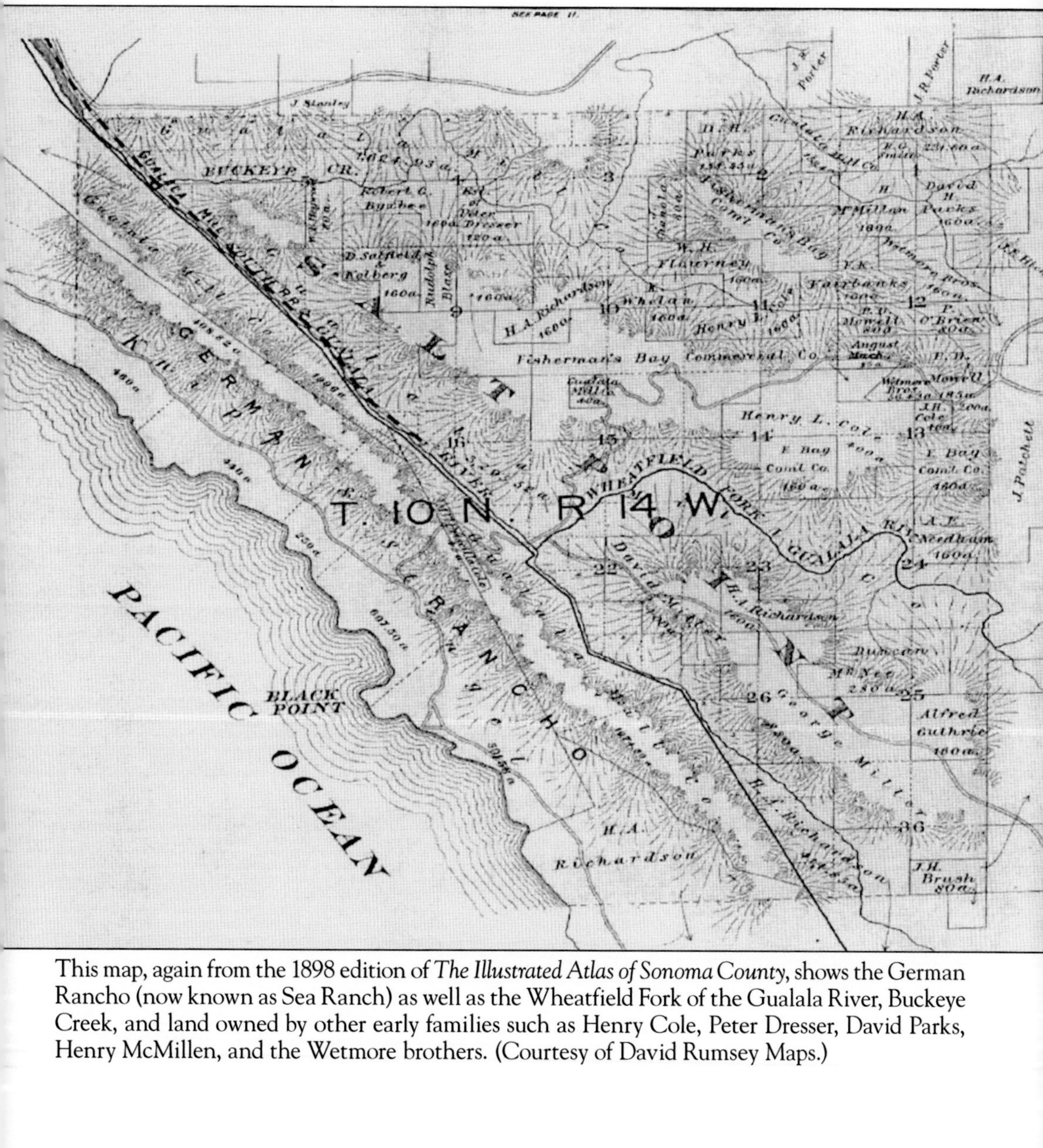

This map, again from the 1898 edition of *The Illustrated Atlas of Sonoma County*, shows the German Rancho (now known as Sea Ranch) as well as the Wheatfield Fork of the Gualala River, Buckeye Creek, and land owned by other early families such as Henry Cole, Peter Dresser, David Parks, Henry McMillen, and the Wetmore brothers. (Courtesy of David Rumsey Maps.)

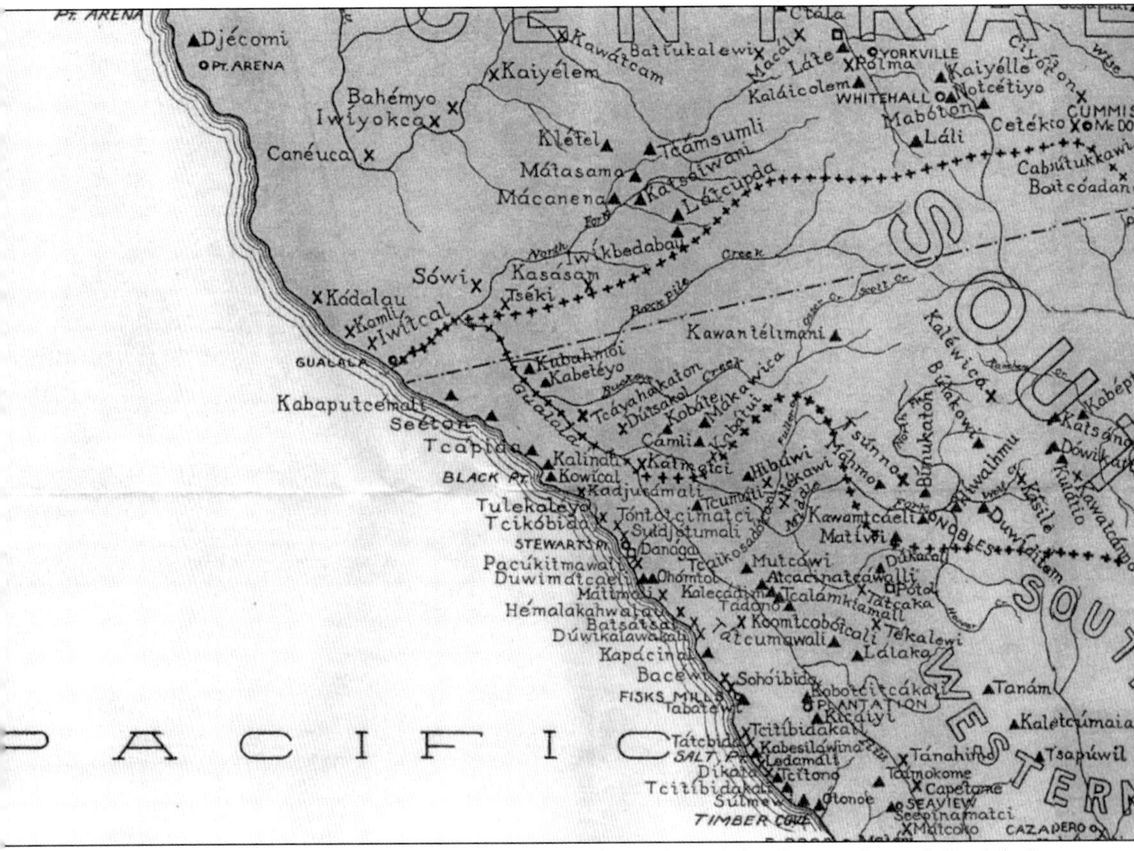

Although the focus of this book is the early Anglo settlers of the Annapolis and Gualala River area, we cannot forget the Annapolis area was originally Pomo land. This area, as well as the coastline, contains many remnants of early Pomo villages and gathering spots. This Pomo language map, dated 1908 from Samuel Barrett, an early Pomo researcher, shows the extensive area that the Pomo inhabited.

ABOUT THE ORGANIZATION

The Annapolis Historical Society is an organization dedicated to the preservation of local history.

Annapolis Historical Society
40049 Annapolis Road
Stewarts Point, CA 95480